Vanwall
Green for Glory

Ed McDonough

Above *Tony Vandervell, in suit and tie, tested the 1956 car before it had been painted. (Ferret Fotographics)*

Vanwall
Green for Glory

Ed McDonough

The Crowood Press

First published in 2003 by
The Crowood Press Ltd
Ramsbury, Marlborough
Wiltshire SN8 2HR

www.crowood.com

British Library Cataloguing-in-Publication Data
A catalogue record for this book is available from the British Library.

ISBN 1 86126 542 5

Dedication
This book is dedicated to Norman Burkinshaw and Derek Wootton

Unless otherwise stated, all photographs from the author's collection.

Typeset by Focus Publishing, 11a St Botolph's Road, Sevenoaks,
Kent TN13 3AJ

Printed and bound in Great Britain by CPI Bath

Contents

Foreword 7

1 Introduction 9

2 Getting Started: The Post-War Years 17

3 Norton Grand Prix? 25

4 Vanwall Under Wraps: Learning with Ferrari 30

5 The First Vanwall 44

6 Enter Chapman and Costin 79

7 1957–1958: Road to the Championship 104

8 Vanwall Legacy 168

Appendix: Vanwall Chassis 186

Bibliography 187

Index 189

Above *Tony Brooks on his way to winning at Spa, 1958. (Ferret Fotographics)*

Foreword

The author explains the reasons for another book on the Vanwall in his introduction, and I am pleased to have the opportunity to record my great regard for its architect, Tony Vandervell, and his remarkable achievements.

This book brings the story up to date and throws some fresh light on it. At this distance in time, it is difficult to fully comprehend the magnitude of Vandervell's achievements and the psychological barrier the British racing car manufacturers were up against in the 1950s. Foreign cars had totally dominated the Grand Prix scene for more than thirty years and it seemed that they had a mystic touch.

The Roger Bannister story provides a valid analogy. At his time it was considered physiologically impossible for man to run a mile under four minutes. Many failed attempts had been made, which created a psychological barrier, but through pain-defying training, determination and perseverance, with the help of a 'pace setter', Roger Bannister finally achieved the impossible – the sub-four minutes' mile. With the barrier down, the time became almost routine for the leading runners of the day.

After more than forty years of outstanding success by British F1 cars since the Vanwall days, it is easy to overlook what it took to achieve the initial successes and to break down that all but tangible barrier. I was very proud to be involved as a driver, but it was the manufacturer that had to have all the commitment, determination and perseverance of a Bannister.

The Syracuse Grand Prix win by Connaught in 1955 was the first Grand Prix victory by a British car and driver since Seagrave in the Sunbeam at Tours in 1923. It could be considered the 'pace setter' for Vanwall, which followed through with the first World Championship Grand Prix victory by a British car/drivers at Aintree in 1957, finally and conclusively exploding the mystic myth surrounding the invincibility of foreign GP cars by winning the World Manufacturers' Championship in 1958.

Tony Vandervell had all but Bannister's physical attributes, and many more a runner would have no need of. It was he who made the Vanwall success possible by creating, leading, motivating and driving the team, his close involvement being a great asset. He was the indispensible catalyst. Without him the team would have been just a group of talented individuals. He attended every race and practice session, bar one, I ever participated in and no-one pulled the wool over his eyes – not for long anyway.

Autocrats can have some infuriating characteristics and make mistakes like everyone else, but they have the power to quickly rectify errors without first having to persuade a committee. His public image was not of the real man. He was very caring, not least about his drivers, kind and fair, but you had to get to know him and earn his approbation and respect.

Vanwall – Green for Glory is an interesting read which I regard as a tribute to Tony Vandervell – a giant among racing men.

Tony Brooks

Above *Harry Schell in the French Grand Prix at Reims, 1956, having taken over Hawthorn's car (VW2/56).*

1 Introduction

Why Another Book on Vanwall?

When people began to hear that there was a new Vanwall book in preparation the comments tended to be of a warning nature and consistently expressed the view that there were already some hard examples to follow. After all, Jenkinson and Posthumus (1975) had told the story, Klemantaski had done a pictorial account (1958), there had been a Classic Car Profile (1967), and even Ian Bamsey's technical treatise in 1990 had added to the Vanwall folklore. So what was the rationale for doing it again?

Aside from commercial considerations of course, there are three main reasons for looking again at the Vanwall story. First, we have moved a long way in motoring literature in the last twenty-five years and the historic racing scene has rekindled interest in every aspect of motor sport history. While 'Jenks' provided what many consider the masterwork, we have a new tradition of digging deeper, of exploring the thoughts and activities of all the central characters, and even the minor ones, in a drama, and we have learned the art of subjecting a period in time to historical scrutiny. We have learned that the modern motor racing fan and historic car enthusiast likes their history, likes it in detail and likes it accurate. We have also learned to question some of the 'given' truths. Jenks listed Jack Brabham as a Vanwall test driver, but Sir Jack recently said to the author: 'I didn't even remember they built a rear-engine car, but I certainly never drove a Vanwall in races or in testing, and I'm sure I would remember that!' It is also apparent that the original literature is not widely available to the newcomer.

Secondly, the Vanwall tale was essentially told as the patriotic account of a single British businessman who attempted to vanquish the 'foreigners' who dominated post-war motor racing. The story largely appeared to end when Tony Vandervell stopped racing and eventually died in 1967. Yet there was more to tell. Vandervell was a difficult and tight-lipped person who spoke very little about his efforts at the time, and there are now people able to cast some light on the motivation, means and methods of this remarkable man. Vanwall and the Vandervell empire lived on, and some of the cars survived, so they can be subjected to scrutiny that was not possible in the days when they were running. There was even an abortive attempt to bring Vanwall back to Grand Prix racing, with World Champion Nigel Mansell to have a role in this! And there was almost a Vanwall road car.

The writer Ernest Hemingway talked about the submerged part of the iceberg hidden away in every story that has managed to make it into print. Much of the Vanwall 'iceberg' has so far not made it into print. The technical rationale for the choices made by Vandervell in the way he developed the odd combination of Norton and Rolls-Royce in the engine left much to ponder. The Vanwall, in 1956 and 1957, was breaking aerodynamic ground that we take for granted now but was largely 'try it and see' back then. Two great names, Colin Chapman and Frank Costin, came on the scene and were integral parts of the machine that brought a World Championship title to Acton/Park Royal in 1958, yet there are numerous accounts of how that came about, and who was influenced by whom. Was Vandervell the autocratic team boss he is often made out to have been, or did he have a tendency to throw his hands in the air and acquiesce to others, warning them that they 'had better get it right'? And who were the members of the team behind him?

The third and perhaps overriding reason, though, for writing about Vanwall is the sheer pleasure there is in immersing oneself in a period of racing which is overwhelming for the giant stature of its drivers and its cars. Look at the drivers of the time: Fangio, Moss, Hawthorn, Brooks, Castellotti and Collins. Not only has the author been fortunate enough to talk to some of the survivors, but also this book is a chance to reappraise and re-evaluate some of the great and almost great. When I was working on *Ferrari 156: Sharknose*, it was clear that the attraction was the proximity to the drivers of the time and the machines they drove, and to go back just that bit further in history was even more tantalizing. And if the cars of the new era, the early 1960s, were enthralling for their technical changes, the cars of the 1950s were no less so, and Vanwall stood out as the car which brought a more 'modern' approach to Grand Prix car design. Ferrari, Lancia, Maserati and Mercedes-Benz were the giants of that decade, until Vanwall came along and changed everything. Though critics of the period tended to see Vanwall, amazingly, as less aesthetic than the 250F Maserati or the D-50 Lancia, historical perspective has tended to shift that view. What is clear is that the hand of Costin led the way to the many changes that followed, and these went against everything the lover of the front-engine Grand Prix car believed in. Fear and disdain for change have

dogged motor racing, so the Vanwall tale is a fascinating account of balancing the proven and the unknown, the utterly reliable and the potentially disastrous. Vandervell often got it wrong, but he had a sense of direction that continually pushed the boundaries until something worked. His own sense of engineering adventure and downright stubbornness must have been an impossible combination to live with, but it flaunted the conventions of the time and succeeded. In historical perspective, there seems to be a strong resemblance to the dogged determination of people like Frank Williams. As you will read in these pages, even the most successful of Vanwall drivers were sharply critical of how things were done, but they acknowledge that 'it worked'.

There was a certain urgency, too, in writing this book. Amongst motoring writers there is often a quiet discussion about getting on with things because the cast of actors is getting thinner. If the heroes of the 1960s are now getting fewer in number, then those of the 1950s are even greater rarities, so the wish not to lose so much valuable experience and knowledge is a pressing one. You will see from this account that the first-hand witnesses are no longer so great in number. That old stalwart Jack Fairman died in the final months of writing this, as did Desmond Titterington who had one race in a Vanwall at Oulton Park in 1955. Many of the Vandervell crew of the 1950s, often mature and experienced craftsmen from within Vandervell Products at the time, are now long gone. Norman Burkinshaw, one of the key figures in the team, close to Brooks and Moss for many years, died on 30 July 2002, shortly after the Vanwall crew responsible for the great victory in the British Grand Prix at Aintree was being celebrated by the survivors and admirers during the forty-fifth anniversary of that groundbreaking event in 1957. That piece of history is passing away and there are still lots of stories to tell. Of the sixteen drivers who raced or tested Vanwalls, eight survive and you will be hearing from some of them in these pages. The others are sadly gone: Piero Taruffi, Mike Hawthorn, Peter Collins, Ken Wharton, Harry Schell, Desmond Tittering-ton, Colin Chapman and Stuart Lewis-Evans.

While this book attempts to be more than a recapping of race reports, it was the reading of those reports that provided another clue to the ongoing interest in Vanwall, which is simply that the Vanwall took part in some of the most exciting and important Grand Prix and non-championship races of the decade. It may or may not have featured in the results or in the lead battles in all of them but it was part of serious racing history. Tony Vandervell's Vanwall precursors, the Thin Wall Special Ferraris, which he used for six years to 'learn the trade', were on the grid for the 1949 British Grand Prix and featured in several major Continental races before the prototype Vanwall Special appeared in 1954. While the Vandervell equipe had a sorry time in 1955, it was on the scene for those mighty Mercedes encounters at Monaco, Spa and Aintree, and for some wonderful races at Spa, Reims and Monza in 1956 before it started really showing its potential in speed that year and in results in 1957. The Vanwall was part of the last 'titanic' decade of motor racing, and its place in history is guaranteed for that alone along with Connaught and Gordini. Taking the first edition of the Manufacturer's World Championship in 1958 just sealed that destiny. I also don't apologize for dwelling on the races because, in those days, and especially in the case of Vanwall, development and progress took place in practice and in the races, with serious and methodical testing being largely still in the future. The Vanwall legend grew on the tracks.

Tony Brooks asked me if I 'had a new angle on the Vanwall story' and the answer was essentially 'no', but we were in agreement that, with a celebration of the forty-fifth anniversary of the British Grand Prix triumph for Vanwall, Moss and Brooks, it was timely to look back at the car and company which led the way in British Grand Prix racing. One of the gaps the author detected in previous writing on Vanwall was that the drivers were never questioned in detail about the car, the racing and the personalities, and so I was very grateful when they agreed to do this, especially Tony Brooks who was very generous with his time and experience, and forthright and open in what he had to say.

Acknowledgements are due to many people in the preparation of this work. It is always rewarding to be able to involve those with first-hand experience of one's subject, and hence grateful thanks go to: Tony Brooks, Alan Brown, Sir Stirling Moss, Maurice Trintignant, Roy Salvadori and John Surtees, all of whom drove a Vanwall at least once. My appreciation also goes to Sir Jack Brabham, Norman Burkinshaw and his family, Ron Costin, Mike Costin and Derek Wootton.

For assistance with photographic material, great help came from Jorg Tomas Fodisch, Steve Havelock, National Motor Museum, Ted Walker (Ferret Fotographics) and Graham White. Peter Collins photographed VW2 and VW14 at Donington when Tom Wheatcroft kindly allowed the author a number of laps in his cars, including VW14, the very last of the Vanwalls. To have been able to drive one of the great line of cars was immensely appreciated and a debt of gratitude is due Tom Wheatcroft and the Donington Collection for preserving the cars and fostering continued interest in Vanwall and other Grand Prix machines. Brian Joscelyne provided colour material from the exceptional collection of photos he has taken over a period longer than he cares to remember. Peter Collins, of course, dug into his archives to find photos of the Vanwalls taken after they finished racing in period, at the same time keeping me focused on the task in hand.

Information, advice and archive material came from a number of sources: Ed Heinzelman, Mike Lawrence and Al Stewart, and

Neville Hay interviewed the principals at the anniversary event in 2002. Without question, Denis Jenkinson and Cyril Posthumus in 1975 wrote the book about Vanwall on which virtually everything since has been based, and while this is sometimes a problem for the later author, they are owed a debt of gratitude for their thorough work. They had unprecedented access to Vandervell files and information for their book and published many fascinating aspects of the story. Howden Ganley, one of the nicest of Grand Prix drivers, shared some of his boyhood enthusiasm for Vanwall with the author. Thanks also to Casey Annis and Dexter Harrison, who learned a lot about Vanwalls for a five-year-old, and to Chris Buck.

Vanwall Remembered

Very special thanks are due to Mike Jiggle. Mike was organizing the forty-fifth anniversary celebrations of the 1957 Vanwall win at Aintree during the writing of this book and was a constant source of support and good humour. To get a feel of the times, we will start by recalling that July day in 1957 as remembered by those who were there. There is something about Vanwall that presses the motor racing enthusiast's nostalgia button every time!

Tony Brooks recalled the period with considerable clarity:

> I remember the Vanwall and BRM days very well. First, in 1956, Mike Hawthorn and I were driving for BRM. The cars were well nigh impossible that year and they retired or didn't start in most of the Grand Prix races. But they did start the British Grand Prix at Silverstone and Mike and I were leading the field for the first few laps and I had the throttle break on my BRM but managed to lash it up and get it back to the pits. They did a repair and I got it back into the race but unfortunately the throttle stuck open in Abbey Curve, which was very fast as Silverstone used to be. My car was

totally uncontrollable if you did anything unpredictable like get a wheel on the grass, which I did, whereas a normal car would allow you to edge back onto the road. But the BRM went completely out of control, hit the outside of the circuit, turned itself over, and did the only decent thing and set itself on fire! Fortunately it threw me out first.

> Things got a lot better the next year, 1957, when I had second place at Monaco with the Vanwall, though the main thing I remember from that race is a very bloody left hand. That was because Monaco was 105 laps in those days, with twenty-four gear changes per lap, and unfortunately my clutch packed up on the fifth lap so I did some one-hundred laps with what was a ponderous, difficult gear change, even if you had a clutch, so at the end of the race my left hand was just like a piece of steak, the result of some 2,400 gear changes. So that is one of my lasting memories. Of course, it was very nice to finish second, which was a reasonably good result for Vanwall at that stage of development and you didn't really need an excuse to finish second to Fangio anyway.

> It was a while before I drove the Vanwall again because I went to Le Mans. My story of the 1957 British Grand Prix started at Le Mans where I was driving the Aston Martin with Noel Cunningham-Reid, who was a very good driver. He brought the car in about three in the morning stuck in fourth gear. I'd had this trouble before with the Aston and managed to free the gear lever on my very first lap I was trying to get it out of gear because we were in second place at the time and I didn't fancy spending twelve hours dropping slowly further and further down the field. On about the third corner, into Tertre Rouge, I was doing what you learn not to do on your first driving test, which is to look down at the gear lever. I was looking down with my hand on the lever accelerating and braking to try to pull it into neutral, and when I looked up I had passed my braking point which was mistake number one. Mistake number two was trying to get round the corner which I very nearly did, but there was a sandbank

Right *The forty-fifth anniversary of the Vanwall win at the British Grand Prix, 1957. Left to right: Roy Salvadori, Stirling Moss, Jack Brabham and Tony Brooks, with a modern version of the streamliner which never raced. (Peter Collins)*

which came down to the edge of the road at the exit of Tertre Rouge, the corner just before the straight. I almost made it round the corner, but then the car started running up to the top of the sandbank and flipped over, trapping me underneath. It was no light-weight! the car. This was three o'clock in the morning and I was beyond the apex of the corner. I lay underneath the car wondering whether I was going to be incinerated, or just run over! Fortunately Maglioli was the next car round the corner and his Porsche knocked the Aston off me. I got up and managed to stagger to the edge of the circuit.

So it was less than a month later that we had the British Grand Prix at Aintree and I was in a bit of a state, really, with a great big hole in my thigh and lacerations over most of the body. Driving myself to Aintree was my first outing since Le

Mans and I wasn't fit to race, but at that time the Vanwall did not have a particularly good reliability record, so I thought we should at least try to get three cars started. I managed to put the Vanwall on the front row of the grid two-tenths slower than Stirling on pole, but doing one fast practice lap and doing ninety laps at competitive speed were two different things. We arranged before the race that if Stirling had any problems with his car, because I wouldn't be able to sustain a competitive speed for the whole race, I would bring my car in and he would take it over. On lap 27, Stirling had already brought his car in and they tried unsuccessfully to fix it, so he brought it in again he took over mine and did fantastically well to win the race. That's a great memory, and it was well worth the effort, but really I shouldn't have been allowed to race that day!

Sir Stirling Moss also remembers well not only the events of that race but the ethos he carried through his racing career, his desire to win rather than to gather points for a championship. The 1957 British Grand Prix in many ways was the perfect example of how he pushed on. He arrived at that particular race for Vanwall following a sinus infection but in fact in much better shape than Tony Brooks:

> I wasn't in great condition for that race either, though I think I had recovered a lot better than Tony. I had got a sinus infection because I was trying to do that fancy thing of turning around on a mono water ski, and when you're on a mono ski and going backwards, a lot of water comes up and unfortunately most of it went up my nose! I got an infection, and it wasn't a very good thing to do. By the time I got to Aintree I wasn't feeling that bad, though I had been in hospital and missed a couple of races. But when you get to the race the race is the important thing and the adrenalin gets going, and you are competing with the other drivers so I don't remember feeling that bad. Poor old Tony was in a far worse state, so when my car gave some trouble I brought it in, and Tony came in and I took his car over and luckily together we were successful. The fillip it gives you to win a race like that with a British car – in England – was amazing, and for us to do it together was terrific.
>
> The good thing I remember from that race was that I knew, having lost a lot of places in the changeover, was that I wasn't going to be blamed if I was racing very hard and broke the car. So you can go like hell and the team doesn't really have a go at you. They wanted me to have a real race then and that was nice. And of course, 1957 was the last year that a team was allowed to bring in another driver to share a car, so in fact Tony and I were the last drivers to share a winning car at a Grand Prix, and that helped to make that Vanwall win even more special.

Roy Salvadori was another of those drivers who was very active in the post-war period, and as the 1950s progressed he found himself driving a wide range of types and makes of racing cars. He drove Maserati, BRM, Cooper, Aston Martin and Lotus cars and of course was a winner at Le Mans. Roy had recognized the potential of the Vanwalls as early as 1955 (Salvadori, 1985) and raced against them during 1955, 1956 and 1957. But in 1957, he came into the Vanwall fold at short notice:

> Tony had hurt himself, and Stirling had done something stupid so they were minus drivers and Stuart Lewis-Evans and I happened to be unemployed at the time. I remember Bernie Ecclestone was around at the time, but he didn't have anything to do with getting us the drives. He was involved with Stuart as he had bought two of the Connaughts when they stopped racing and he had Stuart Lewis-Evans driving for him, and I drove for him in New Zealand. That was the time that Stuart was instructed to sell the two cars in New Zealand or Australia if he could. I remember having breakfast with him one morning and he was looking very content with life and he said he had sold one of the cars, so I asked him how much he had made on the car. So he said 'quite a lot of money – it depends on what the stamp collection is worth.' I said 'What have you done?' and he told me he had taken a stamp collection in exchange for the car and I suggested pretty quickly that he contact Bernie!
>
> That all might have been a bit later, but I was asked to drive the Vanwall at the French Grand Prix at Rouen in 1957, and then again at the Reims GP a week later. The car I had at Rouen was quite a good car, lots of power, and the car I remember from Reims was very dicey. I had some 17in wheels, which were very unusual for that car, and it didn't handle at all. It was very quick. I can't remember driving the streamliner very much, I think I might have done two or three laps, but I don't think either of us wanted to drive it. Nobody seemed to like that car. I was fifth at Reims in a car that was very hard to drive, but if I knew that there might have been a chance to stay in the Vanwall

team, I probably would have worked harder at getting the set-up right. As it was, I drove the Cooper at Aintree when Vanwall won, and managed to
score Cooper's first point in a World Championship race. But the Cooper was easier to drive
than the Vanwall. The Vanwall was a very delicate
car. You had to be very precise with it. It was much
easier to drive a Maserati 250F than it was to drive
a Vanwall. They really needed Moss and Brooks to
cope with that.

While the glory that followed that win at Aintree seemed to set the Vanwall on the road to
overwhelming success, the drivers nevertheless
regarded the car with trepidation. Moss agreed
with Salvadori about the general Vanwall handling, though obviously individual cars dif-
fered from each other. Moss said clearly that:

The Vanwall actually was terrible to drive. It was a
typical Lotus design, which meant it was very sensitive on the steering, the gearbox was a bastard,
there was a bloody awful flat spot until they went
over to petrol. There wasn't very much you could
say for it, except that it won – so therefore it was
very good! In truth, it wasn't a user-friendly car
and I don't think any of us who drove it enjoyed
it like we enjoyed a 250F. It wasn't a nice car, but
it was a good car because it won, and at the time
that was fantastic, but I don't think any of us
enjoyed driving it.

Tony Brooks shared the view:

It was a difficult car to drive as Stirling has said. It
was the antithesis of the 250F Maserati, which was
a car that asked you to throw it around but nevertheless was very quick. You had to be very precise
with the Vanwall. The gearbox was rather long in
movement and rather heavy and it wasn't a car
which liked to drift. You could drift it but you really had to drive it very accurately, very carefully, but
it did the job. If you win races, there is a limit to
the amount of criticism you should apply to the
way in which the car wins the race.

Derek Wootton, one of the very last survivors
of the team who looked after the cars, started
his Vanwall days as an all-round handyman
before he became a key part of the smaller
group who went to the races and worked on
the cars. His memories of course included the
high spots, but there were long-lasting recol-
lections of the many problems Vanwall had to
overcome before scoring a decent result, and
even after the company had started to notch
up some results:

We had lots of problems with minor parts breaking, especially throttle linkages. We increased the
size of them, we replaced them with different
designs, we changed injector pipes, and re-mount-
ed them, and re-bracketed them, and did all sorts
of things like that for what seemed to be a long
time, yet they still broke. Eventually we got it right,
but I remember sometimes just how long it took
to do that, though it was worth it in the end. Of
course, I saw those as good times in racing, when
it was nice to see a driver sitting in a car where you
could actually see the effect of the driver's input to
the car, when he would drift it, and correct it, and
you would see the driver's arms moving, and for us
and for the public I thought it was a much better
spectacle than it is today. And of course our input,
especially at a circuit, was different. We could
change things, but not anything like they do today.
We could change axle ratios, and certain drivers
wanted things changed, like different-sized seats,
but really you did much less changing around once
the car was set up, which was why that was important then. Our drivers were always very nice, and
it was great to be with British drivers who were
prepared to stick with a car with problems and
persevere in order to win with a British car. We in
the team felt that their win at Aintree was brilliant.

Even after the decision to stop racing came
after the end of the 1958 season, there was still a
great deal of enthusiasm for competition. I went
into the technical sales department of Vandervell's
and people used to ring me up and say 'Can you
please get me a set of bearings for this, that and the

Left *Ron Costin (left), son of Frank Costin, presents an award to Derek Wootton at the forty-fifth anniversary. (Peter Collins)*

other', and it turned into a minor competition department. I remember that one of my first customers was Keith Duckworth. I went along to see him at Friern Barnet where he had this Anglia engine and I remember he wanted some bearings with a different clearance and I went back thinking 'How the hell am I going to get this done for an Anglia engine, and Tony Vandervell isn't going to be interested in that.' Well, I eventually went to him and said 'Look, would you make a set of bearings for this Anglia – it's racing at Brands Hatch and I'm convinced it's going to win.' He gave in

somewhat reluctantly. He wouldn't rush into a decision, but he was always interested in new ideas – that was him. So he got the experimental department to make them and the car did win. It grew from there and we were supplying bearings to a lot of competition cars and our department was doing very well. Of course, that was the Ford 105E engine, which was the first engine Cosworth developed, and that was the forerunner of the Cosworth DFV. I always saw it as a connection between the past and the present in racing.

2 Getting Started: The Post-War Years

Though the successes of 1957–58 made the Vanwall name a motor racing legend, Tony Vandervell's name was rarely mentioned in connection with the Thin Wall Ferraris that were an important part of the post-war motor racing scene in Britain, and to a lesser extent on the Continent. In fact, it wasn't until June 1951 that *Motor Sport* mentioned the 'Thinwall Special' at all, getting the spelling wrong on that occasion and not getting it right until November of the following year! Even then, there was an admonition to Tony Vandervell that he had better 'find some new parts'. *Motor Sport* might be forgiven for its problem in getting the nomenclature correct, as the company labelled the cars as 'Thin Wall Specials', but then referred to them in correspondence as 'Thinwall Specials'. Although Alberto Ascari was behind the wheel of the Ferrari at the BRDC International Trophy in August 1950, no connection with Vandervell was mentioned in the press, and this did not occur until Reg Parnell appeared in the car.

In fairness to the serious approach to reporting the racing scene taken by *Motor Sport* at the time, those were not the days of PR reps at every event. Vandervell was secretive, and the Vandervell–BRM rivalry had been brewing for some time. Tony Vandervell, also, was a man who had learned to work very independently, and his sometimes abrupt manner failed to endear him to a curious press. This meant that relatively little was known about him and his endeavours, and this remained a pattern throughout the Vanwall years.

Racing Reignited

Although Tony Vandervell had had no direct involvement in motor racing himself for nearly twenty years, the post-war expansion meant that Vandervell Products Ltd was growing and prospering, and it did not take much to reignite his pre-war enthusiasm. Vandervell was always a strong patriot, and his business pursuits were undertaken with the notion that Vandervell's success was a British success. What would now be viewed as chauvinism was a much simpler concept post-war. What did light the touchpaper for Vandervell was an invitation from Raymond Mays to co-sponsor his effort to build and race a thoroughly British Grand Prix car, with aid in money, kind and development from the motor industry. Mays had a good reputation as a racing driver from his exploits with ERA pre-war, and his fierce patriotism encouraged Vandervell, who was initially a very strong supporter of the British Racing Motors (BRM) project. Like Mays, Vandervell regretted the lack of success by Britain and British cars in international motor racing, and the immediate post-war success of the Italian teams, mainly Alfa Romeo, but also Maserati and then Ferrari stirred something in Vandervell that would soon make him lose patience with the BRM 'committee' car.

The BRM beginnings were in 1945, though Mays and Peter Berthon had set the scene with their successful development of the ERA between 1934 and 1939. In fact, they had

Guy Anthony (Tony) Vandervell

For those who believe in fate, there is perhaps some significance in the fact that Tony Vandervell was born in the same month, September 1898, as the Norton Manufacturing Company was established in Birmingham. Vandervell's father, Charles Anthony, was well on his way to building a lasting industrial concern, turning a small electrical business into one of the leading names in electrical parts and services by the beginning of the twentieth century. By the time Tony's younger brother Geoffrey or 'Ned' was born in 1913, the family had a country house as well as the home in London, Tony was attending school at Lynton House in Holland Park before going to Harrow and father Charles had bought a large share in Norton. The company of which he was chairman, Shelley, was a creditor of the Norton Company, so when the firm came up for sale, Shelley purchased it and 'CAV' had become the chairman of a motorcycle manufacturer.

Young Tony Vandervell became a racing motorcyclist in his teens and was quite successful on a 500cc side-valve BS Norton. He took part in a number of hill climbs, and once had a famous impromptu road race with one Graham Walker, father of Murray, which the sixteen-year-old won from the veteran. Harrow wasn't an exciting place for Vandervell, so at the onset of war he took the opportunity to move on. Giving a false statement about his age, he gained entry to the Army Service Corps where he started as a motorcycle dispatch rider, a suitable job for a bike racer, and advanced to becoming workshops officer with an artillery battery. (Jenkinson and Posthumus, 1975) His search for adventure, boredom with the mundane (which included school), and a pragmatic approach to life were early personality characteristics, which developed rapidly during the war years.

After departure from the military at the end of the war, he returned to his old love, motor cycle racing, and developed his new passion, which was for cars. The acquisition of an ex-Malcolm Campbell Clement–Talbot was an important move. Although father Charles supported Tony's sporting aspirations, Tony did the bulk of the work on this car himself, stripping its cumbersome body and carrying out a full rebuild with the aim of turning it into a successful race car. This he accomplished and was rewarded with victory at the Kop hill climb, beating Campbell himself in the bargain. Into the 1920s, Vandervell raced both cars and bikes, gaining an expertise in race building and maintenance for which he was rarely credited. His later involvement in the hands-on aspects of running a Formula 1 team often drew criticism from outsiders who saw him as a meddler, when in fact he had served his apprenticeship as a race mechanic, competitor and builder to a far greater degree than many of the team members he would employ. Vandervell's later confidence in his ability to construct a sophisticated racing machine had its grounding in the hard work of his early motorcycle and car racing days. The possible 'fatal flaw' might also have been developing in these early days as well – the notion that he should test and try everything himself, and the belief that he knew or ought to know what the car is doing. Hence, Vandervell is often pictured behind the wheel testing a new car, or a different version, and also,

Above *Tony Vandervell.*

continued from previous page

as he did at Spa, driving the car to the circuit against advice, which had costly consequences. This was, indeed, the characteristic which drew many people to him as well often making it difficult for those same people to work with him. Ingrained in him at this early stage was clearly a very strong work ethic.

In 1922, CAV put his son to work in one of his factories where not only his knowledge of engineering and particularly electrical engineering got a significant boost, but where he had some responsibility for a limited range of business activities, something at which he proved to be adept. His father would later reward him with his trust and significant support in investment. While many would later argue that Vandervell was always trying to prove his worth, his early work experience indicates a reasonable degree of self-confidence, and in spite of a fairly light-hearted approach to school, he was soon proving to be a hard worker, in fact someone who believed in hard work for himself and for the people around him. Another formative event at this period was the venture undertaken by CAV's two brothers, who started their own car manufacturing concern known as Vandy. Not only was this reasonably successful, but it had the interest and some investment from CAV. Although the Vandy did not last long, it had been an eye-opener for Tony, as the Vandervell electrical business had been involved in the supply of parts.

Tony Vandervell married in 1925 and upon his father's retirement from full-time business in 1926, the electrical business was sold to Joseph Lucas Ltd where Tony was employed, though his seeming lack of tolerance and wish to pursue business on his own terms saw him leave fairly soon after starting. Despite something of a playboy past, Vandervell was a worker and when his father set him up in the retail business selling radiograms, he made a success of it quite quickly, though the financial downturn of 1929 put an end to the company. This, however, was far from being a bad thing. CAV had bought a small London bearing maker,

O & S Oilless Bearing Co. and Tony was eventually placed in charge as a director, CAV recognizing Tony's need and skill to find his own way of doing things. The attention he had paid to his earlier work in his father's company showed fruit. Tony had a strong and almost compulsive urge to take on difficult jobs and find cheaper and better ways of getting them done. He applied this drive to the bearing business, evolving more effective manufacturing processes for bearings, securing lucrative contracts and expanding the business.

Not long after his start at O & S, Tony came across the new American approach to bearing production, replacing the cast steel, bronze and brass bearing shells with a new process whereby the 'bearings had thin steel flexible backings with a thinner layer of bearing metal, the two being bonded in long continuous coils of strip'. (Jenkinson and Posthumus, 1975, p.23) The two halves could be easily and quickly pressed into their housings, making the whole engine maintenance programme much shorter and easier. Vandervell set off to visit the company in the USA, proposing to gain the permit to produce the new 'thin shell' or 'thin wall' bearing in Britain under licence. An agreement was eventually reached for the UK and European market in 1932 and GAV, as he was now becoming known, set off to sell the idea to British car manufacturers. He had had a relatively easy time selling the idea to underwrite the new tooling and machinery to CAV, who saw great promise in the 'thin wall' bearings. Thus Vandervell Products was established on Western Avenue, Acton, London, with CAV putting up nearly half a million pounds to demonstrate his faith in his son. The operation got under way in 1936, with 200 employees. The number increased rapidly and during the early war years, production emphasis was on bearings for military vehicles and weapons, though Tony Vandervell spent much of his time improving and developing the product, to the point where he was made a director of the original American company in 1942. He travelled regularly to the USA and Canada, and in 1946 set up Vandervell Products (Canada) Ltd.

already started to approach the British motor industry before the war to get support in turning the ERA into a world-beater but were overtaken by events. Mays, Berthon and Ken Richardson developed the BRM Research

Trust, which got its initial financial boost from Oliver Lucas of Joseph Lucas Ltd in addition to services and components. However, more significantly Lucas contacted Alfred Owen of Rubery Owen who manufactured auto components and urged him to support the project, which he did very generously, and in effect took over control of the project. Vandervell was invited to join a board of consultant directors who included some very important companies in the industry: Tecalemit Ltd, Automotive Products, British Wire Producers Ltd, Rubery Owen & Co.Ltd, Specialised Pistons Ltd, George Salter & Co. Ltd and Lucas. (Jenkinson and Posthumus, 1975, p.26) This appeared to be a group of such powerful men that they could have been expected to create miracles, but in fact the composition of such a potent group was virtually its undoing, and it was not long before there were serious rumblings about lack of progress. While Jenkinson and Posthumus' history tends to be somewhat more sympathetic regarding Vandervell's dissatisfaction (perhaps not surprisingly, as Denis Jenkinson was fairly close to Tony Vandervell), Ian Bamsey's 1990 review, *Vanwall 2.5 Litre*, is perhaps inclined to take slightly more account of the BRM side.

The fact that BRM had chosen to go the route of the very complex V-16 engine with its new car made life even more difficult, and slow development and continuing problems in getting parts that worked meant the first car did not appear until late 1949. It was heralded as a world-beater even then, but when it raced for the first time at the International Trophy at Silverstone in 1950, the clutch failed on the line, and it was a full nine years before BRM tasted real success.

However, Tony Vandervell's desire to be on the stage of international motor racing grew rapidly after the project was first announced back in 1945. When the first post-war races began in 1946, he was already keen to see some worthwhile British competition for the mainly Italian runners. His apparent 'dislike' of the so-called 'damned red cars' or 'bloody red cars' has been repeated endlessly over the years. It probably wasn't dislike as much as envy and an impatient wish to demonstrate what he *knew*

the British could achieve – what he thought *he* could achieve. Anti-Italian jingoism was easy, especially in the years so close to the finish of the war, and convenient, but for Vandervell those words also masked an admiration for Italian engineering and workmanship. This admiration was to bring him into a direct business relationship with the one man who should have been his competitive arch enemy: Enzo Ferrari. Here indeed was a clash of two very powerful chauvinists.

Ferrari Connections

That a collaboration should come about between such men is not as surprising as the fact that it lasted some years. Neither man was ever prepared to give ground in public to the other, and the Ferrari fanatics who over the years came to revere Enzo would have been shocked by the lack of apparent regard Vandervell at times seemed to have for the *commendatore*. Unlike Ferrari, Vandervell never worked at promoting himself and creating something of a myth about himself or his products, which Ferrari certainly did. Vandervell believed in the quality of his products and treated Enzo Ferrari as much as a customer as a fellow racing car constructor.

The details of how these two men met has been somewhat lost in time, though Richard Williams (2001) records how Giuseppi Busso, who had been responsible for the construction of the first prototype Ferrari car in 1946, and Luigi Bazzi, who had already been with Ferrari at Alfa Romeo for many years, had begun to struggle in their attempts to produce adequate power for the 1.5-litre supercharged engine that Ferrari was building to contest Grand Prix races. Gioacchino Colombo had designed this engine and Ferrari was planning a serious effort to challenge Alfa Romeo, which had brought its pre-war 158 Alfetta out of hiding after the war, dusted it down and proceeded to win everything.

Giulio Ramponi, mechanic, racing driver and co-driver from the pre-war Alfa Romeo days had moved to England and was doing a thriving business preparing, tuning and repairing a range of cars. He had come across the new 'thin wall' bearings being produced by Vandervell Products and brought a set back to Enzo Ferrari in 1947 to try in the new engine, and they immediately helped it rev more freely, though there was still much to do on that engine. There were those who suspected that Colombo's continued 'moonlighting' (he had his hand in several projects) contributed to the problems with this engine. This, however, was the first significant use of Vandervell's bearings in racing in Europe, and started a tradition that continues today. It also brought Vandervell to Ferrari's notice as the two companies worked more closely on the use of the bearings in the 1.5-litre V-12.

While Enzo Ferrari wanted to build something to beat Alfa Romeo, Vandervell wanted to buy one, as by 1947 he was becoming seriously impatient with the slow and unproductive development of the BRM. While still a director, he proposed to the Trust that they buy an existing Grand Prix car. There was no chance of getting an Alfa Romeo, as they just were not for sale. Maserati was less competitive and Vandervell felt what he knew of the Ferrari meant it would be something that the Trust and the project could learn from. Though he was later portrayed as being considerably 'anti-foreign', he was also pragmatic and thoughtful, and could put aside his short-term feelings to achieve the long-term goal. The other outcome of Vandervell's technical connection with Ferrari over bearing development was of course that he had begun to amass considerable knowledge of how a Ferrari worked.

The existing involvement of Vandervell Products with Ferrari and the fact that the British Motor Racing Research Trust had already established good connections with the government Board of Trade resulted in an import licence being granted in January 1949 to bring the latest Ferrari 125C into the UK. This was by no means an easy task at the time, but numerous representations had been made, as Mays and Berthon had originally planned to import a pre-war Mercedes Grand Prix car. The fact that they saw this as a 'state of the art' racing car nearly ten years after it had been last raced was either a sign of how good it was or an indication that they may not have known where they were going!

Vandervell was stamping his authority on the direction that the Trust, or at least the part of it that wanted to get on with racing, was going, and by putting up the payment for the car himself, he wanted Vandervell Products to receive some publicity from it. The intention was to race a contemporary Grand Prix car and apply the learning to the BRM. But the import licence forbade either racing or use for advertising purposes unless the import duty was paid, which all the principals were keen to avoid doing. Mays and Berthon again called upon their friends in the ministry, as they had done before, and got a waiver to these rules. However, by the time the car finally arrived, Vandervell had decided to pay the purchase tax and customs charges himself, allegedly to be free from any restrictions, though in retrospect it seems likely that he knew then where he was going and wanted a strong claim on the car, which was supposed to be a jointly held asset of Vandervell Products and the Trust.

Denis Jenkinson must have been fairly close to Vandervell or others at Vandervell Products because he was able to record in minute detail the entire saga, including details of the paperwork, up to and including the actual delivery of the Ferrari to Blackbushe airfield where Tony Vandervell was supervising the unloading. (Jenkinson and Posthumus, 1975) Jenkinson appears to have gained access to the team's paperwork and administrative files, possibly sometime in the early 1970s. Fees amounting

Above *Raymond Mays in his unsuccessful drive in the 1.5-litre Thin Wall Special at the British Grand Prix in 1949. (National Motor Museum)*

to more than the car had cost were paid for taxes and customs duties, and an entry had been made for the British Grand Prix at Silverstone on 14 May 1949. The driver was to be Raymond Mays and the reserve – G. A. Vandervell. There were complications as the car was referred to as the Thinwall Special and the RAC took umbrage at a special being entered in its premier event. Vandervell was refused as a reserve driver, and the BRM project's chief mechanic Ken Richardson was substituted. The RAC relented in the face of Vandervell's strongly worded arguments regarding the name of the car, putting it forward as a technical mobile test bed. It was to be prepared by Berthon, and looked after by a combination of Vandervell and BRM project staff.

The witnesses to these first exploits with the Ferrari have often marvelled at how BRM and Vanwall ever came to be successful in the way that they did. The relatively short-chassis Ferrari was a serious handful and Raymond Mays gave a lacklustre performance, handing over to Ken Richardson near the end of the race. While Richardson had done some testing, he had virtually no race experience and very quickly had a huge accident at Abbey Curve, hitting some spectators, although by an amazing twist of fate no one was seriously injured. While Emmanuel de Graffenreid won the race in a Maserati 4CLT, the organizers had learned an important long-term lesson about crowd control as a result of Richardson's crash.

While Brock Yates implies that the car was immediately shipped back to Ferrari as a result of its poor handling (Yates, 1991), in fact the 'test bed' programme for which the Ferrari had been intended got under way back at the Trust's base in Bourne, Lincolnshire, and initially Peter Berthon stripped the car down to bare essentials and prepared a long report, which Tony Vandervell then turned into a very outspoken letter of complaint to Enzo Ferrari. He stated categorically that the car was just not good enough, that it did not have enough power, it was overweight and the short chassis made it oversteer violently on some corners. Furthermore, he proposed that Ferrari assist him in redesigning a longer chassis.

While to some this has always appeared to be an example of Vandervell's lack of tact and his hard-headedness, in retrospect it is very possible that he used this forthright approach in quite a calculated manner, as he knew perhaps more about Ferrari developments than Enzo would have liked. For example, as Jenkinson points out (Jenkinson and Posthumus, 1975, p.30), the Thinwall Special had a single-stage supercharger and Ferrari had been working on a much improved twin supercharger for his own cars. Vandervell knew about this and was determined to use as much new technology as he could get his hands on. While Yates (1991) argues that relations between the British and Italian industrialists suffered a setback, it seems that the opposite may well be true, as not only was Vandervell learning that the Ferrari engine was not something so sophisticated that he couldn't match it, but Ferrari also felt there was something significant to gain from Vandervell's technical know-how in the engine department. This rather seems to be the start of their quirky but often productive technical liaison.

Ferrari was fairly effusive in his response to the letter, pointing to several successes involving the use of the Vandervell bearings in a range of Ferraris during the season, and a number of options of how to proceed were offered. But Vandervell himself conducted a more searching inquiry into the build of the engine that he had been sent, and was critical of both design and particularly of construction, which he duly pointed out in another letter to Enzo Ferrari. Again, the Italian was not outwardly disturbed by the account and after a

series of correspondence, it was agreed that the first 125 should be reassembled and returned with all its components to Ferrari and a new, longer chassis car with two-stage supercharger would be sent. That turned out to be a much lengthier undertaking than any of the parties had envisaged, and it must have passed through Vandervell's mind that he might perhaps be making a mistake in planning a complete and total divorce from the BRM project in the spring of 1950. As it happened, he expressed his views on the lack of progress of the BRM, but made no specific move to depart from the Trust at this stage.

Split from BRM

During the winter, Vandervell had some technical meetings with Ferrari's Aurelio Lampredi, the 'genius' of the large-capacity Ferrari engine. Apparently, unknown to Ferrari himself, Vandervell made trips to Modena to discuss the technical aspects of bearings and engine development with Lampredi. Of course, Vandervell met with Ferrari on some visits, but it seems that Lampredi and Vandervell arranged their own meetings. While Vandervell was keen to get the new car to England in time to prepare it for the British Grand Prix in May 1950, it became clear that the 4.5-litre un-supercharged car was not going to be ready by this date, so Lampredi helped to organize the use of a 1949 1.5-litre Grand Prix engine with two-stage supercharging and four overhead camshafts to be used in the interim. A new chassis would be constructed by Ferrari, but, in the event, this did not make it on time for the premier British race either. By May, the connection with the BRM project had been severed for good. It had now become important for Vandervell to demonstrate that he could operate as a race car entrant, if not a constructor at this point, both to justify his split from the BRM consortium and to satisfy himself.

When the Grand Prix was missed, a second target of the International Trophy at Silverstone in August was set, the 1.5-litre car with Ascari as the driver to be sent in time to set it up correctly. When the entry was again sent in for a Thinwall Ferrari Special, with an Italian as the driver, a number of noses were once more out of joint. The car duly arrived, though with no time for any testing, and it was sent off for the race where it was yet again a major disappointment. The Ferrari, 125-C-02, had a swing-axle rear suspension and the allegedly potent engine, but it could do nothing against the Alfa Romeos and Fangio. This car, which in historical terms is known as Thinwall Special number 2, was neither threatening in practice nor in its heat, and was not running competitively when a heavy rainstorm caught Ascari out and he spun and retired. To add a degree of insult to injury, the engine had arrived with the name 'Thinwell Special' inscribed on the cam covers. In spite of Ferrari's admiration for Vandervell's technical prowess, he managed not to translate that into a correct spelling on the engine!

One thing happened at the Silverstone race which must have lessened Vandervell's disappointment somewhat and that was the fact that the BRM made its racing debut in the hands of Frenchman Raymond Sommer, and had a journey in the race which could be measured in inches. Sommer had the half-shaft break as the flag was dropped and that was the end of some considerable razzmatazz.

None of this stopped Vandervell from carrying out another fastidious post-mortem and the message sent to Ferrari this time was even more vitriolic than the previous year. The total strip-down investigation found the engine to be: 1) not new; 2) poorly put together; and 3) failing to take into account all the technical information Vandervell had passed on to Ferrari regarding the preparation of parts, especially the crankshafts, which were not nitride-treated in the way current practice demanded.

His list of complaints was very long indeed, and Ferrari must have been furious, though his response was tempered by his wish to retain the liaison with the British company. While not accepting most of what Vandervell had said, he did promise a 'spirit of cooperation'. Vandervell had set his sights on the Lampredi 4.5-litre power plant, and ultimately he would get one, though by the time this happened, that engine had progressed further and the British team would remain a step behind. Such was the qualified nature of Ferrari's 'spirit of cooperation'.

3 Norton Grand Prix?

The Norton Engine Project

Well before the events of the 1950 racing season had occurred, there had been a number of other developments in the career of Tony Vandervell that would have a major impact on what was to come much later. Some of these occurrences were known at the time to at least a few people, though probably not regarded as significant in the working life of a man who was an industrious and ambitious worker/director. Some were very little known indeed and one of these was the appointment of Vandervell as a director of Norton Motors Ltd in 1946.

There is no evidence that Vandervell was using his early experience with motorcycles in any conscious way to shape what he eventually wanted to do with his racing cars. But he seemed to have clearly grasped an important concept at an early stage. Setright (1968) contends that the engine which would appear in a Vanwall had been inherited from BRM, and BRM had in turn derived it from the Norton motorcycle company of which Vandervell had been a director. Setright also says (1968, p.366) that Vandervell 'suggested' to the BRM Trust that it might try to develop a 'water-cooled version of the Norton engine as a feasibility study of future potential value'. In truth, Vandervell did something rather more specific than that, and was instrumental in getting a contract drawn up for Peter Berthon to design a four-cylinder racing motorcycle engine based on what he had already learned from the BRM V-16. Berthon performed particularly poorly in his capacity as a designer of the racing motorcycle engine, resulting in this task eventually being largely taken over by draftsman Eric Richter to complete. To give Berthon his due, he was more preoccupied with the fraught BRM sixteen-cylinder at the time. It took from 1948 until 1950 before Vandervell finally took hold of the four-cylinder Norton engine project and pushed it on to completion. He was at this same period arguing with Ferrari, expanding Vandervell Products at Acton, and then building a new bearing manufacturing plant at Maidenhead. In the midst of this, he was also diminishing his contacts with the BRM project, but had made sure that many technical and financial aspects of the Norton engine project were firmly under his control.

Setright points out that Vandervell had recognized that motorcycle engines were at that time well in advance of car engines in obtaining the most power from a limited swept volume, and in fact had been doing this for decades. The long-standing British motorcycle engine with single cylinder and overhead valve design and reasonable capacity had been a force for many years, and of these the Norton overhead camshaft version was by far the best. Using alcohol fuel, the 500cc Norton engine was producing a remarkable 50bhp, though this was substantially reduced when it had to use petrol after the war, a problem that would come to haunt the Vanwall project.

Differences in opinion at Norton about the

four-cylinder project, combined with Norton's own financial difficulties, also kept the project from advancing quickly. However, progress did take place. Setright describes in detail precisely what the cooperative BRM/Norton/Vandervell team achieved:

> An unfinned cylinder barrel of Norton proportions, which were then 82.4mm bore and 94mm stroke, was so contrived that its lower half was spigoted into its crankcase, while seven-eighths of what remained was enclosed in an aluminium water jacket and the uppermost portion was spigoted into the aluminium cylinder head, so that the necessary watertight joint was divorced and remote from the fire joint between barrel and combustion chamber. In every significant respect, the conformation of the shape thus enclosed (as well as that of the ports leading to and from it) was a precise reproduction of Norton practice, as was the layout of valves and overhead-camshaft valve gear; however, the liquid cooling was exploited by putting the water in direct contact with the exhaust valve guide that was finned to present the greatest possible surface area. (Setright, 1968, p.366)

The plans for the four-cylinder Norton motorcycle engine more or less evaporated as the work went into what would become a 125cc single-cylinder unit with dohc that was essentially only a test-bench unit, though it was producing 4bhp more than Norton's own unit at the time, at least in short runs on the bench. It seemed that few people, including Norton managing director Gilbert Smith, were entirely clear what was going on. The late journalist Charlie Rous wrote of motorcycle racer Geoff Duke's disappointment with Smith, who said to Duke in 1951 and 1952 that the four-cylinder Norton would not be ready for 1953, and Duke duly though reluctantly moved to Gilera to race. (Rous, 1990) The truth was that the developments had stopped and the work which was going on was

focused on what would become the Vanwall engine, though it is possible that Smith himself was unaware of this. Certainly, the research and development which had been carried out in relation to the Norton unit over a period of some three to four years remained a well-kept secret.

What had become a clearer concern for Tony Vandervell by late 1951 was what he needed to do to turn his brainchild into something that would work in a Grand Prix car. Though he was learning a great deal about racing with the 4.5-litre Ferrari, it had become obvious that he needed and wanted to build his own successful engine. Though it remains somewhat unclear as to why Vandervell went on with the Ferrari for so long, it was apparent that he was committed to learning everything he possibly could from that venture. Evidence of Vandervell's intentions regarding the engine was the way in which he went about quizzing the competition experts at Norton over who might best solve the problems of converting the test bed single cylinder into a proper engine.

Leo Kuzmicki

Attention came to focus on Leo Kuzmicki who was working in the competition department, but had got there by unconventional means. Kuzmicki was Polish and had served with Free Polish Forces during the war. After the war he was employed in a menial capacity in Norton's Birmingham factory, as he had decided not to return to Poland. He was carrying out his tasks at Norton when one of the race mechanics discovered that Kuzmicki had lectured on internal combustion engines prewar at the University of Warsaw. Geoff Duke credits Kuzmicki for Duke's success in the 1951 season after Kuzmicki had his broom taken away by racing chief Joe Craig and was sent to the competition department. He redesigned the 350cc race engine with his 'squish' piston, a flat-top design instead of the usual much larger dome affair. He achieved a 30 per cent increase in power and Duke started to win in the 350 class again. Geoff Duke in his own book, *In Search of Perfection*, recounted both how he had been kept in the dark about the 500cc engine project and also how Kuzmicki was not sufficiently acknowledged for the amazing work he did on a number of engines. (Rous, 1990)

While Rous (1990) says that Vandervell asked the question of Kuzmicki about how they could make the four-cylinder racing car engine work, and Kuzmicki is alleged to have replied 'Why not build a four-cylinder engine with Manx cylinder heads?', it seems unlikely that Kuzmicki would have had such a simplistic view of the project. According to Jenkinson and Posthumus (1975), the threads of the BRM/Norton project and what Vandervell had got people at Norton to work on began to come together in 1951, and Vandervell suggested this solution, to which Kuzmicki responded politely but with some reservations about the complexity of such a move. One of the factors that compelled Vandervell to push on with the project at this point was that there was an existing two-litre Formula 2 class, and the rumours that Grand Prix racing would be run to the Formula 2 regulations in the near future were gaining momentum. Vandervell was beginning to see his own plan becoming a reality.

Once Vandervell had begun to see the future, there was little hope that he would step back and review the potential problems. His approach was to get on with the job, and deal with the snags as they occurred. While he had many admirers for this style, he also had a number of detractors, especially amongst his staff who knew they would end up having to sort out problems that might have been avoided. However, he also engendered enormous loyalty and the eventual success meant that few people felt he did it the 'wrong way'. He was definitely not a committee man.

Vandervell gave over part of the Acton and Maidenhead factories to the engine development work. Kuzmicki went to work on taking the complex project forward, having now been given access to what the BRM/Norton team had already learned. His knowledge of cams, valve gear and port shapes was invaluable, but he was essentially a specialist in design of the top end of the engine, and his learning curve was steep as he had to consider how the power was to be used in a race car. The 500cc Formula 3 had come into existence, of course, and the Cooper Manx was the chassis/engine combination of choice, though in reality these cars were more four-wheeled motorcycles in technical terms than they were cars. Kuzmicki's solution to the design of the head was to:

> retain the independent construction of the four cylinders but to surround them by a common water jacket. The cylinder head was also a casting common to all four cylinders but it incorporated valve gear that was an exact copy of the Norton original, the upper extremities of the valve stems being open to the gaze of the curious because exposed hairpin valve springs were bearing upon them, as were cylindrical tappets in cam boxes mounted above them. The induction system thus controlled naturally enough incorporated four motorcycle type carburettors – the Amal racing variety, which is of singular efficiency at wide throttle openings because of the absence of obstruction in the bore in that condition. (Setright, 1968, p.367)

If this sounds complex, it probably was in the design, though in the metal it looks less so. In fact, when you gaze upon the final product, the hairpin valve springs look very basic indeed. The author recommends the reader to visit the Donington Collection to look at what Tom Wheatcroft has done to preserve Vanwall posterity, and to look closely at VW2, the reconstructed 2-litre car with the engine exactly as it was first designed! Karl Ludvigsen, in fact, emphasizes just what a 'throwback' the use of hairpin valve springs was, pointing out that they were first used on the 1910 twin-cam Peugeots, where the springs were in the open between the cam cases and cylinder heads. (Ludvigsen, 2001) That writer also quotes Edward Eves on the problems inherent in the design:

> The valve gear was one of the biggest headaches, and all concerned must have rued the decision to use hairpin valve springs. All the British spring makers tried their hand at making springs that would stand the pounding (of the Vanwall's heavy valves), and so did Scherdel in Germany. Exotic materials, finely ground and finished, were used, but all of them failed eventually. The eventual solution was to run every spring on a rig for several hours before fitting it. (Eves, in Ludvigsen, 1998, p.167)

Rolls-Royce Solution to the Bottom End

Vandervell had to face the task of finding the appropriate bottom end of the engine, and, as before and afterwards, he could call upon his many contacts in the automotive industry for help. In this instance, however, help was much closer at hand and his eldest son Anthony made an important contribution to the next phase, when in discussion with his father he suggested the use of a Rolls-Royce bottom end.

Anthony was working as an engineering apprentice at Rolls-Royce at the time and had a good knowledge of the range of Rolls-Royce motors, including the military applications of four-, six- and eight-cylinder units, the B-Series. These economical units used many common parts and were very strong for military use. The four-cylinder engine used a B-40 crankcase of the rigidity that Vandervell felt the crankcase and crankshaft needed to be in order to handle the high power output that the Nor-

ton engine was likely to deliver. Though this unit was made in cast iron, it could be duplicated in aluminium. Thus in early 1952, a discreet order for a B-40 crankcase was made to Rolls-Royce. Though a vast amount of change and refinement was required, the basis was there for a sound engine for the 2-litre Vanwall design. At this point, Eric Richter moved to Vandervell from BRM and had the key task of developing the bottom end of the engine. The crankcase was then cast in aluminium with the cylinder block section absent and this was replaced by the one-piece aluminium water-jacket that had been developed in the Norton/BRM project. This water-jacket enclosed four Wellworthy cast-iron cylinder liners which were spigotted at both ends and sealed into the crankcase, using long bolts as was customary in the racing Norton Manx engine. Thus, the threads of several years' thinking, planning and experimentation were finally coming together, at least as far as the engine was concerned.

There was just sufficient contact between Richter and Kuzmicki to ensure that the work they were doing remained compatible and the bulk of the information they shared came through Vandervell himself, who remained actively involved in many aspects of the design process. Kuzmicki and Joe Craig remained focused on the top end, while Richter was involved in taking the B-40 crankshaft from Rolls-Royce, modifying it slightly and then having it forged with an 86mm stroke and four main-bearing journals. This crankshaft had been around for a sufficient period for everyone to feel it would be reliable and would manage the new task for which it was to be used. Indeed, a number of engine components were being used whose performance and reliability were already well known. Joe Craig's work with Kuzmicki is interesting in that he was almost always 'anti four cylinder', but he seemed to change direction somewhat, as he and Kuzmicki worked very closely to evolve a four-cylinder unit that would not only work but be competitive.

GKN Stampings undertook the forging of the new crankshaft and BTH produced a magneto suitable for a four-cylinder engine reaching 8,000rpm using two plugs per cylinder. Norton ordered extra thick 100mm piston blanks from Hepworth and Grandage and these would be turned down to 96mm. The standard bore size was 86mm and a compression ratio of 12.5:1 was envisaged. The ordering of components by Norton aroused no particular suspicion, though as 1952 developed word began to leak out of Vandervell Products about 'significant' engine work. Vandervell, in his customary short manner with the press, gave away nothing and said the company was only involved in doing further bearing research. There was not really a hint of what was by now a rapidly developing plan.

4 Vanwall Under Wraps: Learning with Ferrari

'Thinwall Special number 3', or 'Thin Wall Special' as it again appeared on the car, was essentially a rebuild of number 2, though an extensive rebuild it has to be acknowledged. A long and detailed correspondence took place between Tony Vandervell and Enzo Ferrari from the end of 1950 through the beginning of 1951, the central aim of which was to secure the very latest in Ferrari technology for Vandervell to use in 1951, and indeed right through into 1954 as he masterminded the design and construction of the Vanwall very secretly behind the scenes. One of the great achievements of this period of Vandervell history concerns Tony Vandervell's ability to keep two very complex projects going at the same time. Cynics would argue that there is evidence that this didn't entirely work, but in the end something very significant was achieved.

As it turned out, this was not the latest technology from Ferrari, though it would be some time before Vandervell would discover that, and at first it appeared that he would get the same 'old' technology. Ferrari agreed to modify the chassis with a new de Dion rear axle among other things, and Vandervell was attempting to get the unsuccessful 1950 two-stage supercharged engine rebuilt as well for 'research purposes' – and because he had paid for it! Ferrari had seemingly agreed to this, though it was to turn into a long-term problem for both sides. It would appear that Vandervell tried as hard as Ferrari to 'maximize' his advantage with a rival.

Thin Wall Special Number 3

Vandervell intended to use the 'new' 4.5-litre unsupercharged car at the Silverstone International Trophy race in May 1951 with Reg Parnell as the driver if he was not being used by BRM, which he was not as things turned out, BRM having considerable difficulty in getting and keeping a car running.

The Thin Wall Special was pretty impressive when it showed up at Silverstone in its dark green paintwork, for all intents and purposes the latest from Ferrari and Lampredi. The impression was sustained through practice and the first heat where Parnell kept on terms with Juan Fangio's Alfa Romeo and finished behind the Argentinian. In the second and final heat, it looked like it was going to be a repeat of the dreadful 1950 race, as the skies unleashed a torrent of rain and hail, but Parnell, unlike his illustrious predecessor, Ascari, was able to work the Ferrari into a lead and was in front when the organizers decided to halt the proceedings after only six laps. Parnell was awarded the victory to his own and Vandervell's great satisfaction, and Denis Jenkinson (1975) reported that Vandervell's words over the public address system as the decision was announced were 'pennies from Heaven!' Though Vandervell had got a Thin Wall Ferrari to the chequered flag, BRM had already recorded two race wins in the latter part of 1950, when the car won two very short and minor races at Goodwood. As minor as they were, however, it is likely that Tony Vandervell winced at the occurrence, as his own car was still a long way away.

The Ferrari, campaigned regularly as the Thin Wall Special, went on to take part in six more race meetings that season, including the first overseas excursion to Reims in July. It is a matter of conjecture as to whether Tony Vandervell had expected to receive the twin-plug head version of the Tipo 375 engine in time for Silverstone. It appears that he expected the latest development but was told after this race that progress was being made on the twin-plug ignition. The twin-plug layout did not finally appear in Vandervell's hands until well into

1952. Meanwhile, the team was determined to make the most of the car with the de Dion rear suspension and rear-mounted transaxle gearbox.

Vandervell, now beginning to be referred to more frequently as GAV, though only to his face by a few, sent good wishes to Reg Parnell who was to race again the following week at Goodwood in the Festival of Britain Trophy Race. Parnell started from pole, won his heat and the fifteen-lap final and set a new lap record for Goodwood of 95.54mph (153.72km/h), and if Vandervell was harbouring any suspicions about what Ferrari had sent him, it seems likely that these doubts were dispelled by the car's performance. For the Ulster Trophy two weeks later at Dundrod, Northern Ireland, Ferrari decided not to send a car to go up against the Alfa Romeo of Nino Farina but

Below *Reg Parnell drove the second Thin Wall Special, the 4.5-litre unsupercharged car, to fourth in the 1951 French Grand Prix. (National Motor Museum)*

himself suggested to the organizers that they invite the Thin Wall Special, as it was a thoroughly up-to-date Ferrari. Thus Parnell again drove for the team, doing well to be a close second to Farina in practice and in the race. While the team felt the car was more or less the equal of the Alfa, Parnell's more limited experience was seen as one factor in not beating the all-conquering Alfa Romeo team. In retrospect this is probably deeply unfair to Parnell who drove hard in a car that was heavier and far less refined than the Alfa. It was also to be something of a Vandervell characteristic not to be too effusive with praise for a driver after a good performance. Tony Brooks would have occasion to notice this a few years later, though it was at the time just accepted as the right of the 'Old Man' to behave the way he wanted to, and of course it was something of a cultural norm in that era.

Nearly a month went by before the next outing, which was the Grand Prix of Europe at Reims, where Parnell turned out to be the driver yet again, against expectations because it was thought he would have to honour his BRM contract. However, BRM withdrew and he was free, somewhat to the relief of the team and the drafted-in replacement, Brian Shawe-Taylor, whose lack of experience would clearly have been dangerous at Reims. Parnell again put in a fine performance against a much tougher opposition than he had faced at Dundrod, with more works cars on the grid. He finished fourth in the team's first real Grand Prix, a longer and harder race than they had done, and it was lucky that the final drive broke just as Parnell was crossing the finish line. Tony Vandervell himself was incensed by the press reports which had fourth place going to a *Ferrari*, instead of the *Thin Wall Special (Ferrari)* as he referred to it in his vitriolic letter. It was another nail in the coffin of Vandervell/press relations.

By this time, however, the exploits of the Vandervell team were not lost on the more astute sectors of the automotive industry, and many offers, recounted in excellent fashion by Jenkinson and Posthumus (1975), came pouring in after the Silverstone race. After Reims, Vandervell went on the hunt for a company which could take advantage of the enormous strides being made in the aircraft industry with disc brakes, and finally Goodyear responded to the challenge, though even that company could not work at the speed the motor racing world was getting used to.

British Grand Prix at Silverstone

In the meantime, there was a two-week break between the Reims race and the British Grand Prix at Silverstone. This was to be the first confrontation between the Vandervell team and the BRM. In retrospect, it is odd that the two teams, which had started as one to garner British glory in the motor racing world, were now fighting against each other, at least in the terms which the public understood, even though one of the cars was distinctly not British. And little was said at that time about Vandervell's so-called disdain for things foreign. In many ways, it makes light of the later emphasis on Vandervell's alleged obsession with beating 'those red cars', as has so often been quoted. Here he was using a 'red car', albeit painted green, to beat another green car! The additional slight complexity at this time was that technically Vandervell was still part of the BRM Trust, though he was increasingly less active and would withdraw entirely within a few months. It remains unclear as to whether members of the Trust still saw the Thin Wall Ferraris as part of the Trust's activities, as the first car had been bought for the Trust's research use. It may well have been apparent to 'insiders' what Vandervell was up to, though it also seems entirely possible that this was just another detail which got lost in the 'loose' administration of the Trust.

Reg Parnell was clearly not going to be

available for this race, so the team faced the prospect of a totally new driver in the car. Peter Whitehead, a capable privateer, had been an early customer of Enzo Ferrari's, and had bought his Tipo 125 at the same time as Vandervell purchased the first similar car in the Trust's interests. Whitehead was reliable and skilful, though not someone who was likely to threaten the leaders. Whitehead's significant contribution, however, was to bring David Yorke along to assist the team at the British Grand Prix. Yorke had been helping to manage Whitehead's ambitious racing programme for a few years and was a thoughtful and well organized person. He was usually pretty serious and his characteristic, outwardly dour manner remained with him through his career at Vanwall, and later at J W Automotive in the Ford GT40 and Gulf Porsche days. He once removed the author from the Gulf Porsche pit at Watkins Glen during a pit stop, even though I was there at the invitation of John Wyer, with proper credentials. Wyer's view was that 'David's the boss!' To his credit, he later relented, grudgingly letting me talk to him about the race. 'Pedro Rodriguez says you're a friend of his – well, I suppose that's okay!'

The British Grand Prix was important for another reason, which was that Vandervell went full tilt at the organizing RAC when it first baulked at accepting the team's entry, arguing that the RAC 'invited drivers' rather than teams or entrants. It gave in under the attack, and Vandervell had established himself in the forefront of entrants and beaten Enzo Ferrari by several years to the tactic of threatening to quit motor racing if he didn't get his way.

The race between the two British teams turned out to be the battle of the back-markers. BRM's Parnell and Peter Walker finished in respectable fifth and seventh places, with the Thin Wall Special in ninth after Whitehead had come in complaining of lack of brakes, which were then adjusted. Doug Nye argues that the 'first round had certainly gone to Bourne,' (Nye, 1993, p.68) but it was clearly a battle of medium size fish in a smallish pond, as the European Grand Prix teams were not challenged by the BRM or the Thin Wall Special.

The Brake Problem

The brake problem in the British Grand Prix reminded Vandervell of the dire need for an improvement. The fact that the team was getting the car to go quickly and last for an entire race made stopping power an urgent requirement. It would be interesting to review the history of Formula 1 teams to see if those with slow and unreliable cars also had a correlating lack of development in the brake department. But Vandervell was keen to compete and go fast, so he used his knowledge of and connection with BRM where they were making progress on brakes. He got an agreement to adapt the Girling three-shoe drum system and Eric Richter supervised the building of these at Acton. Vandervell had planned to enter the Italian Grand Prix at Monza and was pressing Ferrari for the latest brakes. Ferrari apparently was being very cautious about this as he may have suspected the information would be passed on to the BRM team; as far as he was concerned, Tony Vandervell was still an active part of the BRM effort. In addition to an argument with the organizers of the race over start money, Vandervell felt he should concentrate on getting the car running properly and decided not to go to Monza. This incident also made it more important for Vandervell to clarify his relationship, or lack of it, with BRM. Being a generally impatient sort of person, he had become very outspoken in his criticism of the BRM project. Whether he had clearer plans for his own Grand Prix team by this stage remains somewhat unclear, but even though he was building up to a divorce from BRM, he was not beyond using his existing connections to develop his own project, in this case the Thin Wall brakes.

The new Girling brake arrangement appeared on the Thin Wall Special at the Goodwood meeting in late September 1951 and these appeared to work well, though the extent to which they were tested is questionable. Parnell drove the Ferrari to second behind the Alfa Tipo 159 in a short five-lap race, and was second again behind the flying Farina and the Alfa in the fifteen-lap Daily Graphic Trophy. In the final five-lapper, a handicap race, he started with Farina, who won, but did not manage to overtake the HWM of the relative 'new boy', the up and coming Stirling Moss, so he was third. That was twenty-five laps of racing plus practice, so it was a good test for the Girlings, though they were only ever intended to be an interim solution to the braking problem. Vandervell had quite early set his mind on disc brakes, and as many commentators have said, once he set his mind to something, he stuck to it. As infuriating as some people found this, he turned out to be right a sufficient number of times so as not to be dissuaded from his approach.

Two weeks later, Parnell gave the team an end of season victory at a relatively minor but enjoyable Formula Libre race, against fairly limited opposition. Over the next few seasons, Formula Libre would enjoy considerable popularity, as rule changes meant there was an abundance of machinery with no international category to run in, and thus some of these races gathered sufficient competitors to put on a very exciting show. They would be the battleground for the Thin Wall Special and the V-16 BRM, and therefore gained public attention, and kept the motoring press shouting for a proper British Grand Prix contender. The Scottish race at the Winfield airfield circuit also marked the occasion of Reg Parnell's last drive for Vandervell, though that thought had probably not occurred to anyone at that point.

Off-Season Developments

In the 'off-season' – the winter of 1951–52 – a number of events occurred which did not so much shape the future indelibly but certainly pushed things in a particular direction, at least as far as Vandervell was concerned. His interest in developing the power output for the Ferrari engine led him into an ongoing correspondence with Enzo Ferrari that was very productive. They debated various approaches to improving the power including new pistons forged by Hepworth and Grandage. Vandervell had a view that the Weber carburettors could be improved, though it is unclear whether this was purely on technical grounds or a suspicion that he could manage something better than the Italians. An experiment and a series of efforts involving Amal carburettors and the work of Eric Richter came to naught as far as the Ferrari engine was concerned, but this took place in early 1952, at the height of the early development of what would become the 2-litre Vanwall engine, so much was learned in this process. However, to outsiders, and indeed to some insiders, it appeared to be an example of getting sidetracked. This view was the result of a limited number of people knowing how much was going on in the future-planning department. Many were working on projects, but few were aware at this point of how these projects might be connected.

It was during this winter period and in the correspondence with Ferrari that Vandervell declared he was no longer part of the BRM project, and Ferrari appeared to accept this. It was decided between them that Ferrari would acquiesce to Vandervell's demand for a twin-plug, twenty-four-valve head engine for his Ferrari. In further discussions about the deficiencies of the Ferrari chassis, namely it being too short and therefore cramped in the cockpit, Ferrari's eventual suggestion was that Vandervell might consider having one of the 375 Indy chassis, as American regulations allowed a longer wheelbase and this would make the cockpit roomier. Vandervell was happy with this offer, and though work continued on the existing car in the short-term, the plans for 1952 would revolve around a longer chassis 375. Also, during this busy winter period, it had finally been decided that the World Championship in 1952–53 would be run to the Formula 2 rules. With Alfa Romeo deciding to retire after two Championship winning seasons, the Grand Prix scene looked bleak, and with a number of manufacturers already possessing engines to the F2 2-litre limit, this seemed a sensible move. It was a move that pushed Vandervell forward as well because he now had the basis of an engine for this formula, even though there was still a great deal of work to be done. But it was during this period, as Jenkinson and Posthumus (1975) confirm, that Tony Vandervell made up his mind to construct his own Grand Prix contender. Though he shared with Ferrari that he had separated himself from BRM, it seems likely that he did not go so far as to tell him he was going to build his own cars. He allowed the 'Modena wizard', as he saw him, to think he was happy running Ferraris in lesser races. However, as the Acton factory was operating at full capacity and included part of the racing effort, and the Maidenhead factory was now fully operational and able to take on more of the race development, Vandervell knew he had the infra-structure for a Grand Prix team. Indeed, many teams had operated from much more modest facilities in the past and did so at the time, and a number more would in the future.

We will look more closely at how the Vanwall came together in the next chapter, but as all these developments were taking place, Vandervell kept his hand firmly in the racing game by racing the Ferrari, and using the learning from that project to feed into his behind-the-scenes work on the future car, the planned existence of which can probably be timed to February 1952 when the B-40 crankcase was ordered from Leyland Motors, which made the engines under licence to Rolls-Royce. At the same time, Vandervell had been talking to Harry Mundy, who was then the chief designer at Coventry Climax, and had been involved in the early days of the BRM project. He later revealed he was certain that GAV was up to something that he wasn't talking about at the time, but he just wasn't sure what it was. Mundy, in a review of the Vanwall story in 1959, put the date at January 1952 'when this project was put in train.' (Mundy, 1959, p.ii)

The 1952 Racing Season

The 1952 British racing season opened with the Easter Goodwood meeting in mid April. Shortly before this, Goodyear had finally reported back after exhaustive research that it had a plan for the disc brakes for the Thinwall Special and Vandervell told Goodyear to go ahead. This was the Goodyear Aviation Division, as the design had been adapted directly from aviation practice. This did put Girling's nose out of joint to some degree, but by this time Vandervell was actively courting, and getting, more and more industry support, even though he was often abrasive and not easy to work with, as Mundy also pointed out in his 1959 review. Through Ferrari, Vandervell had approached Scintilla for a new design of magneto that was aimed at smoother running rather than more power. This presumably also disappointed Lucas, who offered to design a magneto that was largely rejected by Vandervell. He was certainly less inclined to be rigid about obtaining all his components from British manufacturers, whereas a central ethos of the BRM project was to be entirely British, BRM standing for British Racing Motors and being meant to incorporate the broad contribution of the British motor industry. Had BRM been more efficient in its early days, no doubt the British motor industry would have got behind it more strongly, but as it was, many supporters were starting to drop by the way-side. As a result, BRM began to mean BRM the racing car manufacturer, rather than the original wider symbolic meaning.

At this opening race Vandervell saw his chance to begin to employ drivers of international calibre in his team and contracted the Argentinian Froilan Gonzalez to drive at Goodwood. He won the main event of the day, the twelve-lap Richmond Trophy, and set the fastest lap at 90mph (145km/h), proving to Vandervell that the Scintilla magneto, which ran at half engine speed, worked well and reliably. Gonzalez also took part in the shorter Easter handicap race, but in his exuberance spun off and finished third. When Gonzalez returned to the Goodwood Festival of Speed a few years ago, incidentally to drive the BRM V-16, he sat with the author and recalled that race after being shown some photos in the company of Tom Wheatcroft who had both the BRM and the Thin Wall at the time. Through his son as interpreter, he recalled how he found the car especially responsive and remembered thinking it accelerated faster than the works car and had better handling. Although he knew he was no mean driver in the wet, he recalled not wanting to drive that car in the wet at Goodwood because it was 'quick and felt on the edge – a good but sensitive car.' He remembered meeting Tony Vandervell and thought he was an 'interesting man, very English,' which Tom Wheatcroft thought was not only funny but very accurate! Gonzalez thought he might get to drive for Vandervell again, but it would be some years before it happened.

There was a sideline to that race that shows up another, less familiar side to the Vandervell character, a side which many have remarked on though few could give examples of, and that was his kindness and occasional empathy. It seems that Ken Richardson had been held partly responsible for non-progress at BRM

and had been sacked. He asked Vandervell for a job as a test driver, which was a fairly unusual position at the time. Richardson had done some driving of the BRM, but probably not as a serious and systematic test driver. Vandervell respected Richardson, and wanted to keep him on his side and offered him a drive in the Thin Wall Special in another of the minor races at Goodwood that day. Sadly, Richardson repeated his unfortunate debut experience of a Thin Wall Special, going off on his first lap.

Thin Wall Special Number 4

The new 'Thin Wall Special number 4', the final Ferrari to be run by Vandervell, albeit for the next two years, arrived before its debut at the Ulster Trophy Race at Dundrod in Northern Ireland. This was finally the car with a twin-plug head, chassis number 010–375, and although it was sent presumably as a complete chassis, a great deal of modification was done to it by the Vandervell staff, some of whom by this time were doing some familiarity work on the new 2-litre engine as well as working on the Ferrari. The Ferrari had the longer Indianapolis chassis and de Dion rear axle. The previous chassis is reported as having been broken up in 1952 and this may have been because the car was totally dismantled to use as many components as possible from that chassis on the new one. On the other hand, GAV had asked Ferrari about getting hold of one of the new Lampredi-designed 2-litre engines, a works engine, to install and use in the older 'number 3' Thin Wall Special, so there must have been that chassis available at least at the time of this correspondence in the first half of 1952.

However, there were many problems with the new car. The Girling brakes were adaptable, but many suspension components had to be made, as did other parts, as many from Italy were delayed or did not arrive at all. The car was substantially different to its predecessor,

Above *Italian Piero Taruffi on the grid for the Formula Libre race at Silverstone, June 1952. (Ferret Fotographics)*

with a much roomier cockpit, a cleaner and more effective shape, a new radiator and front end, fairings over the rear suspension and a large carburettor intake, amongst other things. Denis Jenkinson (1975) makes the wry comment that both his own *Motor Sport* magazine and the new *Autosport* totally missed the fact that this was an entirely new car! The longer wheelbase and all the other changes were missed completely.

Vandervell's plan to have Luigi Fagioli drive was tragically spoiled by the Italian's serious injuries in a race at Monaco, from which he later died. Piero Taruffi stepped into the breach for the first of four drives for Vandervell, the last of which would be four years later in a 'proper' Vanwall. In the meantime, Taruffi did a thoroughly professional job of winning the race – at least once he had got going. He had stalled at the start, sat there calmly and waited

for the mechanics to bring out the mechanical starter, waved to them, and viciously accelerated away, recording over 125mph (200km/h) over the first kilometre from a standing start. Vandervell's thoughts, unfortunately, were not recorded!

This was of course the second direct encounter with the BRMs. Fangio's car had been a fraction faster than Taruffi's in practice, but the cars were poorly prepared and tired from a previous outing. Both Fangio and Moss lost their clutches on the line, had to be push-started, Fangio spun to miss a spinning Bira, Moss came upon his spinning teammate, while Taruffi had already got up to sixth, past Fangio. Moss retired the BRM with overheating, while Mike Hawthorn initially led with a Cooper-Bristol, but Taruffi steamed past him and only lost the lead at the refuelling stop. Fangio finally retired when the fuel lines clogged and Taruffi and Thin Wall number 4 won after just over three hours of racing. Alfred Owen, who was by now moving into a leadership position at BRM management, sent a message of congratulations to Vandervell at Acton.

Taruffi was in action again in the Ferrari at the Silverstone Formula Libre race in July, some five weeks after the Ulster Trophy. This was the British Grand Prix meeting, which was of course being run for the 2-litre cars, but the organizers put on a Libre race to satisfy the mainly British enthusiasts who wanted to see the British teams. The two BRMs with Gonzalez and Ken Wharton were on the front row with a works 375 Ferrari for Luigi Villoresi and Taruffi. It was at this race meeting that John Cooper was alleged to have made his famous Vandervell/Alfred Owen comparison: 'At one end of the paddock would be old Vandervell dispensing caviar and champagne from his vast caravan … at the other end would be Alfred Owen with his BRMs, a pack of sandwiches and a bottle of Tizer.' (Nye, 1993, p.69)

Taruffi again did well after a bad start, having found the car creeping, for which he was penalized for a jumped start. This was a tremendous race, in which Gonzalez drove one of his great races after taking over Wharton's BRM. He caught the two leading Ferraris before he was forced to retire, but Taruffi out-drove Villoresi and won in spite of the thirty-second jump-start penalty. On this occasion, Vandervell was uncharacteristically enthusiastic over the performance of his driver. This was in part due to the fact that Taruffi was both a knowledgeable engineer and an experienced motorcycle racer, and also spoke very good English, so Vandervell had a considerable respect for him.

The next outing for the car was at Turnberry Airfield in Scotland, another Formula Libre

Below *1950 World Champion Nino Farina at Goodwood in September 1952. (Ferret Fotographics)*

race, and as Vandervell had been impressed by Mike Hawthorn's driving at Goodwood, he invited him to race in Scotland, which Hawthorn was pleased to do after testing the BRM and finding it not at all race-worthy. However, Parnell's BRM won this minor race, as the transaxle in the Thin Wall Special was having difficulty handling 400bhp, and this would lead to considerable Vandervell modifications of the Ferrari to cure it. It later transpired that Hawthorn, in his own book, confessed that when he heard the terrible noise from the back of the car he looked down and saw that he had revved the engine to 9,000rpm. He told the mechanics that he would get in serious trouble with Mr Vandervell over this and asked them to reset the tachometer. (Hawthorn, 1958)

Plans for Hawthorn to drive in the BARC Autumn Trophy at Goodwood in September went awry when Hawthorn was injured in a Cooper-Bristol testing accident, so another international notable, Nino Farina, joined the ranks of Vandervell's drivers. Farina managed to coast across the finish line second with a stripped crown wheel behind Gonzalez in the BRM in the five-lap Woodcote Trophy, but couldn't start the main race, which went to the BRMs. A new crown-wheel was designed before the next race two weeks later at Charterhall in Scotland and this withstood Farina's aggressive start, but instead the aluminium gearbox casing broke so he was out again, the race being won by Bob Gerard's pre-war ERA. This was a pretty humiliating day for both Vandervell and BRM, and the press, which had been playing up the so-called 'rich man's' rivalry between Vandervell and Owen, started to be critical of both teams' failings. This race also marked the end of the BRM Trust, as the Owen Organization bought the BRM operation. It was also at this last meeting at Charterhall that Tony Vandervell had a close look at the 500cc F3 race, with mainly Cooper chassis and Norton Manx engines.

This led him into a closer relationship with John Cooper, who became seriously involved in the Vanwall project at the end of 1952 and into 1953, but we will come back to that. John Cooper himself admitted that until this involvement began, he had no idea that Vandervell had anything to do with Nortons, although by that time he himself was working closely with them. (Cooper, 1977)

The 1953 Racing Season

As developments for the Vanwall progressed into 1953, the Ferrari would be used five times during the year, producing two good results and a number of mechanical failures. These five races would all feature a confrontation with BRM, which helped to keep races for what were now aging Formula cars on the bill. In spite of some hard words with both Enzo Ferrari and Nino Farina about the conditions under which a Ferrari driver would drive for Vandervell, differences were patched up in time, though not for the first race. Farina and Ferrari wanted to honor their Shell contracts, and it was only because of the company links in the UK between BP and Shell Mex that the Thin Wall could run on BP. During this tense period, however, Ferrari had suggested improvements to the carburation. It came as something of a shock to Girling, after its work with Vandervell, that the Easter Goodwood meeting would see Vandervell's Ferrari show up in the paddock with disc brakes for the very first time. Apparently, Girling expected Vandervell to continue using the 1952 drum arrangement even though it had developed discs for BRM. Goodyear had finally produced a Vandervell-modified arrangement that took many by surprise. Jenkinson (1975) described the brakes as being quite unusual in that the pad caliper was pivoted on one side and only one pad moved, and this pressed on the disc and swung the caliper, and it thereby self-aligned. The new disc departed from tradition by being forged steel rather than cast iron, the disc being drilled in order to save weight and reduce the build-up of heat found in standard discs.

Because Farina and Ferrari did not get their contractual arrangements sorted on time, Vandervell had recalled Piero Taruffi. Taruffi was completely new to disc brakes and the first five-lap handicap race was just not enough time for him to get used to the feel of them, so he was well down in the results. In the main event, the fifteen-lap Glover Trophy, Taruffi had acclimatized and ran a much closer race, though he was still six seconds behind the BRM of Ken Wharton at the end. This result and the fact that the experimental Cooper 500cc car which Vandervell was supporting to try out a four-speed gearbox arrangement was uncompetitive, sent Vandervell away in a less than happy frame of mind. This was another example of perhaps too many projects that the ambitious industrialist had undertaken in which he knew where he wanted to go, but precious few other people did. In the end, however, this experiment would pay some dividends in the relationship with John Cooper.

Nearly two months went by before the next outing, the team's second overseas race, which was the Albi Grand Prix in France, where Ascari was being sent with a works 375 Ferrari to join the Thin Wall in fighting the BRMs. Farina appeared to drive, and the often temperamental Italian was not put in a better mood by a number of problems. The four-choke Weber carburettor set-up had had plenty of time to be sorted out, but it just wasn't working and the team reverted to the twin-choke arrangement. There were two heats and a final scheduled for this event, with one heat for F1 cars and one for F2 machines, and a final for all. Farina ran out of fuel in practice and did one of his characteristic *prima donna* shows for the spectators, and then had an oil pipe split in his heat which meant he was out of the final. He stormed off, having also been made unhap-

py by the lack of first-class hotel and eating arrangements! Vandervell's lack of familiarity and experience with foreign meetings was partially to blame as well, though this time the BRMs only won their heat and wore their tyres out in the final, so Rosier's Ferrari won. The BRMs had put on a good display and the meeting was noted as BRM's best performance so far.

If things had gone well at Albi for BRM, they were certainly different six weeks later when another substantial Formula Libre race was arranged as a support event for the British Grand Prix at Silverstone. While the Grand Prix itself was run to F2 rules, Ferrari entered a 2.5-litre car for the Libre race, and this was considered a foretaste of what was coming in the not too distant future. It was at this meeting that Tony Vandervell admitted that he 'had something up his sleeve' for the next season, and indeed the amount of racing items Vandervell Products were buying in around the country that would not suit a Ferrari had raised suspicions, though Vandervell officially denied it to the press. The author recently quizzed the late Keith Challen about his own attempts to get information from Vandervell. Challen was grudgingly respected by GA' but even he could not get any specific idea of what Vandervell was up to, and that was at a pretty advanced stage of development of the new car.

At Silverstone, Farina was making another appearance for Vandervell as well as driving the Ferrari in the Grand Prix. He drove a good race in the main event to come third behind Ascari's Ferrari and Fangio's Maserati, and in spite of the effort in that race, he stepped into the Thin Wall Special and proceeded to act as if he hadn't just driven in a Grand Prix, setting Silverstone's first 100mph (106km/h) lap, passing the BRMs and Hawthorn's Ferrari and disappearing into the distance. Hawthorn retired early and Vandervell had immense satisfaction in seeing Farina beat the BRMs of

Above *Piero Taruffi about to practise the fourth Thin Wall Special at Goodwood, Easter 1953.*

Below *Taruffi on the grid at Goodwood, Easter 1953.*

41

Above *Mike Hawthorn in the Thin Wall Special at Goodwood in September 1953.*

Fangio and Wharton, and beat them in some style.

Farina was adapting well to the disc brakes at Silverstone and again two weeks later at Charterhall in Scotland for another Formula Libre race, but though he set a new record in practice and led Wharton's BRM easily, the ignition system let the team down and he was forced to retire. Mike Hawthorn returned to the fold in late September for the fifth and last race of the season at Goodwood, where he was entered in two five-lap handicap races and a fifteen-lap Goodwood Trophy race, a major contrast to the fifty-lapper at Charterhall. Hawthorn had serious engine problems in practice, but the car was returned to Acton and repaired – to a degree anyway – and Hawthorn ran away with the first five-lap race, and then won the main race as the engine lapsed on to

eleven cylinders. The Vandervell mechanics, with Norman Burkinshaw in charge, had risen to the occasion and got the car to the line a winner, though it wasn't fit for the second five-lap sprint. Burkinshaw would find himself in this position many times over the next five years, and he became a key part of Vandervell's team of experienced and very hard-working mechanics.

Into 1954

By the time the 1954 racing season commenced, life at Vandervell's had changed enormously as vast effort had been put into the development of the Vanwall, or Vanwall Special as it was first known. In fact, it was never entirely clear why so much effort had been poured into the Ferrari as the new car required a great deal of the team's resources. At the time, it was easy to attribute this to the technical information being gained from racing the Ferrari, never mind being a means by which the crafty Vandervell could keep abreast of what was going on in Italy, and at Ferrari in particular. Denis Jenkinson (1975) theorized that the Ferrari was kept for two main reasons, one being as a means of testing new drivers, and secondly as a familiar test bed for new parts, particularly brakes. Today, of course, we would ask why there wasn't a test car just for these purposes, but at the time Vandervell was fanatical about secrecy. It was inherent in the man that he did not want anyone to know the details of what he was doing, but more importantly he was not about to risk the ridicule that had been heaped upon BRM as a result of the announcement that it had a world beater before the car could get off the start line. There also continued to be some pressure to keep the

Thin Wall Special in races against BRM, and there were clearly a few times where it was wheeled out for Peter Collins to have something else to drive, five times in 1954 to be exact. Peter Collins liked the Thin Wall, so Vandervell felt further justification in keeping it going for a relatively long period.

But we need to go back and look more closely at the drama that was unfolding behind the scenes, as a brand new Grand Prix car was being designed and constructed, while the racing world rarely suspected that Tony Vandervell was doing anything other than running an old Ferrari. Clearly the bulk of the Vanwall story in those days, like Hemingway's iceberg, was well hidden beneath the depths of Acton and Maidenhead!

5   The First Vanwall

As recently as May 2003, *Motor Sport* dubbed the Vanwall a 'radical GP car that sparked a new world order'. There is indeed much truth in that view, though it is a view that seems somewhat influenced by the passing of many years and by nostalgia for the days when 'radical' meant something other than a million-dollar electronic gimmick producing a thousandth of a second advantage. The simplified view of what Vandervell did was that he attached four 500cc motorcycle engines to a Rolls-Royce bottom end with a common crankshaft and called it a Grand Prix engine. In effect, that *is* what he did, but radical was not the term used to describe it in the early days! What was radical about Vanwall was the way Vandervell operated, using existing technology to spark creative leaps in race car design. Much of this approach was inherent in the way the man worked, but much of it was also the result of accidents along the way. Much of what Vandervell produced did not work and it took often radical means to make things work. Innovation occurred, but it seems dubious that Vandervell would have reacted positively if you called him 'radical'! Interestingly, the most radical element of a Grand Prix Vanwall came not from GAV himself, but from Colin Chapman and Frank Costin. However, it was Vandervell's personality that allowed these things to happen, and indeed he fostered them. A point even came towards the end of the story when Vandervell felt some of Chapman's work was 'behind the times'.

By 1951, Vandervell had created a thoroughly professional racing outfit, with the team being a self-supported organization at Acton, where Phil Wilson was responsible for mechanical work and Fred Fox for engineering, and the infrastructure was in place to sort out most of the problems that a serious racing team would encounter. Vandervell's vision of the future developed into far more than beating BRMs, though he was quite happy to do that. It extended to much larger foes which included Ferrari and all the Continental teams. The rapid pace of progress with Joe Craig at Norton helped to encourage this vision, as did the intensity of the team's learning about carburation in trying to cure problems on the Ferrari. Even the experiments with twelve Amal carbs had their value, and Vandervell was convinced of the potential of exploring new approaches to carburettors.

As the Vandervell name became more familiar through the team's racing efforts in 1952, there was even more interest in thin wall bearings in racing engines, and Vandervell was an early consultant to Lancia when Gianni Lancia was working on the D-50 in 1953. This interest brought with it sufficient funds to continue the ambitious developments for a Formula 1 car. While few details of the new car escaped from the racing department, those that did concerned a 2-litre F2 engine, but as 1952 progressed it was clear that 1954 would see the rules change yet again, so at an early stage Vandervell was able to see further into the future, and was already regarding the 2-litre engine being worked on by Norman Burkinshaw and Arthur Pratt as an interim measure.

Links with Cooper

During 1952, Vandervell's relationship with John Cooper strengthened, resulting in the purchase of a Cooper F3 chassis. This was in itself a failure, but it did convince Vandervell that Cooper was capable of building a chassis for the 2-litre engine. While the Cooper-Bristol was the first consideration, it was soon dropped in favour of a fresh design similar to the Cooper-Bristol, but able to take the 2-litre engine and eventually a 2.5-litre unit, as well as suspension, steering and transmission from the Ferrari. The closer that Cooper and Owen Maddock looked at the Thin Wall Ferrari, however, the closer the new chassis began to resemble a product of Modena. While the later Vanwall may well be seen as 'radical', the first attempt was essentially a Cooper–Norton–Ferrari–Rolls-Royce!   Vandervell's cleverness, however, turned it into a car in its own right, and his foresight had produced an engine that could be enlarged to 2.5 litres fairly easily.

Mike Lawrence saw Vandervell as perceiving John Cooper as a 'kindred spirit' and therefore he commissioned Cooper to design a chassis that would have to:

> accept Ferrari-copy suspension, hubs, steering and gearbox, since these were all known elements. Consequently, the car had double wishbone and transverse leaf front suspension and a de Dion rear, also with a transverse leaf, located by twin radius rods. As on the Thin Wall, Goodyear single-pad discs were fitted (in-board at the rear) and the four-speed gearbox, a copy of Ferrari's, was mounted in unit with the final drive. (Lawrence, 1998, p.253)

While we will come back to assess the contribution of Costin and Chapman to Vanwall, L.J.K. Setright, an avowed Chapman/Costin fan, was less than complimentary about the Vandervell-conceived, Cooper-designed and -built Vanwall chassis and body: 'This was the Vanwall, the crude, Cooper-framed Grand Prix sow's ear that Costin and Chapman were consulted about in the hope that it might be made into the silk purse of metaphor.' (Setright, 1976, p.62)

This is an interesting comment in view of the fact that Setright was a great admirer of the Ferrari 375, the chassis of which was being copied, and it appears that he didn't realize that this was what Cooper was copying! Though Setright made these comments with the luxury of hindsight, a very workmanlike process was underway at Cooper's Hollyfield Road factory, where Owen Maddock set to work constructing John Cooper's design for what would be known in the Cooper history as a T-30, a conventional ladder frame. The Thin Wall Special had been sent to Cooper's showroom and Maddock spent hours, if not days, pondering the model for his work, which was to be reduced in scale and incorporate numerous changes. While the body generally followed the lines of the Ferrari, a radiator intake was notable for its absence, and cooling was provided by an externally mounted Clayton-Still 'Wire Wound' tubing affair. (Lawrence, 1998)

This distinctly odd-looking arrangement had been arrived at as a result of the Amal carburettors overheating, and the external mounting took the heat away from the carbs. The Amals had been used as Vandervell had been long convinced of their potential. A great deal of debate had gone on through the latter part of 1952 about trying fuel injection on the car, with various systems considered, but as time went by Amals were used, essentially as an interim measure.

Progress Continues

As Maddock was completing his work in the early months of 1953, Norton Motors was in severe financial difficulty, and the company was bought out. While Vandervell was not involved officially, he maintained his close connection with the competition department. As 1953 advanced, so did work on the new car, to the point where Vandervell considered an entry for the Spanish Grand Prix at the end of the year, but this race was cancelled so the pressure was relaxed somewhat. In September, *Autosport* ran a story about the rumours of a 2.5-litre Grand Prix car with twin overhead cams being constructed by a British firm. The details were wrong, but by now news of the Vanwall was spreading, though this name was yet to be considered. Vandervell's interest in Mike Hawthorn as a driver for 1954 also helped to let the cat out of the bag.

Vandervell had a prolonged business trip to the USA at the end of 1953, and during this time much progress was made on the car. The engine was producing over 200bhp on the test-bench, and further work on a Bosch fuel-injection system was beginning to look more promising. In addition to the original 2-litre engine, Fred Fox was supervising the building of the bigger units of 2.3- and 2.5-litre capacity. A five main-bearing crankshaft had been developed to replace the original four main-bearing crank. It is pure speculation to say that Vandervell's absence helped the team to progress, but it is very likely to be true. While the genius was often productive in coming up with solutions to problems, he certainly also seemed to hinder other people from getting on with problem-solving themselves. Nevertheless, he inspired a true sense of commitment in the group of workers, who were now beginning to see something important coming out of their hard work. In early March, Vandervell was clearly pleased and excited when he wrote a note to Leo Kuzmicki: 'We have done what I always wanted to. Put four Nortons together. I can now tell you without a shadow of a doubt that it can be done. We pulled 235bhp at 7,500–7,600rpm, with straight exhaust pipes 29 inches long.' (Jenkinson and Posthumus, 1975, p.66)

Throughout early March 1954, there was intensive work on both the chassis and mechanical components. The Thin Wall Ferrari was now being regularly employed as a test bed, with several variations of fuel and oil tanks being built by Marston Excelsior, tried on the Ferrari and then adapted for use on the new car. The fuel tanks that eventually appeared on the car came from another company. It was an indication of Vandervell's dedication to relative secrecy that he would not let his industry suppliers (some of them close associates) see what they were making components for. Even Cooper only supplied the very basic tube chassis and did not see it as the mechanical parts were adapted and fitted. Some companies advised on these components, but Vandervell would often go to another firm to get them made. However, as March progressed, the fact of the car's existence was generally well known, if not any of the details, and as March came to an end, Vandervell let it be known, rather than announced, that he would have the 'Vanwall Special' ready for Easter.

'Bloody Red Cars'

It transpired that Vandervell had made an entry for two cars for the Easter Goodwood meeting in April, and had already engaged World Champion Alberto Ascari to debut the new Vanwall Special – described as a 1953/54 2-litre F2 car – as well as the Thin Wall Special. Gianni Lancia had originally agreed to this, but later felt that Ascari was needed to practise for the Mille Miglia. The BARC failed to notify the press that Ascari was not going to show up at Goodwood, nor was the Vanwall Special, so the fans were upset when they discovered that on race day. This brought serious criticisms of Ascari and Lancia in the press, which Vandervell attempted to mollify. This certainly did not help Vandervell's attitude to the press, but a more important aspect of this is that he acted to help Gianni Lancia and Alberto Ascari, and it certainly was not Vandervell who was intensely anti-foreigner at this period. The so-called dislike of the 'bloody red car' was as much a product of the press and a sentiment that had emanated from BRM's early days.

It is something of a moot point, but Denis Jenkinson reported on this episode, acknowledging that Vandervell had a good personal and business relationship with Gianni Lancia. While it may be true that Vandervell at times did not distinguish between the daily press and motoring journalists, it also seems true that Jenkinson distanced himself from many actions of the press. This, of course, is nothing new as today's media blithely report that problematic situations are caused or encouraged by 'the press' or 'the media', skipping over the fact of their own membership of that group. Even the reporting of this long-past event has a touch of 'spin' on it and the author acknowledges the speculative nature of these comments. Nevertheless, virtually every story on Vanwall and Vandervell for the last forty-plus years has made reference to those 'bloody red cars', in spite of the fact that there is little actual evidence that Vandervell regularly used that phrase, and some evidence that he never used it. There is no attempt here to change the view of Vandervell's 'rugged patriotism', and the fact that he was committed to a British victory in a British-made car, but he was also pragmatic, and knew the value of foreign markets, the skills of foreign drivers, and that Grand Prix racing was a world sport. One of the consequences of his reluctance to converse with the press is that he did not leave a legacy of other quotable quotes, and so this one has stuck.

It was probably just as well that the Goodwood entry did not materialize as the Vanwall Special had not been tested, and in fact it did not get its first test until it appeared at Odiham Aerodrome near Basingstoke in May 1954, only a short time before it was due to appear at the International Trophy at Silverstone.

While the car had been prepared, the Vandervell organization seemed to have been somewhat lax in respect of signing drivers for the season. Vandervell certainly had his eye on Mike Hawthorn but had not approached him. In one of Vandervell's many informal conversations with John Cooper, Cooper suggested that he might consider trying Alan Brown, who had reasonable experience and whom Vandervell already knew as it was he who had the job of driving the abortive Vandervell-run Cooper 500cc F3 car. John Cooper was perhaps reticent to make this suggestion to GAV, as he was always conscious of the difference in status, wealth and power between the two men, although he also felt that they somehow had a comfortable relationship with mutual self-respect. (Cooper, 1977)

Vandervell did ask Alan Brown to test the car, and to drive it in its first race, as the testing was considered successful. Alan Brown told the author how it came about:

I found Tony Vandervell a brilliant technician who was well aware of the current technical knowledge. He was an extremely receptive and very friendly person. It was indeed John Cooper who suggested that I should test the modified Norton engine. This engine was incredibly smooth and although the rev limit was slightly higher than a normal 'double-knocker', it did lack the gutsy torque of a production unit. Nevertheless, it had enormous promise which we quickly realized. Initially, we tested the car at Odiham on a circuit which we laid out on the airfield. Tony was personally involved in all aspects of the testing. We spent many hours at Odiham and if Tony was not there, David Yorke was always present. I cannot remember the names of the mechanics, but we formed a very friendly relationship. Testing was done over a period of weeks. It was at one of these sessions that Mike Hawthorn was also testing his Cooper-Bristol and I remember commenting to Eric Brandon that there was a future star – how right I was! I was very happy to be asked to drive the car at Silverstone. I had no contract and although weather conditions were far from perfect, we were convinced that the car had a future.

I could find no faults with the handling, considering the bad weather. Naturally, I was disappointed not to be asked to drive the car again, but Tony explained that he wanted a younger driver. I think it is worth mentioning that the team was 100% enthusiastic.

Alan Brown

Alan Brown was thirty-four years old when he drove the Vanwall Special. He had been one of the stars of the post-war 500cc F3 racing scene. He had worked as a sales representative for the trucking firm of Dennis Motors in Guildford, and, driving his Cooper, he established himself with an impressive win in the 1951 Luxembourg Grand Prix for F3 cars. He was fifth in the Swiss Grand Prix in a Cooper-Bristol in 1952, and competed in a total of eight Grand Prix races. He accompanied John Cooper over a period of years to international F3 and sports car races, and their adventures were not limited to the racetrack. He was one of many so-called 'journeyman' drivers of the period who attained a good degree of success, often in quite difficult cars, who were then overshadowed by the next generation of drivers, many of whom were pure professionals. Alan Brown, now eighty-four, lives in Malaga in Spain.

Above *Alan Brown got the Vanwall Special going quickly on its first outing.*

Denis Jenkinson (1975) said that the car had also been tested at Goodwood but Brown did not remember this, though he did recall the effort going into making the car look serious and professional.

The Vanwall Special Makes its Debut

When the Vanwall Special arrived at Silverstone on 15 May, for the BRDC Daily Express International Trophy, very little was known about it, and there was a view that it was another too-little, too-late effort, something that had been built for the F2 regulations that had now come to an end as this race was run to the new international 2.5-litre rules.

Above *Alan Brown debuts the Vanwall Special at Silverstone, May 1954, with the first version of the radiator.*

This car was known simply as the Vanwall Special, a prototype with no further chassis number. [Chassis numbers for the Thin Wall Ferraris and the Vanwall Special and Vanwalls in this book are taken from Sheldon and Rabagliati except where otherwise noted.] The press and the public would both be surprised by what Mike Lawrence referred to as 'the superbly made Vanwall,' as in his opinion a characteristic of all Vanwalls was that they had been beautifully put together. (Lawrence, 1998, p.253)

Ian Bamsey described the car as it first

appeared at Silverstone, recognizing that Vandervell's foresight meant that by departing from the supercharging route and developing a four-cylinder engine used in conjunction with the potent fuel brews of the day, he would have a competitive car with plenty of future development left in it. Of course, Ferrari was now going the four-cylinder route as well, and indeed both manufacturers had been watching each other over the last two years, with Vandervell more the watcher than the watched. Bamsey says:

> The new Vanwall chassis was clearly derived from the stable's green Ferraris. It featured a conventional tubular ladder frame, wishbone front suspension, de Dion rear with leaf springs both ends and a four-speed gearbox mounted in unit with the differential. All this was Ferrari practice and Maddock had been asked to incorporate Ferrari suspension, steering and transmission parts. The single-seater body was conventional and the most unusual aspects of the chassis were the Goodyear-designed disc brakes, as already seen on the Thinwall Special, and an arrangement of external gilled tubes which acted as the radiator. (Bamsey, 1990, p.14)

Setright (1968) further describes the chassis as having two robust tubular longerons to carry the unequal wishbones at the front, the de Dion suspension at the rear, and the leaf springs at both ends. Setright also comments on the engine as it appeared in its first 2-litre form as having been an unnecessary handicap that could be overcome by means of boring out the cylinders to 91mm, which would easily increase capacity by 10 per cent, which indeed happened very shortly after the first race. Several experiments were done in cooperation with Shell Mex & BP to find an appropriate methanol mixture for the engine, it having been realized many years previously in motorcycle racing that methanol/alcohol fuels burn much cooler than petrol, and this was especially significant to the Vanwall as the engine was essentially employing motorcycle principles. This knowledge did not particularly help the team to avoid numerous cooling problems, which were the team's recurring nightmare for some time.

The cylinder head as it finally appeared on the car was a single-piece casting in alloy, and it had been designed around the shape and dimensions of the Norton valve gear, port shape and combustion chamber. The liners were enclosed by a cast-alloy water jacket, and the liners were sandwiched between the crankcase and the head. Inlet and sodium-filled exhaust valves actually stuck out of the top of the head casting, each with the double hairpin spring, with the legs of the spring crossed over each other. Separate housings contained the camshafts, with the housing rather uniquely mounted on a sort of pedestal the length of the head. The gears in a separate housing located on the front of the engine drove the camshafts, which operated the valves through the tappets. Engine oil was forced to the cam boxes with a drain return to the sump, and an intricate arrangement of carefully machined and fitted tappets in the camshaft casing kept oil leakage to a minimum.

The June 1954 issue of *Motor Sport* carried three interesting pieces of news. One was the protests of a number of readers over the scandal of Ascari not showing up at Goodwood, a further one was the report of the Mille Miglia where Ascari had justified Lancia's decision to have him practice in Italy by winning the prestigious Italian event and the third was the report of the International Trophy race at Silverstone. In spite of a considerable build-up to the first appearance of a Vanwall Special in this race, the report briefly acknowledged Alan Brown's good attempt and the car's failure with a broken oil pipe, and that was all. Given the fact that the Vandervell vision was beginning to become reality, it must have crossed Vandervell's mind to ask what he needed to do for his cause to be acknowledged, though it is likely he would deny that.

In fact, the team had a very positive introduction to racing the new car. While the results hailed Gonzalez's triumph in the Ferrari, both in the International Trophy and the accompanying sports car race, Alan Brown had put on a good performance. With 90,000 fans in attendance, the organizers had bolstered the field with 2-litre F2 cars, of which the Connaught was the initial favourite, but Brown was a full three seconds quicker in the first practice, sharing fifth place with Reg Parnell in a 2.5-litre Ferrari. Four other full F1 cars – Gonzalez, Behra, Moss and Trintignant – were the only ones quicker than the 2-litre Vanwall Special. It has to be said that Brown was getting additional practice as he was also taking part in the seventeen-lap sports car race in a Cooper-Bristol and he won the 2-litre class, a race in which C. Chapman won the smallest class in a Lotus-MG. Of course, a number of other drivers were in more than one race, but Brown was on very good form, enjoying the smoothness of Vandervell's engine in practice.

The real sensation was in the second day's practice when heavy rain poured on to the circuit and Brown slid the green Vanwall Special round to fastest time of all, leaving Gonzalez behind, and demonstrating just how potent the smaller-engined car was by putting in on the front row for his heat alongside Moss, Behra and Gonzalez. It was an amazing debut for the car and the racing hadn't even started.

As the first fifteen-lap heat began on Saturday, the conditions were dreadful, but Gonzalez got the 2.5-litre Ferrari into the lead ahead of the 2-litre Connaught of Tony Rolt and the Vanwall Special of Brown. Though he was overwhelmed by the likes of Moss and Behra, Brown held sixth until he spun in a huge pool of standing water at Woodcote Corner, but he got going again, and because Rolt had also spun, Brown came home sixth and was the first

2-litre car. The second heat for the remaining cars ran in the dry, and as the field lined up for the thirty-five-lap final, Brown and Rolt were side by side on the fourth row. On a dry track, Gonzalez disappeared into the distance. Brown had moved from eighth to fifth by lap twelve, and looked to be heading for a 2-litre-class win in spite of one cylinder cutting out, but at the halfway point Brown saw the oil pressure gauge read zero, as an oil pipe had broken, and sadly he headed for the pits. Jenkinson (1975) reported Vandervell as being reasonably happy with this first result, and later reports indicate that some members of the team were nearly delirious, as they had done far better than they had expected. Press comment was limited but the Vanwall Special had arrived, and it was a serious, professional-looking entry on to the racing scene.

The 1954 Racing Scene Continues

Peter Collins entered the Vandervell camp on 29 May, when he was invited to drive the Thin Wall Special in the Aintree 200, another Formula Libre race which saw a lighter, shorter BRM Mk II. Author Chris Nixon (1991) argues that Vandervell had Collins in mind as a Vanwall driver as well as Mike Hawthorn, and the races in the Thin Wall Special were perhaps something of a try-out for Collins if that was the case. Nixon, like others, also mistakenly assumes that the Thin Wall Ferrari was the original car Vandervell bought in 1951.

The race was being run in the opposite direction to what was customary. It was an immensely wet day, but Collins rewarded Vandervell's decision to try him out with a brilliant pole-winning position in practice. He dominated both his heat and the final before water caused a serious misfire and the car had to pit on both occasions. *Motor Sport* (July 1954, p.370) reported that 'Tony Vandervell was billed by one newspaper as Tony Vanderbilt. He personally assisted in changing the

Thinwall Ferrari's many plugs after the car had become fluffy towards the end of Heat 1.'

Collins showed what a good wet weather driver he was and he found himself back in the car a week later for the BARC's Whitsun Meeting at Goodwood and again he was on pole, ahead of the two BRMs, which led initially before Collins displaced them and set fastest lap on his way to winning in this fifteen-lap event. Chris Nixon also reports that in response to newspaper comments about Collins not having done National Service, he stated in an interview that he was part of Tony Vandervell's effort to build a winning British Grand Prix car to beat the Italians. (Nixon, 1991, p.142) Collins had come under some criticism as a so-called draft-dodger, but not nearly as much as Mike Hawthorn had. Some elements of the daily press made it clear they didn't see motor racing as a patriotic activity in any shape or form.

After the International Trophy race in May, feverish activity was going on at the Vandervell headquarters, where the 2.3-litre engine was already up and running. The new five main-bearing crankcase was finished, as were new crankshafts with their internals so that the 2.5-litre unit was almost, but not quite, ready to race. However, Vandervell had planned his programme in evolving stages so that the car itself was fully set up to accommodate all three engines with very limited modifications. So when the second evolutionary development – the 2.3 or 2,236cc to be exact – was needed, the bore was increased to 91mm to achieve this as the programme continued to modify the crankshaft for the final version. The 2.3-litre engine spent many hours on the test-bench. Vandervell had hoped he would have a fuel-injection system ready for the British Grand Prix but ran out of time to achieve this, though Bosch was working on the design of a system to be ready before the season was over, and turned its attentions to matching this up to a 2.5-litre engine.

British Grand Prix at Silverstone

A field of thirty-one cars showed up for the British Grand Prix at Silverstone on 17 July, and as at the International Trophy, the crowd of nearly 100,000 was soaked by a deluge. The Mercedes-Benz team was making its first appearance in England since attending Donington in 1937, and for that reason alone thousands of fans flocked to the circuit. The Mercedes came with the all-enveloping slip-streamer bodies, which had been suitable at Reims but were much harder for Fangio and Karl Kling to drive at Silverstone. Nevertheless, Fangio broke Farina's lap record that had been set in the Thin Wall Special. Gonzalez and Hawthorn had their Ferraris on the front row with Fangio, along with Stirling Moss in the 250F Maserati, while Peter Collins had got the Vanwall Special on to the third row. An entry had been sent to and accepted by the organizers of the French Grand Prix at Reims on 4 June, but the 2.3-litre motor had not been completed by this time and Vandervell did not want to swerve from his plan by using the smallest engine again.

Motor Sport was now referring to the car as the 'Vanwall', and noted that the car had a strange cowling to cover the tube-affair radiator with which Brown had raced. This cowling was a simple alloy sheet ducting for better aerodynamics, and to concentrate the flow of cool air on to the tubing.

Peter Collins was again impressive, this time in the Vanwall Special for his first drive, and qualified eleventh on the third row, fastest of all the non-2.5-litre cars, and faster than several of the 'proper' F1 cars. He was running well up the field amongst the bigger cars until his seventeenth lap when a gasket failed. This was caused by a leak in a cylinder head joint, which caused concern amongst the team and suppliers of parts. The engineers at Wills who provided the head gasket were of the opinion that the head might be moving on the pressure

Peter Collins

Peter Collins was a dashing and friendly young man of twenty-two when he had his first drive for Tony Vandervell at Aintree. He was another of the many graduates of the 500cc F3 school of driving and his career ran parallel with that of Stirling Moss, who was his teammate in the HWM team in 1952. He had won a number of 500cc races from 1949 through 1951 in Coopers and the JBS, and scored several good placings for HWM, then drove for Aston Martin in a DB3 and DB3S in 1952 and 1953, winning the Goodwood Nine Hours in 1952. He had nine races for Vandervell, all in 1954, in both the Thin Wall Special and the Vanwall Special. He drove the BRM in 1955 in Formula Libre and Formula 1 races, as well as a Maserati 250F, and also drove for Aston Martin, coming second at Le Mans, before going to Ferrari in 1956 to drive the Lancia D-50 and the Lancia-Ferrari, taking his first Grand Prix victory in Belgium, and winning again at the French Grand Prix. All of his races in 1957 and 1958 were in Ferraris except for a drive in a Ferrari-Healey at Nassau in late 1957. He was killed at the Nürburgring in 1958 when his Ferrari 246 Dino crashed into the trees. He had been battling with Hawthorn's Ferrari and the Vanwall of Tony Brooks. He is widely remembered for his close and friendly relationship with Mike Hawthorn and for handing over his car to Juan Fangio in the 1956 Italian Grand Prix so that Fangio could take the title which Collins would himself have won.

Above *Peter Collins portrait, shown with Tony Brooks.*

rings and set about manufacturing a thinner gasket for future use. Their enthusiasm over the project was also being reflected by other suppliers who were keen to help Vandervell. Gonzalez had led Hawthorn home in the two Ferraris in the Grand Prix. It is interesting to note that Denis Jenkinson did a detailed profile of the Mercedes for *Motor Sport* in the August 1954 issue, but he had yet to get round to paying attention to the Vanwall Special and it doesn't seem possible from his writings to see why this was so, given his later serious interest in the car.

Vandervell sent an entry for the Swiss Grand Prix on 22 August, at Bremgarten, for what would turn out to be the last Swiss Grand Prix after the Le Mans disaster the following season, and Vandervell did actually attend this race to meet his colleagues and do some Vandervell bearing business, as so many teams were using his product by now. However, the entry had been turned down, evidently on the grounds that the car or the team was not significant enough, so Collins was sent off to a minor race the previous weekend at Snetterton with the Thin Wall Ferrari. Collins would not have been able to do the Swiss race anyway, so Alan Brown was the likely substitute. Chris Nixon wonders what Collins was up to that weekend because he wasn't racing anywhere! (Nixon,

1991, p.143) This was also seen as a way for the team to keep active, though with all the developments going on at Acton, they must have felt that they didn't need the favour. Collins drove another exceptional race from pole position in the forty-lap Formula Libre race which saw him lap Flockhart's BRM before half distance. The Goodyear brakes on the Thin Wall Special were excellent, while the Girlings on the BRM just didn't work and Flockhart went off the circuit several times.

Italian Grand Prix at Monza

The next race for the Vanwall Special was to be the Italian Grand Prix at Monza on 5 September, where the car was being entered by Vandervell Products Ltd rather than the customary G.A. Vandervell, and it had been hoped that the 2.5-litre engine would be ready for this important race. The 2,490cc unit was being tested at Maidenhead during August. At virtually the last minute a valve failure on the test bed was catastrophic and it meant the 2.3 would have to be used in Italy. The 2.5-litre engine now had a bore of 96 mm with a modified combustion chamber shape differing from the first two designs. To manage this, the valve angle had been reduced to an included

angle of 60 degrees. The original 2-litre motor had also self-destructed during the testing programme and that had been discarded. There was speculation but no confirmation of what went wrong in the testing. It apparently was not the hairpin spring arrangements, which to some people were suspect. These springs had a lower inertial weight than coil springs and provided good reliability, though the manner in which they were made seemed to make them possibly prone to breakage as they were subject to direct bending when made. According to Bamsey (1990), the engine operations were very efficient in spite of their somewhat old-fashioned appearance, with the camshafts running in plain bearings, being gear-driven off the nose of the crankshaft. The strange radiator/cowling arrangement had been replaced during August by a much better looking conventional set-up, though few people knew that the core of the new radiator was from a standard Morris Oxford, and was quite large but effective for the job in hand.

The *Motor Sport* report was effusive in its

Vanwall 1954–5 2-litre F2 and 2.5-litre F1

The first Vanwall ran once with the 2-litre engine, twice with 2.3★ and four times with a 2.5★★, all in 1954, and the 2.5 was used all through 1955 and 1956. The single 1954 chassis was used throughout 1954, and three more of these were built in 1955, and replaced in 1956 by the Chapman/Costin design.

Layout and chassis
Multi-tubular space frame chassis

Engine
Type	Norton top end, Rolls-Royce Type B-40 bottom end
Block material	Aluminium alloy crankcase
Head material	Aluminium alloy
Cylinders	In-line four
Cooling	Water, externally mounted radiator on first car only
Bore and stroke	86 × 86mm
Capacity	1998cc
Valves	Two per cylinder, exposed hairpin valve springs
Compression ratio	n/a
Carburetion	Four Amal carburettors
Max. power	200bhp
Max torque	n/a
Fuel capacity	25gal (114ltr)

Transmission
Gearbox	Four-speed Vandervell-adapted Ferrari
Clutch	Vandervell multi-plate
Final drive	In unit with the gearbox

Suspension and steering
Front	Unequal length double wishbones, transverse leaf-spring
Rear	de Dion, transverse leaf-spring, twin radius rods
Steering	Vandervell worm and wheel
Tyres	Front, Dunlop 5.50 × 16; rear, 7.00 × 16
Wheels	Borrani 16in wire wheels

Brakes
Type	Goodyear-Vandervell single front disc; rear single disc
Size	12in disc front, 11.75in disc rear

Dimensions
Track	
Front	4ft 5.75in (1,370mm)
Rear	4ft 3.75in (1,315mm)
Wheelbase	7ft 6.25in (2,300mm)
Overall length	13ft 9in (4,200mm)
Overall width	n/a
Overall height	n/a
Unladen weight	1,370lb (620kg)

Performance
Top speed	155mph (250km/h)
0–60 mph	n.a

★2.3 litre engine
Bore and stroke	91 × 86mm
Capacity	2236cc
Maximum power	235bhp

★★2.5 litre engine
Bore and stroke	96 × 86mm
Capacity	2490cc
Power	260bhp

The chassis layout and mechanicals remained the same for the 2-, 2.3- and first 2.5-litre cars praise of the Vandervell effort, and this appeared to be the first time the team was fully recognized for the professional and potentially competitive nature of its approach:

> Mr Vandervell deserved full marks for putting the car in the thick of the opposition, and though the four Amal G.P. carburettors were being somewhat bothersome, Collins was by no means outclassed by giving away nearly a quarter of a litre in this battle where every c.c. was going to count. Knowing the Italian climate and the conditions of running at Monza, the Vandervell *equipe* wisely fitted a normal radiator to the car as they had not had sufficient experience with the surface-type one to try it under such extreme conditions. A small point this, but at least it showed a healthy appreciation of the job in hand and augured well for the future of the Vandervell team, for we have seen too often the results of lack of thought before leaving the home base when going to a big Continental meeting. (*Motor Sport*, October 1954, p.577)

Lawrence (1998) says that it was in relation to solving the cooling problems that Frank Costin was first involved with the team, suggesting the relocation of the radiator and also a higher wraparound perspex windscreen which was used, and also designing shrouds for the front suspension that could not be made on time. None of the other writers mention Costin's work at this stage.

Collins qualified sixteenth, five seconds off Fangio's pole time, but he had impressed everyone by the way he was hurling the car around the circuit to compensate for the handicap of smaller displacement. Whereas the journals by now were dismissing the Gordini team, the Vanwall was seen as the real up-and-comer. The 2.3 engine was able to compete well with many of the others and was fastest of the non-2.5 engine cars, but Collins was more than making up for the deficit. This led to some questions about the handling, Jenkinson and Posthumus (1975) seeming to suggest problems, but the totally sideways Collins was making it handle differently than it had been asked to so far. The attention in the race was mainly on the fierce battle at the front between the Mercedes of Fangio, the Ferrari of Ascari

Left *Peter Collins managed seventh place at the Italian Grand Prix at Monza in September, 1954. (Ferret Fotographics)*

Above *Collins watches the opposition in practice with Tony Vandervell, 1954 Italian Grand Prix. (Ferret Fotographics)*

and Moss' Maserati. At twenty laps Moss was lapping Collins who had moved up five places from the start, but the Vanwall Special engine was running sweetly and Collins was not over-extending it. By three-quarters distance his consistent driving had brought him up to fifth. On lap sixty-three he had to pit, as the cock-pit was flooding with oil from a fracture on the oil pipe to the pressure gauge – it was repaired by flattening the pipe. He dropped back but regained places to finish seventh, as Fangio secured the 1954 World Championship.

The press celebrated the news that a team of 2.5-litre cars would appear the following year, not knowing that this engine would race much sooner than that. The engine had performed flawlessly, the new cooling system surpassing the team's hopes. Though the water

Above *Peter Collins at the Goodwood Chicane in the Thin Wall Ferrari, September 1954. He also drove the Vanwall Special, which he shared with Hawthorn. (Ferret Fotographics)*

pump was circulating the water at 2,500 gallons per hour at 6,000 rpm, no water was lost and the temperatures remained steady through the nearly three hours of Grand Prix racing. Though Collins' drive in the race was less spectacular than his practice, he did well to beat all the Maseratis, which must not have gone unnoticed in the team.

Goodwood Trophy

Progress on the 2.5-litre engine was being made according to schedule and it was decided to run it at a small end of the season meeting organized by the BARC at Goodwood. The team would bring both the Vanwall Special for Collins and the Thin Wall Ferrari, and would also give Mike Hawthorn a drive in the Vanwall Special in the Libre race. By this time, Norton had changed considerably and Leo Kuzmicki had moved to London to take up the position of research engineer for Vandervell Products and would work at both Acton and Maidenhead, while his colleague Joe Craig was moving in the direction of retirement after a long career in the motorcycle racing business. Vandervell was also pleased to have a chance to run both Collins and Hawthorn in his team at the same time, even though it was a relatively minor meeting.

Collins was in the Vanwall Special for the twenty-one lap Goodwood Trophy race, and the race was purely and simply a battle between Moss in the Maserati 250F and Collins who had the crowd on its feet by driving at the very edge of adhesion to try to keep Moss in sight. He didn't succeed, but he had the tail hanging out at St Mary's Corner and his performance got him on the cover of the November *Motor Sport* and the Vanwall Special received the recognition Vandervell felt it deserved. In the ten-lap Woodcote Trophy Formula Libre race, Collins ran away to a sixteen-second victory in the Thin Wall. Ken Wharton was second in the BRM, just ahead of a fierce struggle between Moss in the 250F and Hawthorn, who was enjoying himself immensely in the Vanwall Special. Rumours after this race had not only Collins and Hawthorn on the Vandervell payroll for 1955, but Stirling Moss as well!

Below *Collins in the Goodwood Trophy race where he was second. (Ferret Fotographics)*

Aintree

The team was immediately off again up north for the *Daily Telegraph*'s meeting at Aintree on 2 October. Moss won three of the races on that occasion, and one C.A.S. Brooks won his class in the saloon/sports car event in a Porsche. Tony Brooks distinguished himself in that race by standing on the brake instead of the clutch at the start and then had to drive through the field to win, something that Tony Vandervell noticed. Moss led the seventeen-lap Aintree Trophy race from the start, but was chased hard by Hawthorn in the Vanwall Special, who in turn was pursued by Harry Schell in a Maserati and by Behra and Mantovani. Schell got past by virtue of some hard driving, though Hawthorn re-passed him to take second in another fine show for the Vanwall Special, and it also seems that Harry Schell's determination didn't go unnoticed either. Hawthorn described the car as oversteering, which really handicapped him on the corners, and he also felt the revs rose too slowly, with the power only coming on at 4,500rpm. He felt he might

have overtaken Moss on the last lap if he hadn't grabbed third gear instead of second. (Hawthorn, 1958, p.126)

There was also a Formula Libre race of equal distance, which Collins led, but the engine was tired in the Thin Wall and retired after nine laps. Hawthorn again drove the Vanwall Special, this time having a big spin while chasing Sergio Mantovani and filling the oil cooler with dirt, which of course made the oil temperature rocket and the pressure disappear, so he too retired. This was not a disappointment to Vandervell, who felt he had a chance of securing the services of both British drivers for the following season. At both Goodwood and Aintree, the two drivers felt that the Vanwall Special's handling could be improved and they encouraged GAV to take this as seriously as he had the work on the engine. Hawthorn's experience of running in the wheel tracks of Moss and the 250F Maserati left him impressed with the forgiving nature of the Vanwall Special, and it was a valuable lesson for the team, as surely there was no better measure of a Grand Prix car's handling than the 250F driven by Moss. Vandervell recognized this and a few months later bought a 250F chassis for comparison purposes.

The Aintree race was notable for the fact that the Libre race cars were now showing their age, and though Collins had led, Moss was quicker. The BRM was well down, and though the BRMs would race for another year, the Thin Wall Special Ferrari was retired and did not race again. It had been the fastest racing car in Britain for some time, and had served Vandervell well as a mobile test bed for his F1 project.

Spanish Grand Prix at Pedralbes

The Spanish Grand Prix took place at Pedralbes on 26 October, and the front row of the grid had Ascari on pole in the new Lancia D-50, with Fangio alongside in the Mercedes W196, then Hawthorn, who had finally got Ferrari's 553 Squalo working well, and Harry Schell in his own Maserati 250F. But there was no Vanwall, as it was called on the entry list, though Vanwall Special was still written down the flanks. Valve spring breakages were plaguing the team, but the engine had been tested over many hours and the team was looking forward to seeing how the 2.5-litre engine could perform in a 'real' Grand Prix. Arthur Pratt was responsible for the testing work and had his hands full trying various types of steel for new springs as well as experimenting with numerous new brews of fuel from Shell Mex & BP. The search was on for an effective fuel which would have a cooling influence on the valves and be both potent and get good consumption figures. The valve head failures also led to new types and shapes being developed. Problems with the valves would be something the team would become very familiar with.

There was a great deal of anticipation as the car appeared for practice at this difficult street circuit, but Peter Collins was caught out. According to Nixon (1991, p.145), he was just going too quickly into a corner, had the Vanwall turn over and hit a tree with some considerable force, seriously damaging the back end. Within a few minutes, Stirling Moss got his feet in a mess on the pedals of his 250F (the throttle was in the centre) and went off in the same place, though with less damage. Hawthorn gave them both a hard time when Moss and the sheepish Collins returned to the pits, something he regretted as he did the same thing in the same place a few minutes later, denting the rear of the Ferrari. Both the Moss and Hawthorn cars could be repaired, but Collins had been fortunate not to be injured. Vandervell is thought to have referred to Collins as a 'silly young sod', but was philosophical about the incident. In retrospect, it is unthinkable in today's Grand Prix racing that a relatively minor accident would send the team home. But in the 1950s, there wasn't a

Above *Mike Hawthorn, also at Goodwood, in the Woodcote Cup race which Collins won, and Hawthorn was fourth. (Ferret Fotographics)*

spare car, nor did a spare chassis even exist, and there is no evidence that any thought had been given to building one. In spite of the time and resources going into car development, no one had thought of this expedient, and it just wasn't part of the scene at the time.

No lap time seems to have been recorded for Collins in practice, so it was difficult to compare him with the opposition. The fanfare accompanying the new Lancia D-50 with its impressive throaty exhaust note would probably have stolen the Vanwall Special's thunder anyway, and Ascari put in a stirring drive until the new Lancia faltered.

1954 had been a good year for the new 2.5-litre formula, with five manufacturers taking part, and some of the best drivers ever were all racing in the same category. The competition between Mercedes, Ferrari and Maserati had been close and hard, the newer drivers were improving and looking like future championship material, while the older drivers seemed to be getting better, with the possible exception of Gonzalez, who was badly affected by the death of his close friend Onofre Marimon. As the new year approached, it looked less and less likely that Gonzalez would continue as a force in Grand Prix racing.

Preparing for the 1955 Season

With even the daily papers now urging Tony Vandervell to sign Moss, Hawthorn and Collins for 1955, he took the team home to plan the new year. The Vanwall Special was stripped back at base, to find that the chassis was damaged beyond repair, as were the de Dion tube and assembly, as well as the wheels and several ancillary parts. Much of the body-work and undertray were wrecked, but, as was his custom, Vandervell sent the bill to his insurance agent, as he had insured both cars for every meeting throughout the season, the premium being less than £140 for both. Thus the Vanwall Special was scrapped as it was no longer GAV's intention to build another Ferrari copy. He did, however, buy a great deal of machine tools from Maserati, which was famed for its production of milling machines, and took the opportunity to buy a rolling chassis to have a closer look at the best handling of the contemporary Grand Prix cars. This was chassis 2513, which remained a rolling chassis for many years and is now on the historic motor racing scene.

While work proceeded on the building of two new chassis, presumably with the Maserati 250F now as the model rather than the bigger, older Ferrari as had happened the previous year, a supply of parts was designed and manufactured, much of it in-house. While the first thought was to use the original Ferrari copies, these were abandoned, though there is no absolute evidence that the Vandervell team used the 250F in the same, more or less direct copying manner as it had the Ferrari.

While the team went straight into preparations for the cars for 1955, Vandervell set about signing up his drivers, believing that he had the services of Collins pretty much guaranteed but getting Mike Hawthorn would be a harder task. This turned out not to be the case. Mike Hawthorn had done very well at Ferrari, but disliked living in Italy. It had been in Italy in

1952 that Hawthorn was first introduced to Ferrari, and Vandervell had facilitated that introduction and got him his first test drive. He had enjoyed driving the Thin Wall Special and liked Vandervell. At the end of 1954, when he was undergoing medical treatment for injuries and burns he had received at Syracuse, he felt he wanted an easier season and respite from the activity of Ferrari. Vandervell offered him a contract and a reasonable retainer, which was all the inducement he needed as he very much wanted to spend more time in England. The further offer of a sports car drive at Jaguar cemented Hawthorn's plan for 1955.

An interesting aside to Hawthorn's signing was that *Motor Sport* (January 1955) praised Tony Vandervell for putting the Thin Wall Special to one side once the Vanwall Special was due to be raced. This was not only inaccurate because the Thin Wall raced several more times in 1954, but it also indicated that the best racing journal of the time apparently had no idea what Vandervell had been using the Thin Wall for. This was not a fault of the magazine, because those were the days when journalists limited how much they pushed teams for information, but it does raise a question about just how much access Denis Jenkinson had to the team at the time, compared to what he was able to learn about them much later after they had stopped racing.

Signing up, or attempting to sign up, Peter Collins proved to be much more difficult, which came as a surprise to GAV. The reasons behind this remain unknown, as Collins never told anyone what his thoughts were when Vandervell made him an offer to drive. There was a long period, from November until almost the start of the 1955 season, when Collins was either out of touch, could not make up his mind, or was saying he was about to make a decision. A number of difficulties were put forward as to the reason for these delays, one being conflicting oil contracts. In January 1955, *Autosport* announced that Hawthorn

Mike Hawthorn

Mike Hawthorn was twenty-five years old when he signed to drive the Vanwall early in 1955. In spite of some ongoing health problems throughout his life, he developed a formidable reputation as a single-seater and sports car driver in the early 1950s. He started with a Riley sports car, having been encouraged by his father who had been a motorcycle racer. When a Cooper-Bristol was made available for Hawthorn to drive in 1952, he started to build a strong reputation with fourth places at the Dutch and Belgian Grand Prix events, and these and his introduction from Vandervell got him up the first rung of the Ferrari ladder. In 1953 he went to Ferrari full-time and made the reputation that sustained him for the rest of his career with a monumental battle with Juan Fangio at the French Grand Prix at Reims, a race which is often cited as the best 'duel' of all times. He developed a large and enthusiastic following,

though in more recent times he has also been seen as one of the many 'playboy' racers of the period, perhaps with a streak of arrogance. He was severely criticized for avoiding National Service, and was originally blamed for the Le Mans disaster of 1955.

Hawthorn decided to leave Ferrari after the death of his father and after being injured at the Syracuse Grand Prix. He went back to Ferrari in 1955 for a short spell after a poor period with Vanwall, went to BRM in 1956, and returned to Ferrari for 1957 and 1958, when he won the World Championship from Stirling Moss by the tiniest of margins, although that would not have happened had Phil Hill not waved him past at the Moroccan Grand Prix. The death of Peter Collins earlier in the 1958 season affected him greatly and he had decided to retire at the end of 1958. It is considered to be one of the great ironies of motorsport history that Hawthorn was killed in a road accident a very short time after he was crowned champion, albeit in a 'race' on public roads with the late Rob Walker.

Below *Mike Hawthorn.*

had signed for Vandervell, to drive what from now on would be known as the Vanwall. That announcement also included the statement that Collins would be in the team, because it had been widely assumed that this was the case. Oddly, there was also another item in that same issue which did not indicate what Collins had in mind for 1955. He was known as a very easy-going person, but Chris Nixon theorizes, quite rightly this author believes, that Peter Collins was less enamoured of the idea of being in the team with Hawthorn than anyone at the time thought, and as history has drawn a kind of special bond between these two drivers, the real motives were not questioned. Nixon argues that Collins may well have thought that he was in line for the number one driver slot in the Vanwall, but with Hawthorn there that would not be likely, as Mike was much more experienced. Even as late as March, the journals were saying Collins would be in a Vanwall at Pau, but by the time a Vanwall first raced in 1955, Collins had become a BRM driver. It is not clear whether Collins ever discussed this with Tony Vandervell. He certainly never drove for him again.

While GAV was attempting to sort out his drivers for 1955, he managed to get Peter Whitehead to agree to let David Yorke come to work as team manager for the Vandervell team, and he was apparently quite glad to switch his emphasis to Grand Prix racing as Whitehead was now mainly involved with sports cars. During this period Vandervell thought he might recruit Robert Manzon if Peter Collins couldn't make up his mind, but by the time he asked, Manzon had signed for Gordini.

Testing of the new car took place in early April, and when it appeared it was apparent that the final form of the chassis was more akin to the previous year's Cooper/Ferrari look-alike than had originally been intended. There is some evidence that more radical ideas for the

chassis were put aside in favour of concentrating on getting the engine right, and for Vandervell, this meant fuel injection. The chassis was modified to accept front coil springs in the suspension instead of the leaf springs. By this time, all suspension and steering parts were being made 'in-house' to avoid dependence on outside suppliers and to ensure quality. Setright's view was that the overheating problems and related cracking of the cylinder heads had been put in the past with the new radiator layout. (Setright, 1968, p.368)

Vandervell himself made visits to Bosch in Stuttgart to keep up with the progress on the all-important fuel injection. As he felt he now had the valve spring reliability problem solved, he was anxious to get everything he could from the engine. Early problems were encountered in obtaining the correct amount of fuel delivery, so Vandervell designed his own mechanical linkage between the throttle slides in the air intake and the fuel feed rack of the Bosch pump. (Jenkinson and Posthumus, 1975) This effort to get the injection system right meant that the team decided to pass up the early season races and concentrate on getting to Silverstone in May.

It seems that the first testing by Hawthorn at Odiham airfield used the 1954 carburettors, the injection being fitted slightly later. In a second session, Hawthorn found the injection not that impressive:

> I found the injection system was still producing a large flat spot – or rather a complete depressed area – between 4,000 and 5,500rpm and although there was plenty of power above 5,500, the car was obviously not in a condition to perform well on the Goodwood circuit, so it was withdrawn and efforts were concentrated on getting it ready for the Monaco Grand Prix on May 22. (Hawthorn, 1958, p.137)

Nye (1993, p.87) describes the injection system:

Vandervell's preferred fuel-injection induction system had been applied, the injection pressure pump being driven off the cam-drive and gears and mounting therefore on the front of the engine. The injector nozzles screwed into the underside of the inlet ports, directing their mixture spray onto the back of the inlet valves. Slide throttles and inlet bell mouths were provided by retained Amal carburettor bodies, stripped of their jets so that on full throttle, a wide open unobstructed path was provided. The four slides were opened by short cables, run over quadrant segments on a cross-shaft carried by the inlet cam-cover.

In spite of the effort of Bosch to perfect the system, several obstacles had to be overcome. One was the objection by Daimler-Benz to Bosch developing a system for its rival, but this was dealt with between businessmen as a trade-off for the continued supply of Vandervell bearings to Mercedes. The second, and more important issue, according to Setright anyway, was that the four-cylinder Vanwall engine was a much more difficult engine on which to employ fuel injection:

> The engine of the Mercedes-Benz W196 had eight cylinders and was therefore an eminently suitable, well-balanced and smooth-running unit. The same could not be said for the Vanwall's four-cylinder engine, for it could not be said of any in-line four, since the acceleration of the pistons descending from top dead centre is different from the other two climbing from bottom dead centre. The vibration inseparable from such an engine wrought havoc with high-pressure fuel lines, and was also responsible for a number of irritating derangements of the throttle linkages. However, even when all was running well, the car remained at a disadvantage because its capacity was 12 per cent less than that of its rivals, and it became clear that this was something that would have to be remedied as a matter of urgency. (Setright, 1968, p.369)

However correct Setright's view was in hindsight, it was an achievement that Vandervell was quite happy with at the time, having got the injection system ready for the first race, along with improved disc brakes, which Goodyear had developed with a view to making the rear brakes in-board to reduce the unsprung weight. The disc brakes had worked well from the outset, while numerous other teams were still struggling with them, and remained slightly suspicious of discs as well. Of course, the problems with the fuel systems and throttle linkage were to come, and when they did, Vandervell had to pull another 'cat out of the bag' to compensate for them. But as the 1955 season was about to start, the prospects looked good for the team. Whatever the criticisms of the four-cylinder engine, the Vanwall was producing some 285bhp at 7,400 rpm on methanol and some 308bhp with a nitro-methane additive, the best power of any of the mid-1950s teams with such an engine. (Ludvigsen, 2001, p.165)

The Vanwall's 1955 Season

In Flames at the International Trophy at Silverstone

As the BRDC International Trophy at Silverstone approached on 7 May, Vandervell signed the Smethwick driver Ken Wharton to pilot the second car. Vandervell knew Wharton, who had had a number of races in the BRM V-16 against the Thin Wall Ferraris and was a straightforward person with some flair as a driver. Vandervell also felt that enough progress had been made on the fuel injection to race some weeks before the Monaco Grand Prix, as Hawthorn had been able to do further testing at Silverstone.

Alberto Ascari had won the Valentine Grand Prix in Turin on 27 March 1955, and Jean Behra the Pau Grand Prix on 11 April, Ascari's

Ken Wharton

Wharton was thirty-nine years old when he drove for Tony Vandervell in 1955. He had been a regular BRM driver in the V-16, but his racing had started much earlier in an Austin Seven before the war. He was an accomplished rally driver, excelled at hill-climbs and had a long sports car career as well as taking part in a total of fifteen Grand Prix races. He established a garage business at Smethwick after the war, which propelled him into further competition and also provided a place for him to build his own cars. In the late 1940s he won the RAC Trials championship two years in a row, and also won the Tulip Rally three times in the early 1950s.

He won a hill-climb championship in 1951 with a Cooper-JAP 1100 and started driving the BRM in 1952, and also drove Cooper-Bristols, Frazer-Nash, ERA and did long-distance events for Jaguar. He was leading a sports car race in New Zealand in January 1957 in a Ferrari Monza when he crashed and was killed.

Below *Ken Wharton made his debut in the Vanwall at the International Trophy race at Silverstone, where he had a serious crash. (Ferret Fotographics)*

new Lancia D-50 looking like it would give the Mercedes some very tough competition. Behra won again at Bordeaux two weeks after Pau.

The International Trophy was something of a disaster for Vanwall. The cars appeared with the word Special absent, and were numbered one and two in the programme. There was considerable praise in the press for the British teams constructing cars to battle with the Continentals, commenting that the BRM copying Maserati and Vanwall doing the same with Ferrari was no bad thing. This represented something of a change of tune, but the papers were being extremely patriotic in praising the achievements of two Englishmen in winning the Mille Miglia (Moss and Jenkinson), although they did it in a Mercedes. The patriotism would however suffer something of a blow at Silverstone.

Hawthorn was in the new VW1 and Wharton in VW2. A number of the F1 drivers were, as usual, taking part in the sports car and saloon races, so they had plenty of practice in both atrocious and sunny conditions over the weekend. Hawthorn won the Touring Car Race in a Jaguar and Wharton was fourth in a Ford. Practice saw Hawthorn get the Vanwall on to the front row with Moss and Salvadori (Maseratis) and the amazing streamlined Connaught of Jack Fairman. Hawthorn and Salvadori had been equal quickest in practice. Hawthorn was pleased with the practice performance, but less so in the race:

> Our cars had gone well in practice and I found myself on the front row at the start, having tied with Salvadori for fastest lap in 1min 48sec With us were Moss and Fairman on the new streamlined Connaught. However, I was in trouble early in the race with oil sweeping back over my visor owing to a fault in the oil supply to the valve gear. This had worried me during the test driving and the gearbox had been checked for leakage. It was eventually found that the oil was dripping from the engine into the undertray, from where it drained back and got onto the drive shafts, which flung it forward into the wind and by this roundabout means sprayed it all over my face. I struggled on for a time, but had to give up. (Hawthorn, 1958, p.137)

This was on lap 15. Hawthorn was in a good fourth when he stopped, and Ken Wharton came into the pits and had a plug change and attention was given to the throttle linkage, then he went back out having lost ground, though he had been well up the grid. As a fierce fight took place between Salvadori and Peter Collins, who was driving the ORMA (Owen Racing Motor Association) Maserati 250F which the BRM team had bought while they worked to develop a new BRM, Wharton came back into the pits for a nineteen-minute stop. The throttle linkage was fouling

on the bonnet so a great deal of work was done on rearranging the layout, and a hole was cut in the bonnet to allow access. The team really wanted to give the car a chance to show its merit, though it had lost some eighteen laps, and this turned out to be an unfortunate decision. While *Motor Sport* contends that Wharton lost control, Jenkinson and Posthumus (1975) say he was forced off line at Copse Corner by another car. At the time, he was going as quickly as the leaders with the throttle working well, but his excursion saw him strike a marker board and this 'threw the car into the air, the broken de Dion tube ripping the under-shield and fuel tank, so that the car burst into flames. Wharton jumped out with considerable burns and a fractured wrist'. (*Motor Sport*, June 1955, p.338) Vandervell later denied that the de Dion tube had actually broken.

It seems unlikely that Tony Vandervell was paying much attention to the International 500cc race that followed, in which Stuart Lewis-Evans was on pole position and set a new lap record. Vandervell was looking after his injured driver and car. VW2 was seriously damaged in the fire, as the marshals decided to put out the fire in the grass before attending to the car.

Hawthorn's view was that Wharton had been trying to un-lap himself from Salvadori when he went off. Hawthorn also reported that Vandervell had gone to the corner and raved at the fire brigade. (Hawthorn, 1958, p.138) Roy Salvadori remembered the incident with Wharton well:

> Resigned to finishing I slowed a little and Peter Collins pulled further and further into the distance. I then noticed Wharton's Vanwall in my mirrors; he had lost a lot of time in the pits and was several laps behind, but was now lapping very fast, apparently trying to set a new lap record. We became involved in quite a dice, he tried to overtake me on braking for Copse, got on to the grass and in my mirrors I saw the Vanwall bounce off a

corner marker, slew across the grass and catch fire. I was fortunate not to have been involved. The Vanwall was almost completely destroyed, but, luckily, Ken escaped with fairly minor burns. (Salvadori and Pritchard, 1985, p.84)

Injury was compounded by insult when Peter Collins won that race in the BRM-owned Maserati, fuelled by BP, the company which supported Vanwall and for whom Collins said he could not drive as he was contracted to Esso and Castrol! There was some compensation from the insurance for the damage to Wharton's car.

The day after the International Trophy, the Gran Premio Napoli was run on the Posillippo circuit at Naples, and Ascari scored another win for the Lancia D-50, with Villoresi's similar car third behind Luigi Musso in a 250F. Posillippo is a twisty and spectacular street circuit on the outskirts of Naples and was a real test for the Italian cars, and the Lancia and Maserati were looking formidable as the early season progressed. All the major teams, however, would show up at Monaco in two weeks for the first serious Grand Prix of the year.

Monaco Grand Prix

Ken Wharton was clearly not going to recover in time for Monaco so his entry was scratched, and only VW1 was sent for Mike Hawthorn. He had done more testing at Silverstone after the International Trophy, but the flat spot was still there, though he had learned to keep the revs up and lapped very close to the circuit record. Hawthorn then had the engine blow up in the test session after recording these times, as a circlip to locate a gudgeon pin had been left off and the piston moved, twisting the head off the connecting rod. This meant that the engine had to be taken out of

Wharton's car and installed in VW1 and sent to Monaco without a spare.

The predictions for the Monaco Grand Prix, the first race run there since 1952, were that the battle would be between the Mercedes-Benz W196 and the Lancia D-50. This turned out to be accurate, though doesn't tell the story of the race at all. Mike Hawthorn missed the first practice as the cross-channel ferry had been delayed, and two Mercedes and two Lancias led the first session in the order Fangio, Ascari, Moss and Castellotti. Hawthorn was an early starter for the Friday practice, which began at 6 a.m., and the Vanwall was sounding crisp and going cleanly, something of a surprise as it would take all of Hawthorn's skills to keep the revs up at the tight little Monaco circuit. He found the steering lock too limited and he struggled to get round the Station Hairpin, and for once the brakes were not working as well as they had, Goodyear experimenting with a ventilated disc. These required heavy pedal pressure, but too much pressure locked the brakes and

Hawthorn frightened himself a couple of times. However, his best practice lap got him on to row four, twelfth fastest, though a long way from the leaders. There was a furious pace being set for the first twenty laps, and the two Mercedes moved away into a good lead, but Hawthorn's Vanwall had the throttle linkage break on lap twenty-three and he was out.

The linkage between the throttles and the injection pump, a complex arrangement to start with, broke when a ball joint came apart for no visible reason, though the team suspected some part of it was under excess stress, though they were unable to find the cause at the time, and clearly this linkage was proving to be, quite literally, a weak link in the fuel system.

Of course, Monaco was not famous for the Vanwall result, but for Alberto Ascari's plunge into the Mediterranean. Fangio had stopped

Below *Mike Hawthorn had his second unsuccessful 1955 outing at Monaco. (Ferret Fotographics)*

and Moss was on his way to winning when his Mercedes also ground to a halt at the pit. This put Ascari in a position where he only needed to finish lap 92 to go into the lead when he made a slight error at the approach to the harbour, and into the water he went. He would have been remembered for this event alone, but a few days later he was killed while testing Castellotti's Ferrari Monza 750S. The Ascari legend became history, as the ultra-superstitious Italian, who never would drive without his own helmet, asked to borrow Castellotti's, and off he went, to die within one or two laps for reasons never fully understood, though it is now believed a course worker may have run across the track and Ascari attempted to avoid him. At age thirty-seven, the same age at which his father had crashed to his death, one of the great drivers was gone. Mike Hawthorn had rated him as faster than Fangio at the time. The poor financial state of the Lancia company also meant that it was the end of the road for them, and their resources and cars were soon passed over to Enzo Ferrari.

Almost for the first time, Tony Vandervell was despondent and angry at the state of the results, as the things that had gone wrong were not serious but neither had they been sorted. Mike Hawthorn was also not one to keep his opinions to himself and was clearly having second thoughts about driving a British Grand Prix car. If the Monaco debacle was not bad enough, it got worse at Spa for the Belgian Grand Prix.

Belgian Grand Prix at Spa

On the first day of practice, Hawthorn, in an optimistic mood for he liked the long, daunting Spa circuit, was taken by surprise when he found himself getting drenched – and it wasn't raining. The header tank had split and the water was getting round the bulkhead into the cockpit, joined by an amount of leaking oil as well. On Friday, the gearbox selectors started to tighten up and Hawthorn felt there was a gearbox seizure imminent so he stopped. Work proceeded through the night so that the gearbox was in good condition for mid-afternoon final practice on Saturday. Then Vandervell showed what many would consider a major lapse in judgment. He decided to fire up the car in the centre of Spa and drive out to the circuit. To put this in some perspective, this was not all that extraordinary for cars were often driven to a circuit. But Spa is a long way from the circuit, and it is an uphill journey. VW1 had been fitted with high gear ratios for the long, high-speed track, and GAV hadn't gone far before he was bogged down in traffic and slipping the clutch in the high first gear. By the time he got to the circuit, the clutch was finished. Hawthorn only had to do a few laps to find that out, so essentially all the practice sessions had been problematic. Hawthorn didn't learn the truth until after he had stopped. He seems to have controlled his temper at the time, but there were many reports of 'dark murmurings' that evening, as the team repaired the damage, and Hawthorn avoided Vandervell. Vandervell for his part sheepishly remarked that 'it was his car', but he knew what he had done. Hawthorn later revealed that he spoke to Vittorio Jano that day and Jano said it would be possible for him to return to Ferrari, which was going to run the Lancias.

Chief mechanic Norman Burkinshaw was a loyal Vanwall team member, but he reported much later that Hawthorn was furious at the stupidity of GAV's action. Jenkinson and Posthumus (1975) say Hawthorn was 'rather displeased', but that was something of an understatement. Burkinshaw knew that if a mechanic had done this, they would have been heading for the door, and there even seems the possibility that some venom was aimed at the mechanics for not stopping Vandervell!

Castellotti had pressed both Lancia and Ferrari to be allowed to have a D-50 at Spa, even though Lancia had officially said it had stopped racing. He drove spectacularly well, though he had to retire. Though he was on the fourth row, Mike Hawthorn was a full fifteen seconds behind Fangio's pole time, and after nine laps of the 14km (8.7 miles) circuit, he was well back, with oil blowing out of the gearbox as a result of Vandervell's indiscretion. As Hawthorn stood on the side, he apparently pondered how good the Lancia D-50 was, and how well he could be driving it. While Fangio and Moss were first and second, Hawthorn went back to his hotel and later told team manager David Yorke in no uncertain terms what Vandervell could do with his car. He had also frightened himself driving the car so quickly on full fuel tanks, the front end getting light and making steering very difficult. As his vision failed under the flood of gearbox oil, and thinking the gearbox would seize, he knew he was having his last ride in a Vanwall. Vandervell did not object to Lancia's direct approach to take Hawthorn, and the deal was done the evening of the race.

Norman Burkinshaw had this to offer about Hawthorn's spell in the team:

> He joined us at a bad time. The car wasn't really race-worthy, we were still developing it and everything went wrong for Mike. He was quite mechanically minded, but he was a bit cheesed-off with the way things were going, so he didn't help us much. Once he got out of the car he just used to disappear – he liked the girls, did Mike! But the main thing was that he'd been driving for Ferrari before he joined us and was used to a fairly reliable motor, whereas we were still developing the car and going through a bad spell of breakages. Mike had won a number of races with Ferrari and he wanted a car that was going to win. (Nixon, 1991, p.110)

As Hawthorn left Spa, he headed for Le Mans where he was to drive and win for Jaguar, in a race that became the darkest day in motor racing history with over eighty people killed in the crash of Levegh's Mercedes, an accident for which Hawthorn was held responsible in many quarters for some time. Hawthorn returned to Ferrari for the next race, the Dutch Grand Prix on 19 June, where he was seventh in the Ferrari 625, not the Lancia that he thought he would drive. Before June was over, he would send Tony Vandervell a cheque for part of his retainer, and pointed out to Vandervell what he believed were the car's deficiencies. Vandervell responded with a reasonable defence, saying that the car had in fact set a record for 2.5-litre cars at Silverstone, but the end had come and the contract was cancelled.

When the daily newspapers said that Vanwall would not be at the Dutch Grand Prix due to a shortage of drivers, Vandervell was inundated with offers to take the wheel. He went through a period of substantial doubt about what he saw as a righteous action in forming an all-British Grand Prix team, but two drivers had let him down and a third was still in hospital. He made numerous contacts to see who might be available, casting about for Castellotti, Trintignant, Taruffi and Schell. The 'non-professional' applicants included many racing drivers with more or less experience, and many people who had never even driven a car!

Vandervell was by now busy attempting to find drivers, dealing with what became a long-standing problem of leaking rubber fuel tanks, and was also trying to discover a solution to the unreliable throttle linkage. The fuel tank issue was resolved by reverting to alloy tanks. Leo Kuzmicki was also tackling a redesign of the cylinder head to fit larger valves. The engines had encountered valve pick-up problems, with high running temperatures causing the head to distort and damage the valves. Relatively small cylinder heads meant that temperature was more critical than in so-called more traditional heads. A number of engine problems, including fuel pump breakages, were traced to a high-frequency vibration. Vandervell and

Bosch worked quite closely on this difficulty because it took some time to determine whether the vibration was coming from the injection system or elsewhere in the engine. It was during this very busy period before the British Grand Prix that Vandervell had also started casting around for someone to design an aerodynamic body for certain circuits, having taken notice of the Connaught streamliner at Silverstone at the International Trophy. This idea had merit, but as no one was located instantly, the idea was put aside, and GAV starting thinking maybe he would put the Vanwall engine in the Maserati 250F chassis that he had. When he realized the work involved in this diversification, he also shelved that notion, and got back to finding drivers for his existing car. Though it is difficult to confirm, this must also have been the time when he realized his own chassis left a lot to be desired, as it had not changed substantially from the Cooper/Ferrari copy of 1954.

Aintree

Ken Wharton had recovered sufficiently to be entered for the British Grand Prix at Aintree on 16 July, and Vandervell had also secured an agreement from Harry Schell to join the team, leaving the ranks of the privateers to join a proper works team. Schell was another of those drivers who Vandervell felt comfortable with. He was somewhat like Wharton – no great ace but a hard worker and an especially pleasant person. In fact, Vandervell thought Schell's playboy nature and good humour would be an antidote to the gloom which had set in during the early part of the season. He didn't realize just how good a choice Schell would turn out to be.

The Vanwall team arrived at Aintree with VW2, Wharton's rebuilt Silverstone car, for Harry Schell and the new VW3 for Wharton himself. A great deal of effort had gone into testing the engines in the week before the race

in order to insure reliability. It did not take long for the message to be clear that no one was going to touch the four Mercedes. Schell had the Vanwall ahead of the Ferraris in the first session, which came as a relief to the team. Behra managed to get his Maserati amongst the Mercedes in the second practice, and Schell was on fine form. His 2min 03.8sec put him behind only the German cars and the works 250Fs of Behra and Roberto Mieres. Two rows further back was Hawthorn in the Ferrari 625, while Wharton in the second Vanwall was three places behind Hawthorn. All this was something of a pick-up to Vandervell, who was pleased not only with his choice of new driver but with the fact that his car was beginning to look promising again.

His heart must have missed a beat at the fall of the flag when Schell made a mess of the start and stalled the engine, thus allowing the entire field to get away ahead of him. He then drove with complete abandon, absolutely loving the handling of the Vanwall, which he literally threw into every corner, passing Hawthorn and the other Ferrari drivers to Vandervell's joy. However, not only did Schell push the car, he pushed the throttle pedal off its mounting and had no throttle at all, which caused him to retire. In the meantime, Wharton had found he had perhaps returned to Grand Prix racing a bit earlier than he should have, and was taking it easy. He suffered a fractured oil pipe which was repaired, but at the pit stop Schell took over Wharton's car and went straight back to driving on the limit. The car ran beautifully and though he was well behind, he finished ninth, the only British car to do so. GAV, in his customary gruff manner, only had praise for the invincible Mercedes team, an effort he really aspired to, though it was Schell, rather than Vandervell, who had put some spark into the team that day. Moss became the first British driver to win the British Grand Prix in a race that lingers with some questions hanging over it. Did Fangio let Moss win that race? Moss

Harry Schell

Schell was almost the perfect stereotype of the playboy racing driver. He was thirty-four when he drove the Vanwall at the British Grand Prix and he was in his sixth season of Grand Prix racing. He had been born in Paris of American parents, and his father had been the patron of the Ecurie Bleue Team which raced Delahayes before the war. His father was killed in a road accident and his mother Lucy took over the team, entering René Dreyfus at Indianapolis before the war. After service for the US Army during the war, Schell started racing in 1949 with a Talbot saloon, and then a 500cc Cooper-JAP in 1950. He had a number of good results which saw him get an entry at Monaco in 1950, though he was in a first-lap accident. He drove Maserati 4CLs in the Swiss and French GPs in 1951, the same car in four Grand Prix events in 1952, and then seven races for the Gordini factory team in 1953. He entered his own Maserati A6GCM – the precursor to the 250F – in several 1954 races before buying a new 250F, and

he had occasional works drives for Ferrari and Maserati before joining Vanwall in 1955.

He returned to Maserati after the 1956 season with Tony Vandervell, and then went to BRM for 1958 and 1959, buying a rear-engine Cooper T51-Climax at the end of 1959, which he ran at the US GP in 1960, before joining the Yeoman Credit Cooper team. He was killed at Silverstone while practicing for the International Trophy. Through the years he had also had a very busy sports car career with many notable drives and crashes, especially in the Maserati 450S in South America. He never managed a Grand Prix win in fifty-six starts, though he was second in the BRM at Zandvoort in 1959.

Below *Harry Schell made his Vanwall debut at the British Grand Prix at Aintree in 1955, but broke his throttle pedal. (Ferret Fotographics)*

says he still doesn't know, and even if he does, he isn't likely to say now.

The fall-out from the Le Mans disaster meant that a number of races were cancelled, and some countries debated banning motor sport, and indeed Switzerland did. The September issue of *Motor Sport* carried an editorial suggesting that there were too many race meetings anyway, and perhaps a return to the pre-war pattern of a race every two or three weeks as had happened at Brooklands would be a good idea. The editor was also predicting that racing would soon return to Donington and that open road racing was about to be allowed in Britain! What the change of schedule meant for Vanwall was that Tony Vandervell decided to do some lesser meetings to keep the team active, and no doubt to ensure that the

Above *Schell in the pits at Crystal Palace, 1955, with mechanic Norman Burkinshaw, young journalist Mike Tee, David Yorke and Tony Vandervell. (National Motor Museum)*

linkage problems had been solved. Vandervell had at various times said that he was not going to do any more minor meetings, but equally often changed his mind on this, thus allowing the growing contingent of Vanwall fans more opportunities to see the cars.

Minor Meetings

The first of four relatively minor meetings that the team went to in 1955 was the BARC International Trophy Meeting at Crystal Palace, the main event taking place in two ten-lap heats and a fifteen-lap final, though the entry was hardly 'international'. Mike Hawthorn was there driving Stirling Moss' Maserati 250F, and won his heat from the 250Fs of Salvadori and Gould, with Fairman in a Connaught and C.A.S. Brooks in an F2 Connaught. Harry Schell in VW2 easily won the second heat from Paul Emery in his Emeryson-Alta and Jack Brabham in the 2.2-litre Cooper. Earlier in the year, Paul Emery had attempted to convince GAV that he should put the Vanwall engine into the Emeryson chassis, an offer Vandervell politely turned down. In the final it was a straight fight between Hawthorn and Schell, the Maserati pulling out a gap of 1.4sec and holding that to the end. The Vanwall had a trouble-free race and practice to everyone's relief.

Two weeks later, Vandervell had entered Schell (VW2) and Wharton (VW3) for the Redex Trophy F1 race at Snetterton, and Schell in the Formula Libre race at the same meeting. As the heat win at Crystal Palace did not count as a race win, a small portion of history was made at Snetterton when Schell took the very first race victory for a Vanwall. This was a very wet race day at the Norfolk circuit, but even so 40,000 fans turned out. In the Redex F1 race, Schell adopted his usual driving style and 'went for it', with Wharton a steadier and smoother second. The field had been joined by Rosier and Volonterio to represent the Continental drivers, but the Vanwalls were untouchable, Schell pulling away from his teammate who kept comfortably ahead of Moss. Stirling Moss must have wondered about what was going on with his own Maserati as Hawthorn had won with it two weeks before, but here he struggled to keep the Vanwalls in sight. He did, however, offer an explanation:

We entered the car for Lance Macklin, Mike Hawthorn, Bob Gerard and John Fitch to drive when I was committed elsewhere and I did not race it again until 13 August at Snetterton where the immense difference in character between my Mercedes and this traditional Italian oversteerer seemed really vivid. I was slower in practice than the Vanwalls of Wharton and Schell and on race day found myself in a huge dice with an Australian named Jack Brabham driving a centre-seat Bobtail Cooper with a rear-mounted 2-litre Bristol engine. He spun at the hairpin with four laps to go, and I finished third. A plug electrode had fallen into No. 1 cylinder and we had the axle ratio wrong. At least I managed to set fastest lap, despite the problems. (Moss and Nye, 1987, p.104)

Harry Schell looked like he was heading for another easy win in the Formula Libre race, and pulled away from the field until the jinx of the leaking fuel tanks struck again, forcing his retirement, which disappointed the team on a good day as so much effort had gone into making the fuel tanks work. The race meeting was also notable for the presence of other up-and-comers Cliff Allison in the 500cc F3 race and Alan Stacey in the sports car race, while on the same weekend in Sweden at Karlskoga, a certain R.K. Tyrrell was winning the 500cc F3 race in a Cooper.

Italian Grand Prix at Monza

There was now a month's break until the Italian Grand Prix at Monza. Four chassis had been built up for the 1955 season and three complete cars would be ready for Italy, Schell in his regular VW2, while Wharton was to drive the newer VW4. The team had improved its internal organization and planning, and this meant that a spare car was ready to go with the team for the first time, as well as complete and generous sets of spare parts. Effort had gone into standardizing the parts being manufactured so that the parts were interchangeable for all the cars, though Derek Wootton told the author that even then some bits which should not have been there got into the parts bins!

Sadly, the Italian race was not to represent

a major stride forward for the team, and certainly the banking at Monza was so rough that it found all the weaknesses in the two Vanwalls.

The cars appeared with tidier cockpit cowling, and the fairings for the suspension had been fitted. Vanwall was the only British team present for Mercedes' farewell race, the company having decided to retire after Le Mans. Mercedes made it clear that it wanted to win and three of the silver cars were on the front row. Schell was trying hard but was bouncing all over the banking, and some modifications were made to most cars' suspension to provide greater ground clearance. Schell was on the fifth row, well amongst the Ferraris and Maseratis, and only a shade slower than Collins, who was in a works 250F for the occasion. Mike Hawthorn was a further row back in the Ferrari 555 Super Squalo, while Wharton was in the middle of the seventh row.

Wharton did not even complete a lap as the fuel-injection pump mounting broke, the bracket having come adrift, and the pump fell off. Schell tore off in pursuit of the leading bunch of ten and for eight laps was the quick-est amongst the second group of cars, but he had been nine seconds slower than Fangio in practice and that was a huge gap. His fiery drive came to a sudden end when the de Dion tube in the rear suspension fractured, presumably as a result of the pounding it had taken in practice during Schell's heroic efforts to get a good time. The intention was to investigate the breakages back at base, but the question was raised as to whether the spare car should have been used or a new de Dion tube fitted after practice. Fangio and Taruffi had finished one–two for Mercedes and Castellotti had soldiered on into third in the Ferrari 555, also a serious handful on the banking at Monza.

International Gold Cup at Oulton Park

Three cars were entered for the International Gold Cup at Oulton Park on 24 September, as the 1955 season drew to a close. Schell was to be in his usual VW2 and Wharton in VW4, with the Irish driver Desmond Titterington in VW3. Wharton did not show up for Oulton Park as he had injured himself again in a

Left *Wharton drove well on the banked Monza circuit in 1955, but retired on lap one with a broken injection pump mounting. (Ferret Fotographics)*

Right *Harry Schell practises the Vanwall VW2 at Oulton Park, September 1955.*

multiple crash at the Tourist Trophy at Dundrod, so he begged off. Titterington was seen as his replacement but this was not the case, as Vandervell had entered three cars, and had been working hard to get Farina or Taruffi back into his team. When this was not possible, Titterington was available, though relatively little was expected of him in a Grand Prix car, as this was his F1 debut. He had had considerable sports car experience and would go on to become an important part of the Jaguar sports car team. He also drove for Connaught in F1 before retiring fairly suddenly at the end of 1956.

Oulton Park was, and still is, a fine road racing circuit and the entry of works Maseratis and the Lancia D-50s sent by the Scuderia Ferrari was highly welcome. There were eight Connaughts, the Vanwalls and three Coopers to keep up British interest, plus the debut of the new BRM P25 in the hands of Peter Collins. The BRM was a real departure from previous form, though its potential was not realized at this early stage. Schell did a determined job in qualifying VW2 fifth behind

Hawthorn, Moss, Musso and Castellotti. Hawthorn was finally in the Lancia D-50 and showing just what a mistake it had been not to put him in this car earlier, while Castellotti was also making the most of a return to the D-50. Desmond Titterington surprised not a few people when he qualified just behind Schell for the fifty-four-lap race. All the British runners now had disc brakes, though some of the Continentals had yet to change.

Moss took an early and surprising lead and started to open a gap, while Collins upset GAV by pushing the BRM in front of Schell. Titterington had by his own admission over revved the Vanwall to 8,000rpm, but it held together. Collins retired with no oil pressure on lap 10 in fourth spot, and at seventeen laps Schell was now fourth behind Moss, Musso and Hawthorn, who was driving well despite having tonsillitis, when the bolts on the driveshaft coupling on Schell's Vanwall broke. This had moved Titterington up to fifth behind Reg Parnell, which became fourth when he simply out-drove Parnell. When Musso retired with no gears, this then brought Titterington

up to a surprised third place, an impressive debut for the Irishman, as he had achieved it by merit as much as by luck. In one of the supporting races, C.A.S. Brooks won the standard saloon car 25-mile event.

1955 Draws to a Close

The 1955 racing season came to a reasonably positive conclusion for the Vandervell Products establishment at their last race meeting, again a relatively minor event at the Castle Combe circuit, an ex-WWII airfield circuit still in regular use today. Two cars were sent for Schell and it was essentially a testing outing for the team. Schell drove VW2 in the Avon Trophy F1 race and VW4 in the Empire News Trophy for Formula Libre cars. The entry looked promising for essentially a club meeting, but the two D-50s were withdrawn, including one for Hawthorn, and the BRM was also pulled out. Schell led from the outset of the 101-mile F1 race ahead of Gould's 250F and Collins ran well in the ORMA 250F until that blew up. C.A.S. Brooks won the 2-litre division in the F2 Connaught. In the Libre race, Flockhart led the opening lap in the V-16 BRM but Schell was soon past in VW4, going more or less at the same pace as he had in the F1 race. Les Leston was in Moss' 250F and Schell won from

Flockhart. The second place driver in the Up to 2-litre Sports Car race was about to have a significant impact on the Vanwall equipe, one Colin Chapman. Three weeks later, that now familiar C.A.S. Brooks caused a sensation by winning the Syracuse Grand Prix in Sicily in a works Connaught, and became the first British driver in a British car to win a Grand Prix. Nevertheless, it still didn't get the press to call him Tony until sometime later!

Leo Kuzmicki had been working on a number of engine developments throughout the season, and in September he revealed his substantial list of twenty points to be accomplished from October through December, and these included doing tests to determine whether carburettors would be more effective than fuel injection. Vandervell would not have it, and many of the twenty points came off the list. The main thrust of the winter work then became focused on redesign of camshafts, cylinder head design, the control and operation of the fuel injection and exhaust systems, and that in itself was an ambitious programme. (Jenkinson and Posthumus, 1975)

6   Enter Chapman and Costin

According to Mike Lawrence, who knew Frank Costin well, Costin's serious involvement with Vanwall particularly in relation to the chassis came about over some drinks on the eve of the Oulton Park race, 23 September 1955 to be precise. (Lawrence, 1998) The story according to Lawrence is that GAV asked Costin what he thought about the car, and his response was characteristically straight: 'wonderful engine, horrible chassis'. Vandervell asked him rather defensively if he thought he could do any better, to which Costin said he thought he could, but that Colin Chapman could do it even better. The argument goes on that Derek Wootton had been pushing for Chapman's involvement for sometime, so Vandervell invited Chapman to Acton, whereupon he looked disparagingly at the Cooper chassis and went away with a commission to design a new frame, and Costin to design a new body.

It was in pursuit of the answer to the question, did Costin bring Chapman or was it the other way round, that a number of tales unfolded. Derek Wootton, who we have mentioned earlier, was officially a driver for Vandervell, often driving the transporter in the mid 1950s. He carried out a number of other tasks, and was one of those men trusted by Vandervell. He gave his account of his involvement:

My early interest in cars centred round the Austin Seven and I joined the 750 Club in the days when it used to meet at 'The Red Cow' in Hammersmith. I was elected to the Committee, and got to know, amongst others, the people involved in the early success of the Lotus company. I helped Colin Chapman complete his Austin Seven special which he called the Lotus. Peter Ross was my passenger in mud plugging trials. Mike Costin was a fellow de Havilland apprentice with Peter and was a neighbour in Harrow. Through them I met his brother Frank Costin who designed the first streamlined body for the Lotus, the Mk VIII, which beat the Porsches at Silverstone in 1954.

By then I was working part-time for Peter Whitehead who was racing a Jaguar, having done an apprenticeship with Ray Martin who had been preparing the Cooper Norton 500 for Stirling Moss, and then built his prototype Kieft 500 which had been designed by Ray Martin, John 'Autocar' Cooper and Dean Delamont (of the RAC). David Yorke, who was Peter Whitehead's Racing Manager and friend, was approached by Tony Vandervell to join him as Racing Manager for the Vanwall Team, and David asked me if I would like to join the company too. I said that would be fine, and I would do any job he wanted. So I joined the Vanwall Team in 1955 as Transport Driver, Mechanic and Assistant to David Yorke. David knew that I knew Colin Chapman and Frank Costin, and noticed that I was making a lot of critical comments about the Vanwall design and suggesting that the Lotus cars seemed to have the solutions to these problems. He asked me if I would approach Colin to design a new chassis for the Vanwall, and Frank to design a new body.

This they did, and the new Vanwall used a space frame chassis and a rear suspension and wheels similar to the Lotus Mk IX sports racing car. With

Frank's new body it appeared at Silverstone in early 1956 and easily won in the hands of Stirling Moss. This was before Stirling was signed up as a regular Vanwall Team driver, and it was Harry Schell and Maurice Trintignant who were to drive the car at the Monaco Grand Prix in May. This tight circuit was well known to exaggerate any cockpit cooling problems, and Tony Vandervell insisted that I arrange for Frank Costin to come down to Monte Carlo to supervise any additional cooling improvements to his shiny new body-work.

Frank assured me that he would arrange everything and gave me his flight arrival time at nearby Nice airport. Unbeknown to me, Frank was prevented at the last moment from coming, and telephoned Peter Ross to go in his place, briefing him on the modifications that should be made if the drivers found the cockpit too hot. Peter was a lowly employee of British European Airways who could travel for next to nothing if there was an empty seat on departure, but had brought his bicycle with him to save the cost of the taxi fare. Mr Vandervell told me to take the enormous chauffeur-driven Cadillac to meet Frank, and to bring him immediately to the restaurant where the 'Old Man' would be found. I was very surprised to see not Frank, but Peter, get off the plane, and the chauffeur clearly did not appreciate having to load a bicycle into the back of his immaculate car.

Tony Vandervell was none too pleased at the substitution, and ordered Peter to be at the garage at six sharp the following morning before the first practice, ready immediately to supervise the cooling improvements. Peter set to work the next morning with the mechanics to create a slot at the base of the windscreen to allow cooling air to enter from a high pressure point, but without spoiling the beautiful lines of the body. Now we had to see if the modifications had worked, and in the practice session both drivers came in at once, their faces were cool, but their bodies were not. 'What are you going to do?' demanded Tony Vandervell of Peter, 'You are supposed to be an aerodynamic expert.' Peter, who had never claimed to

be anything of the sort, mumbled something about a NACA duct, but was immediately told to supervise the cutting of two huge holes in the sides of the body and rivet on a large air scoop. He protested in vain that Frank would not like it. 'Frank is not here – get on with it.' We did, and it has to be admitted that the Tony Vandervell ducts worked very well and solved the problem!

The other incident I remember well was later, after the Italian Grand Prix in 1957, which Tony Brooks won in a Vanwall, when Tony Vandervell noticed one of the Maseratis driven by Willy Mairesse had a much lower seating position as a result of a new five-speed gearbox/final drive unit they had designed and fitted. He decided he wanted to look at one to see if he could get any ideas for the Vanwall. We had an early 250F Maserati chassis and four-speed final drive unit back at the racing stable at Acton. So I was summoned to his hotel, the Excelsior Galia, probably the best hotel in Milan. Still wearing my mechanic's overalls I was directed to the bar where the Old Man was installed and giving out orders. 'I want you to drive to Modena and buy one of the new Maserati gearboxes,' he said. 'But they only have three of them altogether,' I protested. 'See what you can do,' he replied.

'Alright,' I said, 'I will go first thing tomorrow morning. They won't have got back from Monza before then.' 'You will go NOW,' he insisted, 'and be there before they arrive. There is no time to waste.' So I set off in the Fiat 1100 that we rented as a team runabout, and drove slowly through the night to Modena, arriving at the Maserati factory at six o'clock in the morning. It was closed. I waited. At quarter to eight a cyclist arrived at the gates and unlocked them. He asked me what I wanted, and I explained that I had come to see Omer Orsi (who ran the Maserati factory) to see about buying a Maserati gearbox. He turned out to be the Company Secretary, and invited me to wait outside Orsi's office. He eventually arrived at about nine o'clock and invited me into his office. I explained that I had come on behalf of Mr Vandervell to buy one of the five-speed gearboxes.

Above *Harry Schell in the French Grand Prix at Reims, 1956, having taken over Hawthorn's car (VW2/56).*

Right *Vanwall engine showing bracing from engine to chassis. (Brian Joscelyne)*

Unless otherwise stated, all the photographs in this colour section depict the 1957 Italian Grand Prix.

Right *Team Manager David Yorke at the team transporter, which now belongs to Tony Merrick. (Brian Joscelyne)*

Left *The complex fuel injection of the 2.5 Vanwall engine. (Brian Joscelyne)*

Below *Brooks's car gets new plugs before practice while Italian boys take a look. (Brian Joscelyne)*

Above *Moss's car gets a gearbox check. (Brian Joscelyne)*

Left *Moss's car is fuelled for practice. (Brian Joscelyne)*

Above *Roy North had his own garage but acted as mechanic at the races. (Brian Joscelyne)*

Right *Tony Vandervell himself presided over the fuelling at the pumps. (Brian Joscelyne)*

Below *Norman Burkinshaw, far right and back to camera, speaking to Roy Sayers, as they line up the cars to practise. (Brian Joscelyne)*

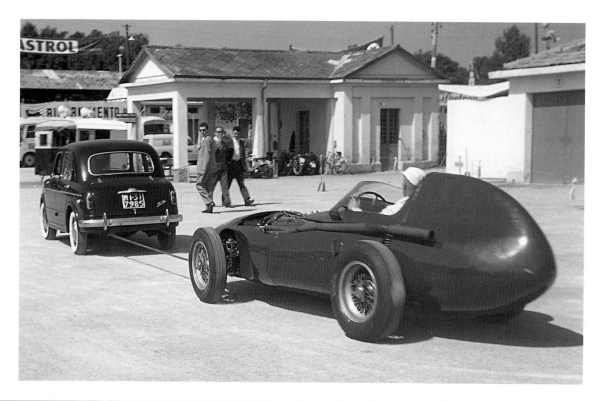

Above *A Vanwall gets a tow start from a Fiat 1100! (Brian Joscelyne)*

Left *Stirling Moss chats in the paddock. (Brian Joscelyne)*

Below *Close-up of Lewis-Evans's car. (Brian Joscelyne)*

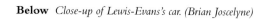

Above *Stuart Lewis-Evans looks on as his car (left) gets attention. (Brian Joscelyne)*

Right *Checking the fuel level. (Brian Joscelyne)*

Below *Just before practice at Monza. (Brian Joscelyne)*

Above *The engine in Tony Brooks's car before practice at Monza. (Brian Joscelyne)*

Right *Stuart Lewis-Evans, centre, and David Yorke, lower left. (Brian Joscelyne)*

Below *Moss confers with Brooks and mechanics as practice starts. (Brian Joscelyne)*

Above *Tony Brooks on his way to winning at Spa, 1958. (Ferret Fotographics)*

Below *Tony Brooks at Goodwood, 1960, with VW5. (Brian Joscelyne)*

Above *Tony Brooks at Goodwood, 2002.*

Left *This is the engine of the car constructed by Norman Burkinshaw and was raced at Silverstone by Tony Merrick.*

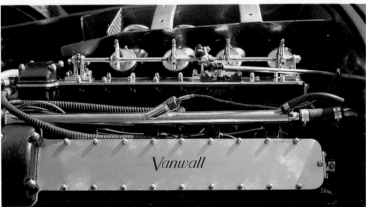

Below *Part of the fabulous Donington Collection of Vanwall history. (Donington Collection)*

'But we only have THREE!' he said. 'Yes,' I replied, 'Mr Vandervell appreciates that, but he only wants one of them.'

Orsi looked blank, relaxed back in his chair, not knowing what to say. At that moment the phone rang, Mr Vandervell was on the line, asking if his man was there. The receiver was handed to me, and I explained how far the conversation had reached. Orsi then asked how the gearbox would be paid for. This I relayed to the multi-millionaire Vandervell, who exploded: 'Doesn't he trust me?' I had to think quickly; if I relayed the message in those exact words the gearbox sale would be out of the window. So I said that Mr Vandervell had a very well respected position in the Motor Industry and felt that his credit was good, he had also bought Maserati milling machines in the past, and was interested to buy some more for the tool room at the bearing factory. This seemed to be well received, and Mr Vandervell rang off, after exhorting me to do my best. Orsi had a series of telephone conversations in Italian which I did not understand, and after some delay I was told to go to the workshop where I would be given the gearbox. Being slightly suspicious, I wanted to be sure it was really the new five-speed box, and fortunately caught sight of Bertocchi, the Maserati chief mechanic. I saw him at every race meeting and reckoned he would tell me the truth. Pointing at the gearbox and raising five fingers I asked him if it was what I had been told, and he confirmed it, so I loaded it into the back of the Fiat 1100 and set off back to Milan.

Arriving in the hotel, still in my racing overalls, I was again directed to the bar, where Mr Vandervell asked me how I had got on. 'Not too badly' I replied. He looked a bit glum and said 'Well, tell me what happened then.' 'I've got the gearbox in the back of the car.' His eyes almost popped out of his head. 'Don't leave it in the car, bring it in here!' So in came the gearbox, still covered in the grime and grease from the race at Monza, and was laid on the thick carpet of the Excelsior Galia bar for everybody to see. I tore myself away with the gearbox as soon as possible to have a good wash and an early night before driving the transporter back to the UK in the morning.'

Exploring the Costin/Chapman/Vanwall connection led to a number of interesting views about the central parties. Frank Costin's son Ron felt overall that his father's achievements across a wide range of motoring and aviation projects were not recognized for their value:

A lot of that was due to himself, because he was a purist. I was trained by him, and the view was always that if something wasn't right, we would change it and put it right, and the cost, the money, was irrelevant. The people we were involved with might consider the improvement we could make was not relevant. Frank would say, 'well, you are not interested then,' and this would lead to problems, but what was always at the bottom of Frank's work was doing it right. His philosophy, and he always said this to me, was 'If you can't make it quicker, better, faster, then don't bother.' He would measure the coefficient of friction of three different wing mirrors he was working on, and there might be something like .003 less drag on one than another, but that was the one he had to have. If something needed money spent on it, then he would. The problem is that you also have to consider how much development you are looking for, but the people whom he worked with knew he was a perfectionist. He rarely made money on his projects, especially when you think how much work he put into them. Many people were not interested in paying to do the very best job. One example of this was his use of canopies over the cockpit of racing cars. The first use of this had been on the Lotus 11 in 1955, and Moss drove it. They would put more and more layers of masking tape and build it up until Moss said that was enough. The same process later was done with the Vanwall, with holes being cut into the perspex at an exact angle so the air blew over the top of the driver, not into his face. That was the kind of detail Frank worked to. You had the trailing edge just right on the canopy to make sure there was no drag. He refined this work even further in the 1960s on the Protos F2 car, and he designed the canopies so they would pop off if there was an accident. Very few other manufacturers would go to the trouble to do this, though Vandervell would allow this kind of experiment. It was this approach that got Vandervell to listen to him, and because of that, Vandervell listened when Frank said he should bring Chapman in to do the chassis for 1956.

Mike Costin, the 'Cos' in Cosworth, was Frank Costin's brother, and of course Ron's uncle. When asked about the Costin/Chapman link to Vanwall, he spoke of how Chapman and Costin first got interested in aerodynamics:

Colin and I were going to build an 'aerodynamic' car, and Colin had a buck made for this, the Lotus Mk VIII, and it arrived and Colin asked me what I thought of it, and I said I didn't think much of it at all. It didn't look at all aerodynamic. I said 'Look, I'll send them up to my brother Frank for a look.' He was in charge of aerodynamic tests at De Havilland. He wasn't an aerodynamicist but he knew what aerodynamics was about, and when all the theoreticians and academics had all failed to sort projects out, the chief of aerodynamics, a chap called Clarkson who knew Frank contacted him. Frank was working at Airspeeds down on the South Coast and this had been taken over and was part of De Havilland. At the plant where they were making Vampires and Vampire trainers, they had an apron full of aircraft the RAF wouldn't accept because they couldn't meet the flight test requirements. Clarkson got hold of Frank and said, 'Could you go up and try to sort this out, because no one else can seem to do it, and there is a range of problems that needs somebody like you to sort them out.' That's how Frank got into specifically aerodynamic work, because before that he was in the design office and the stress office. So I sent the buck up to Frank and asked him what he thought of the aerodynamic shape of this car. Of course, he

had already asked me why I was 'buggering about with all these motor cars' because we were both in aviation. I was working with Colin while I was still employed at De Havilland. He took the model and went away with it and came back in two weeks, having cut it about, reshaped it with plasticine, and had the final body for the Mk VIII. Colin invited him down and they discussed it and Colin wanted him to do more to the shape, but Frank refused. He said anything else done to that shape would make it slower because it would detract from the drag coefficient. In the end, Colin gave in and Frank went back and did all the lofting, drawing out all the lines in full size. That was 1954, or even the end of 1953. That was how they started together, and that car was made totally by amateurs.

Peter Ross was very much involved in all that. In 1954 Frank did the Mk IX, that became the Mk X, and then the Eleven and Eleven Series II. So this was then about the time the Vanwall project came up, late 1955 and early 1956. I am not absolutely certain whether Frank brought Colin into the Vanwall project or whether it was the other way around. I think Vandervell talked to Chapman about the chassis and I presume Chapman got Vandervell to organize Frank to do the body. And as with all those kind of deals, 50 per cent would have dropped off as the deal passed Colin! I was aware that Colin was talking to Frank about Vanwall at the time. I know Derek Wootton was around at the time, and now that I think about it, I believe Derek had said that it was Frank that put in the word for Colin. Derek always knew everything that was going on, and the Old Man used to refer to him as his 'scruffy Wootty', something like that. Everyone knew that if Vandervell wanted something, Wootty could get it for him. As far as structure was concerned, Frank was just as good as, if not better than, Colin and he knew a vast amount about chassis. I learned about structures and how to think about structures from Frank, especially when we built a glider in 1948. If Frank had seen the old Vanwall chassis he would have said 'What a lot of crap that is'. Colin had a

lot to do with formally designing the chassis, but the type of body Frank came up with meant that you couldn't divorce the work on the two. I expect Frank may have done a lot more on the chassis than he got credit for. You know, Colin didn't always give credit for Frank's work, or other people's as well – you know, 'Plagiarize, let no one else's work evade your eyes,' to quote the Tom Lehrer song!'

Whatever the exact details of how the collaboration came about, it is clear that a significant move forward came from the work of Chapman and Costin. Setright sums up the 1956 project thus:

> The chassis had been completely revised by Chapman, who, acting as a consultant, devised a multi-tubular frame whose components were straight, varied in size according to the load they were bearing, and constituted in sum a proper space-frame. The engine, although another big four, was not *just* another: being based on the experience of those who had been involved in Norton, Rolls-Royce and Bosch developments, it embodied a number of uncommon features from which we may single out here the exposed valve stems, hairpin valve springs and high-pressure fuel injection. At least as significant was the body design, contrived by the aerodynamicist Costin

who had previously worked in association with Chapman; presenting an unusually smooth if bulbous body, it had none of the excrescent air scoops and louvres that were common wear among the racing cars of the time. Instead, properly shaped apertures were let into the body surface at points calculated to be subjected to relatively high air pressure, while conversely areas of low pressure were used as points of exit for waste air. (Setright, 1968, p.36)

On the driver front, a great deal had taken place from the end of the 1955 season into the beginning of 1956. When Vandervell had heard that Stirling Moss had not yet signed a contract for another team, he approached him, and

Below *Frank Costin shown working on an aerodynamic Sprite project. (Ron Costin)*

Moss agreed to try the Vanwall, driving VW2 at Oulton Park on 12 November 1955. Moss recounted his first Vanwall drive to the author:

> The first car I drove for them was the original Cooper-designed car and I must say that I thought the handling was quite good but I wasn't so impressed by the engine. It seemed to be flat below about 4,500 to 4,700rpm and at higher revs it had a misfire. I thought the car had potential, but overall it wasn't that good. I drove a BRM on the same day which was considerably quicker. Ten days later a test of all three British-made cars was arranged at Silverstone. I really wanted to drive a British car if it would be competitive. Cars came from Vanwall, BRM and Connaught and I drove them all on both Dunlop tyres and Pirellis. The BRM was quicker than the Connaught, but the Vanwall was quicker than both by several seconds, and wasn't much slower on full tanks, which we tried as well.

I was very impressed with the Vanwall and with the team. I later decided that I would join Maserati for 1956 but I told Mr Vandervell that I would drive for him when my other commitments allowed, and he was happy with that.

Denis Jenkinson was at that test day at Silverstone:

I was able to spend a memorable day at Silverstone when one of our top drivers had three different Formula 1 Grand Prix cars at his disposal to test and see if he would like to drive one of them in the 1956 World Championship series. Moss put a great deal of time and effort into trying to convince himself that one of Britain's Grand Prix cars was ready to help him become World Champion. In one day alone he drove nearly a full Grand Prix distance, jumping out of the Vanwall into the Connaught, out of the Connaught into the BRM, and then back into the Vanwall again. He drove on a dry track and on a wet track, he tried with full tanks and with empty tanks, he went to Oulton Park and risked his neck on wet leaves, and he went back to Silverstone in pouring rain. He really wanted to convince himself that he should drive a green car in 1956, but in the end he signed for Maserati for one year. (*Motor Sport*, January 1956, p.36)

Jenkinson himself seemed to give the edge to the Vanwall for its good handling, though he commented that it still had bits and pieces falling off. He saw the BRM as unreliable and the Connaught, sadly, at 'the bottom of the barrel'.

Moss had contact with Vandervell before he made his final decision and expressed some concern that Fangio might be in the Vanwall team, a rare indication that perhaps Moss, for all his respect for Fangio, really saw little hope for himself in the same team as the 'maestro'. However, he then decided to go to Maserati, and Vandervell redoubled his efforts to get Fangio or someone of his stature. Stuart

Lewis-Evans made an approach, but was told he would be considered. As 1956 dawned, GAV had more or less decided that he would not run a three-car team, and as it had begun to look like he would sign Harry Schell again and Maurice Trintignant, he had to tell Ken Wharton there was not going to be a drive for him, which was not easy as Wharton had been so easy to get on with.

Work Begins on the New Chassis

Following Colin Chapman's first visit to Acton to view the 1955 chassis and meet with Vandervell, during which he got the commission for the new design, he went away to work on it through January and February. Up to this point, the team had been doing modifications to the existing chassis, and when the decision was made to have a new one, they concentrated their efforts on the mechanical problems that still needed to be sorted. Further improvements were made to the brakes, and many of Kuzmicki's twenty points were then acted upon.

Chapman didn't entirely go away and do a chassis design and have it built. Rather, he conducted a number of what Mike Lawrence calls 'chassis design master classes'. (Lawrence, 2002) Jabby Crombac interviewed David Yorke not long before Yorke's death, and he had said there wasn't an engineer at Vandervell's with a clue about chassis design: 'Colin came to our racing shop in Acton and he literally scribbled a rough sketch for our engineers and explained to them the principles of the space frame. For the rear suspension he advised us on a Watts linkage location for the de Dion axle.' (Crombac, 2001, p.67) Lawrence described the Chapman approach in more detail:

Colin clearly knew his stuff and he held a master class in chassis design for the Vanwall team. He didn't design the new car so much as show Vanwall the

Above *The cockpit of the new car with ancillary gauges mounted on the water rail. (National Motor Museum)*

way it should go. It did not end there, because Peter Ross remembers drawing a jig for the Vanwall de Dion rear axle and visiting Vanwall with Colin to do other detail work. The de Dion rear axle layout of the 1956 Vanwall was pure Lotus Mk.9, which in turn derived from the Mk. 7 'Clairmonte'. Peter reckons that the Vanwall chassis was, at heart, very similar to the Clairmonte car. He thinks that it is even possible that Colin passed over copies of the drawings he made for the MK.7. Furthermore, Colin followed the design during its evolution and construction and he and Peter Ross worked with Vandervell's own team on it. Colin made the difference between Vanwall being another British no-hoper … and becoming a world-beater. Frank Costin made up the rest of the dif-

ference. His body for the car was probably the first true aerodynamic body in Grand Prix racing. (Lawrence, 2002, p.55)

During February, improvements on sodium-filled valves were high on the agenda of engine work. New fuel tanks from Italy of riveted aluminum were to be used, and arrangements were made with Porsche for the design and building of a Porsche-style synchromesh five-speed gearbox cluster to fit the existing external casing. The manufacture of parts was by Vandervell Products and Getrag in Germany. As March arrived, the chassis and body were nearly complete, and Jenkinson and Posthumus reflected on it with considerable enthusiasm:

Chapman's spaceframe was clearly lighter, stronger and finer than the old one, while the Costin-designed bodywork was sensational, breaking new ground on almost all points. George Gray's firm made the aluminium bodyshell to Frank Costin's drawings, and a smoother, sleeker racing car had yet to be seen. The long tapering nose had a very small aperture at the front, all the cooling air being carefully ducted through the radiator, and the bonnet had a sunken duct to take air into the fibreglass box in which the Amal carburettor body inlet trumpets were situated. The cockpit sides were extremely high and blended into a high bulbous tail that reached up to the top of the driver's head. A single piece wraparound perspex windscreen enclosed the cockpit, only the upper part of the driver's helmet protruding. Without the wheels and suspension units this new Vanwall would have made a good basis for an aeroplane! (Jenkinson and Posthumus, 1975, p.96)

In March, first testing of the unpainted, unfinished car took place at Goodwood, with GAV exercising his right to drive, in spite of the Spa episode, but he was merely going for a ride and there were no problems other than the issue of getting a large man of fifty-eight into and out of a Grand Prix car. Chapman and Costin were present, Frank Costin there mainly to confirm that the aerodynamic ideas worked in practice, testing out the airflow over the car in a number of places while Harry Schell did the driving.

Schell had a hand in convincing Maurice Trintignant to join him at Vanwall, and also convinced Vandervell that he should sign him. The view of both these drivers at the time was respectful, though they were seen as second-rank drivers. While this was factually true, it was somewhat unfair in that they both had some good results, and could be counted on for good performances, though they were clearly not up to the standard of Fangio, Farina or Moss. Thus it was a great boost to

Below *Tony Vandervell, in suit and tie, tested the 1956 car before it had been painted. (Ferret Fotographics)*

Vandervell and the team when it became clear that Moss would be able to drive the Vanwall at the International Trophy on 5 May. Vandervell had already announced to the team that the 1956 activities would be limited to Grand Prix events, with the exception of the International Trophy, with the result that the team only contested six events during the year. Vandervell was now focused more clearly on the task of running a winning Grand Prix team.

Vandervell did not consider sending entries to the early F1 races of 1956, the Argentine and Buenos Aires Grands Prix, nor the Gran Premio Di Siracusa, never mind the lesser British F1 races. The former were far too big an effort for the team at that stage, but more importantly the car was still under construc-

---

Maurice Trintignant

The French driver Maurice Trintignant was born in 1917 and had already had a long career when he signed for the 1956 season with the Vanwall team, when he was thirty-nine years old. He had a Grand Prix victory behind him, winning the 1955 Monaco race after Ascari took his plunge into the sea, and he still had another ahead of him for Rob Walker in 1958. He took part in a total of eighty-two Grand Prix races, as well as many lesser events and even more sports car races. He started his career before World War II, following three of his four brothers into racing. Louis was killed in a Bugatti in 1933, and in 1938 Maurice drove that same car to fifth at the Pau Grand Prix and won the Chimay GP des Frontières the following year. He had a very serious accident in the 1948 Swiss GP of 1948, in which three drivers were killed, but he recovered fully and drove for Gordini from 1950 to 1953 in some twenty races. He was a stalwart of the Ferrari team in 1954 and 1955, went to Ferrari again after leaving Vanwall for 1957, before becoming a regular Rob Walker pilot in Coopers from 1958 to 1960. He ran his own BRM in his final year in 1964, but by then was struggling to get results. In 2000 he showed up at the Monaco Historics and drove his old Cooper very quickly in the practice session. Trintignant was known by his nickname *Le Petoulet*, which is French for rat droppings, a name given to him in the 1930s when his Bugatti retired because there were the droppings of these rodents in his fuel tank. He also was the mayor of Vergèze for some years and had a reputation as a wine grower. His wine was named *Le Petoulet*.

tion, so the debut of the new car at Silverstone was early enough. When Maserati decided not to enter the International Trophy, Vandervell was eager to provide a car for Stirling Moss and Maurice Trintignant obliged by stepping aside for Moss.

The 1956 Season

The International Trophy at Silverstone

Moss was entered in VW2, which was not the chassis raced in 1955 with the same numbering but one of the brand new Chapman/Costin cars. Schell was in VW1, which was also brand new. The official factory records list these two cars as VW1/56 and VW2/56, which

makes it clear that a new numbering system was being used. Many of the mechanical and suspension parts from 1955 were used on the new cars, but the chassis were largely dissembled in the early part of the year in case they were going to be modified, but with the new design they were redundant and scrapped, though a recreation of the 1954 VW2 was built up from many original parts and can be found in the Donington Collection.

When the cars rolled out of the transporter for the first practice sessions, many people were dumbfounded by the change in the Vanwall. Although Schell had been testing, very few people had seen the cars. The cars weighed in at the minimum of 1,346lb (610kg) dry, some 100lb (45kg) lighter than the Lancia-Ferrari, which for Silverstone were still the original Lancia D-50s. Though both cars used

Right *Harry Schell retired at the 1956 International Trophy, which Moss won. (Ferret Fotographics)*

the Chapman chassis with small diameter tubes, VW2 had thinner gauge tubing than VW1. The front suspension was pretty much as 1955 with double wishbones and coil springs, but an anti-rollbar had been fitted. The rear set-up still included the de Dion with high-mounted transverse leaf spring and negative camber on the rear wheels. A transverse Watts linkage located the de Dion, which ran behind the gearbox and differential. The de Dion tube was located fore and aft by double radius rods at each end. Not only was the appearance impressive, but Schell dominated the first session and unofficially broke the outright circuit record, quicker than Fangio, Hawthorn and the rest; in the second practice Moss equalled this. The sight of two Vanwalls going round Silverstone quicker than the rest of the impressive entry was nothing less than stunning. The fans were ecstatic, though the cynics said the cars would never last. It needs to be added that *Motor Sport* (June 1956, p.359) suggested that the Vanwall body shape was functional but not aesthetic:

> It would be hard to design an uglier shape for a Grand Prix car. However, close inspection reveals some pretty sound reasoning, for the long tapering nose provides excellent initial penetration, the tiny

air entry is carefully calculated to pass the right amount of air to cool the radiator, the passage being beautifully ducted, with a ducted exit behind the radiator to an opening under the car; the header tank is in the scuttle.

There were other comments that later echoed Jenkinson's sentiments, though it appears that the critics may have taken the lead from him. Tony Brooks later told the author that he recalled this and felt it was just the usual response to something different. Subsequently, there are very few people who don't see the Vanwall as one of the most beautiful Grand Prix cars of all.

The Vanwalls were on the front row with the D-50 of Fangio and Mike Hawthorn's BRM P25, as the Englishman had decided to try another British team for 1956; fifth was Collins in the other D-50.

Moss was impressed with the new car, which he described thus:

> The new car was not only sensational-looking and really exquisitely well-built, but also 100lb lighter than the rival Lancia-Ferrari V-8s. Its fuel-injected engine could produce a great deal of power – up to 290bhp at 7,500rpm on alcohol by the end of '57 – but its long stroke and separated valve gear

Left *Moss on his way to his first Vanwall victory at the Silverstone International Trophy race, May 1956.*

made it very tall. Only 12 inches behind its front axle-centres the cambox already stood 26 inches above ground, and the driver's seat was perched above the bulky gearbox so its underside was $12\frac{1}{2}$ inches above the road surface. This meant that the driver's head when seated was 4 feet high so the Vanwall had an inherent frontal-area disadvantage, and the only way to minimize it was to adopt an exceptionally low-drag body – which Frank Costin had now provided. (Moss and Nye, 1987, p.157)

The British cars sparkled as the flag dropped, Hawthorn making the BRM surge past Fangio's Lancia D-50 with Moss in close attendance. Only the Connaught's prestige suffered dramatically as Parnell's car ground to an immediate halt. Then Schell's spirited driving saw him get past Moss; Hawthorn had the magneto drive break on lap 14, so he was out. Moss got into his stride and the lead by one-third distance, but Schell had come in for a plug change, retiring a lap later with a broken pipe in the fuel injection, so the cynics started to think they would be proved right. At the halfway point of thirty laps, Moss had over two minutes in hand, the Vanwall running smoothly and under no pressure. Both of the Ferrari entries had retired with broken clutches, and Moss set a new outright circuit record, as Archie Scott-Brown and Desmond Titterington followed him home in the two Connaughts as the others fell by the wayside.

The engine improvements Kuzmicki had suggested seemed to have worked well despite the 'Achilles heel' in the injection system. Work continued through this early season period to replace the front main bearings with larger ones, and before Silverstone there had been a visitation to Acton from the Royal Aircraft Establishment at Farnborough, its aerodynamicists' report suggesting several changes to Costin's detailed location of ducting on the body. After the Silverstone result, there was little inclination to heed this report.

Tony Vandervell's enthusiasm wasn't exactly overflowing, though he acknowledged to the team that this result had been what he was after. There wasn't vast praise for the team or the driver, but everyone knew he was happy. However, the Vanwall had flattered to deceive and it would only get one halfway decent result for the rest of the year. But Silverstone had impressed everyone and Moss was subjected to considerable questioning the following week as he returned to Maserati for the Monaco Grand Prix. Meanwhile, the contingent of drivers who did not go to Silverstone went to Naples instead, the D-50 drivers Castellotti and Musso hoping to pick up relatively easy spoils, which they failed to do when they both retired, and although they had been four and a half seconds quicker, the win went to the Gordini of Robert Manzon.

Over Before It Had Begun at Monaco

The full field, however, showed up at Monaco, and it seemed likely that the twisty street circuit would be a severe test for the Vanwall, a car which already looked like something for the high-speed venues. Trintignant was in Moss' Silverstone-winning VW2 and Schell again in VW1. Schell had a throttle link fall off in the first practice, but that was repaired and he was going very well, though the Vanwalls were over-geared for Monaco. Trintignant had complained about not being able to see over the screen and wanted it cut, something Frank Costin would not hear of, and so a cushion under the Frenchman's backside was the answer. This worked and he was second quickest to Collins in the second session. In the final practice, Schell was in clutch trouble and Maurice was still peeking over the screen. Louis Chiron had been lent an old Centro Sud 250F, but all he could do was spread engine parts and oil round the circuit, and so he didn't start. Schell was on row two and Trintignant row

Left *Start of the 1956
Monaco Grand Prix,
Schell (16) is behind
Castellotti (22).*

Below *Harry Schell
(16) at the Gasometer
Hairpin at Monaco,
1956, with Moss (28),
Castellotti (22) and
Fangio (20).*

three, both ahead of the sick-sounding BRMs and Collins as well.

Both Vanwall drivers had enough experience to know how the start of the Monaco Grand Prix can easily be the finish, but the Frenchman still flattened his nose against another car and started an overheating problem, which cracked a head and put him out on lap 13, and Schell became embroiled in a sensational battle. Even Fangio seemed to have lost his cool and spun at Ste Devote, so Musso and Schell had to swerve to avoid him. Schell hit the wall, deranging the suspension and the worm wheel and shaft in the steering box, so he had managed only two laps. Moss went on to win his second race in a week, ahead of Fangio, and must have felt that being in a different team to Fangio was the right decision for him.

In the two-week break between Monaco and the Belgian Grand Prix at Spa, new pistons were fitted in the engines. The first Hepworth and Grandage pistons had been replaced by those produced by High Duty Alloys, but collaboration between Vandervell and Daimler-Benz led to investigations undertaken by the German Mahle firm, which came up with a design for a stronger piston. Vandervell had modified these slightly, but it was an advance on the technology they had been employing, and was Vandervell's way of making good use of his industry and racing contacts. It also was an indication of just how well he got on with people like Rudolf Uhlenhaut of Daimler-Benz. This was also at a time when Vandervell was often rushing off to the USA and to Canada to look after the Company interests there.

Good Performance at Spa

With Schell and Trintignant in the same cars as at Monaco, and with some 280bhp now available from the engines, the team was in an anticipatory mood at Spa, and there was to be no repeat of GAV driving the car to

Above *Maurice Trintignant was forced to retire from the Belgian Grand Prix after eleven laps. (Ferret Fotographics)*

the circuit, nor indeed would anyone even mention it within his hearing.

Stirling Moss told the author that 'Harry Schell left my Maserati for dead on the straight at Spa, the straight-line speed was so impressive.' Despite the top speed, the handling of the Chapman/Costin package had not been sorted out for such high-speed circuits, and Schell was a significant ten seconds slower than Fangio's pole time and just over four seconds slower than Moss. He would blow past most of the cars on the long downhill Masta Straight, but had to give way at the corners. Interest in the Vanwalls had been somewhat pre-empted by a fascinating occurrence in Thursday practice. Moss had got tantalizingly close to the first ever 200km/h (124mph) lap time, and when Fangio went out at the end of the session to challenge Moss' time, he was on the circuit alone and nothing else got done as everyone watched and listened. When he slammed the Lancia D-50 past the pit wall 4min 9.8sec later, he had averaged 203.49km/h (126.24mph), a stunning performance.

On Friday, both Vanwalls struggled with the wrong fuel mixture, which saw the return of the high-end misfire that had been noted by Moss. This was cured for the final Saturday session, but was replaced by oil surge so both cars had to run on minimal oil. Schell and Trintignant went round in tandem and went quicker and quicker, until Schell broke off to pick up Francesco Godia whose Maserati had blown up, and he came back on the tail of the Vanwall. Towards the end of practice Schell was doing some very committed driving and

produced a time that was good enough for the third row, with Trintignant behind him. Hawthorn and Brooks didn't have a drive as BRM failed to appear, so Hawthorn offered his services to Maserati and Ferrari, accepting a drive at Maserati without telling Ferrari he had done so, causing considerable bad feeling. Ferrari put André Pilette in a D-50 painted in bright yellow Belgian colours and he was, sadly, hopeless, though guest-driving journalist Paul Frère was back, this time also in a D-50 and he was just slower than the second Vanwall.

At the start, on a damp track, Moss led the three Lancias of Fangio, Castellotti and Collins, with the two Vanwalls leading the rest. Trintignant passed Schell until the mixture problems in the fuel-injection system returned and he pitted and eventually retired at one-third distance. Harry Schell and Paul Frère had a superb and close duel for many laps until the

Below *Schell and Trintignant lead up Eau Rouge at the 1956 Belgian Grand Prix. Schell was fourth.*

Above *Harry Schell approaches La Source at Spa in one of his many spirited Vanwall drives. (Ferret Fotographics)*

Below *Schell exits La Source hairpin at Spa, 1956. (Ferret Fotographics)*

Right *Schell drove the Vanwall better than anyone expected. Spa, 1956. (Ferret Fotographics)*

Belgian began to pull out a gap on the Vanwall. There was drama on lap 10 when Moss lost the drive to the rear wheels and then a wheel itself going up Eau Rouge. He sprinted back to the pits to take over Perdisa's car, while Fangio led. As Moss caught Schell, the Vanwall driver did well to stay with Moss as the car was a real handful, especially over the bumpier parts of the track. Moss passed Schell at Malmedy, but it was going down the Masta Straight when he was shocked to see Schell going past so quickly he couldn't stay in the Vanwall's slipstream. Fangio's transmission broke on lap 24 and Collins led to the end from Frère, Moss in Perdisa's car and Harry Schell a lap down.

By now it appears that Vandervell had decided to run three cars during the 1956 season, and as the team was not doing any minor races, it was felt that this was achievable. However, arrangements for drivers remained somewhat problematic, as Trintignant still had

a contract to drive the rear-engine Bugatti if and when it should ever appear, and because contracts were much looser in those days, decisions were often made at the last moment. As it turned out, the Bugatti was going to be ready for Reims, and it looked like Vandervell was going to be able to get Farina to drive. Stirling Moss had recommended that Vandervell should consider the car's designer, Colin Chapman, who was a good driver, or Wolfgang von Trips. Vandervell was reluctant to use a German driver. Chapman was given a trial at Goodwood in June and Vandervell and David Yorke were impressed with his ability and speed, but then Farina injured himself in an Italian sports car race. BRM's unreliability meant it had withdrawn yet again and Mike Hawthorn was at Reims for the 12-Hour Race. Vandervell approached him and the bad feelings of the previous year seemed to have been forgotten – and perhaps Hawthorn realized how good the Vanwall had become.

Schell Scares Ferrari at Reims

If you go to Reims today, the bulk of the original circuit is still there, although a new dual carriageway has changed the layout of the straight down to Thillois Corner. But the ruins of the pits and the grandstands are still there, and on a summer evening, you can evoke some of the best motor races that ever took place. The results of the 1956 French Grand Prix would not, on the face of it, make it look like one of Vanwall's greatest, but it probably did as much for Vandervell's and the team's sense of determination to win than any other event.

On the first evening of practice, the Vanwalls of Schell (VW1) and Hawthorn (VW2) were absolutely dominant. Schell was suddenly

Below *French gendarmes guard the grid at the start of the 1956 French Grand Prix at Reims.*

threatening the 200km/h (124mph) lap time as Fangio had done at Spa. Then Hawthorn actually did an average of 203km/h (126mph) for his lap and the Ferrari team seemed worried for the first time. Collins was sent out in the D-50 and improved the time, so Schell borrowed VW3 from Chapman, who had been running-in a new engine, and improved his time, though not quite matching that of Collins. The significant fact was that the Ferrari was using far more revs than it should have and was well over the limit, while the Vanwall was running within its capacity.

In the second day's practice, disaster struck – or nearly struck. All three Vanwalls were on the circuit, and Hawthorn had just gone out and was driving around to warm up the car. Chapman was on his first flying lap and hadn't recorded an official lap time as his previous day's times had been credited to Schell. Chapman was flying down the straight towards the

tight Thillois Corner and locked a rear brake … or had rear brake failure … or locked a front brake (depending on whose account you listen to), and drove straight into the back of teammate Hawthorn, who was rudely shoved up the escape road towards Reims centre, while Chapman veered off and hit a small but stout concrete post. Both cars were damaged, and only Hawthorn's car could be repaired for the race. Chapman's F1 career was over. Later on, when a film of the crash was being shown and Hazel Chapman was present, she announced that her husband would not be driving other people's cars. There isn't even a lap time to say how quick he was, but Vandervell was relieved, as he didn't want to be responsible for killing the head of Lotus!

Below *Schell seen here in Hawthorn's car, which he took over in the French Grand Prix, with Castellotti ahead and Collins behind.*

When the time sheets came out for the final grid, Chapman had been credited with a time just slower than Schell's, 2min 29.8sec, but this time was discounted as a mistake, but it didn't matter as Chapman was out. A realistic time for him was probably 2min 36sec, which was quite respectable. Fangio, Castellotti and Collins lined the Lancia D-50s up ahead of Schell, the absent Chapman, Hawthorn, Behra and Moss. Trintignant's Bugatti was twenty seconds off the pace. In the race Schell broke second gear on lap 2, and dropped from fourth to ninth, then he over-revved the engine using first gear, and had to pit. He went out once more but the engine was finished, so he came back in again the following lap. Hawthorn was cruising in fourth, but on lap 10 he was called in and the car handed over to Schell. Hawthorn was not bothered by this: 'I made a good getaway and got into fourth place behind the Ferraris but I felt drowsy and was making little mistakes, which can lead to

Above *The Vanwall's speed at Reims amazed everyone; this is Schell at the end of the pit straight.*

Below *Schell's VW1 gets attention during practice for the French Grand Prix, 1956. (Ferret Fotographics)*

Above *Team Manager David Yorke drives the Vanwall through the Silverstone paddock, British Grand Prix, 1956. (Ferret Fotographics)*

big trouble on that very fast circuit. I had said that if Harry Schell's car ran into trouble I would hand over to him, and therefore when I saw him standing at the pit I pulled in and thankfully gave him my car.' (Hawthorn, 1958, p.186) Hawthorn's exhaustion from the 12-Hour Sports Car race gave Schell the chance to show what the Vanwall could do, in spite of the front end feeling a bit light in Hawthorn's estimation, and nor did he think much of the brakes which required too much pressure.

None of this bothered Schell, who worked his way back into sixth, and then a few laps later into fourth. The Ferrari pit thought he was a lap behind instead of just twenty-eight seconds. He moved up behind Collins before the Ferrari team realized that Schell and Vanwall were challenging for the lead, and they turned to pretty rough tactics to stop him from

passing. In spite of their efforts he got through and onto Fangio's tail, being markedly quicker on the straights. Schell set a new lap record, and then Fangio improved on it. Collins and Castellotti then slowed in front of Schell on the pit straight and Fangio escaped. On lap 37, a ball-joint in the throttle linkage to the injection pump broke and the car was forced in, but repairs lost him far too much time to make up. Then Fangio had a fuel pipe go and he stopped, while Collins and Castellotti fought it out, Fangio rejoining to come fourth behind his teammates and Jean Behra. Schell suffered further problems with a weak fuel mixture and slowed as the valves burned, finally coming in tenth, but having driven the race of his life and frightened Ferrari silly. The Vanwalls had been timed at nearly 290km/h (180mph) on the straight, fastest of all the Grand Prix cars by a long way, and the handling had seen an overall improvement. Vandervell did not have much to say to Schell after the race, but shortly afterwards sent him the cheque for all of his car's starting money, rather than his contractual 50 per cent.

Downcast at Silverstone

A new car was built up in the period between the French race and the British Grand Prix to be held at Silverstone on 14 June, as VW3 had been very badly damaged and didn't race again. As we shall see, the 1956 cars were then used as a basis for the 1957/58 cars in improved form.

Schell was entered in VW2, Trintignant in VW4, the new car, and VW1 was to be entrusted to the veteran Froilan Gonzalez, who was convinced by Vandervell and some very attractive start money to have another race at Silverstone where he had always gone so well. The results of the French race had not had a dramatic impact on the British race-going public, and very few of them knew just what a heroic job Harry Schell had done at Reims, so not a great deal was expected from the green cars. Schell went well in practice and was on

row two with Gonzalez very close on time. He complained about the feel of the front of the car, thinking that it wandered, and to some extent Trintignant agreed and was three rows back. Gonzalez repeated the old BRM trick of not getting off the line as a drive shaft broke. However, the new BRMs were in the lead with Hawthorn and Brooks. Schell pitted before long with a broken shock absorber, and then returned to the fray. Trintignant was having yet more trouble with fuel feed, something the team had just not been able to cure, though several people had advised them to use aircraft components for their fuel system. The BRMs faltered, Hawthorn retiring and then Tony Brooks having his terrible crash which he described earlier in this book. Schell finally stopped with a broken fuel pipe, near the end, a similar problem stopping Trintignant at lap 49 of the 101 laps. Fangio won from de Portago.

Right *Trintignant at Becketts Corner, 1956 British Grand Prix, where he retired with more fuel system problems. (Ferret Fotographics)*

Disappointment Continues at Monza

Careful investigation after the race at first seemed to indicate that fuel impurities had caused the problems for two of the cars, but after exhaustive work, it was discovered that silicate sealant had been used to seal the joints in the fuel tanks and this clogged the filters. Despite resolving some of these problems, Vandervell and the team were downcast after the Silverstone race, and it was decided not to go to the German Grand Prix, so the drivers were released for that race. As the next event would be the Italian Grand Prix at the beginning of September, attention was focused on sorting out the myriad minor problems that dogged the team. It was beginning to dawn on Vandervell that one thing he lacked was a driver who could improve the car, and that no matter how hard Schell and the others tried during a race, they had little to offer in development terms. Of course, testing was a relatively rare commodity in those days, especially in comparison to today or even to the way teams worked ten to twenty years ago.

Below *Fangio leads Schell and Collins at the 1956 Italian Grand Prix at Monza. (National Motor Museum)*

The tradition was to sort out problems at the factory, and hope they wouldn't appear at the races. Vandervell knew he would have to do something about this if the team was to progress.

Despite the work, the Italian Grand Prix was again disappointing. Vandervell had got Piero Taruffi back into the team to drive VW1, with Schell in VW2 and Trintignant in VW4. VW3 was brought along as a spare. The de Dion tubes had been remade with thicker gauge steel to prevent fractures imposed by the banking, and bump stops were altered in the rear suspension to allow more travel. Fangio, who had won the German race, was on pole. Taruffi had done well in practice to be on row two with his teammates two rows and five seconds further back. When the flag fell, the fiery Schell reappeared once more and he was suddenly in third, pushing the leaders hard. Then it was Moss and Schell, the Franco-American leading the Maserati on the straight and Moss going past on the banking, where Schell was forced to lift as the car flew all over the road.

Taruffi came in on lap 9 with oil covering him, and two laps later Schell was in the lead, which had the Italian crowd on its feet. Trintignant retired with a broken front spring mounting, and Taruffi went out and then came back in, covered in even more gearbox oil. A short rain shower allowed Moss to move away from the brave Schell, who came in for fuel on lap 28, where it was noticed that he too was coated in gearbox oil, and the valiant Vanwall ground to a halt a few laps later, having once again given Moss something serious to think about. Moss won a fine Grand Prix that again highlighted the serious potential of the Vanwall.

Piero Taruffi gave a detailed description of the race in his biography:

> There was much discussion about this circuit, which some people held to be dangerous owing to the strain on tyres and suspensions imposed by the steep banking. These overloads often amounted to double the weight of the vehicle and put a corresponding strain on every component – including the driver's spinal column, which, as in bob-sleighing, took some frightful jolts where the banking itself was uneven. For this reason I felt some uneasiness about taking the Vanwall on to the second banking at full throttle: the difficulty was not the driving itself – simply the thought that owing to an unforeseen stress some part of the transmission – or steering – might come adrift. Each time around I held my breath at the thought of what could happen. (Taruffi, 1964, p.159)

Denis Jenkinson (*Motor Sport*, November 1956) reviewed the 1956 season, expressing disappointment over the performances of the British teams and harking back to his early predictions that either Vanwall, BRM or Connaught would come to the fore during the year. He rather castigated the teams for not living up to his expectations, though in retrospect putting money on either BRM or Connaught would have been a long shot at best. He did rightly point out that the fuel system problems at Vanwall had persisted over a long period, and the lack of a solution to this difficulty did seem to be a chink in the Vanwall armour. 'Jenks' raised several valid points such as the use of second-rate materials, and lack of technical sophistication, but had backed away from his earlier argument that a team required a top-line driver, as Hawthorn hadn't accomplished much with BRM. In a later issue, 'Jenks', who had asked the British teams to explain their failures, acknowledged a full formal reply from Connaught (who held parts suppliers responsible for ten out of eleven failures), and an informal response from some Vanwall team members (who held themselves responsible), while nothing came back from BRM! Whether Vanwall responded with action to Jenkinson's pressure is unknown, but things would certainly change in the new year.

7   1957–1958: Road to the Championship

In the next issue of his magazine, Jenkinson was pleased to announce that Stirling Moss had tested the Vanwall and had signed to drive for 1957.

Tony Vandervell in fact had wasted no time after the Italian Grand Prix getting his plans together for 1957. Serious work on giving the hairpin valve springs more strength had been undertaken, and by the end of the year they had been substantially modified with a higher grade of chrome vanadium wire. Yet more work had gone into sorting the fuel mixture problems. Joe Craig was brought out of retirement to assist in this, and Leo Kuzmicki, who had left to work at Humber, was retained as a technical consultant on this project.

Moss and Brooks are Signed for Vanwall

But the big splash for the public was the signing of new drivers which took place at the end of October. Stirling Moss recounts how he came back to Vanwall:

> I remember when I won the International Trophy in 1956 that the Vanwall was not an easy car to drive, even though it was quick. The engine had improved from the first time I tested it, but the aerodynamic advantages were only really significant on fast circuits. The gearbox was not the best and the handling needed work, but I had been very proud to win that race in a British car, even though I went to Maserati for the rest of the 1956 season. I did several further test sessions at Silverstone, Goodwood and Oulton Park before deciding that I would drive for Vanwall in 1957. There were still some reliability problems, but I thought the car was bloody quick and the best 'green' car I would get a chance to win in. I made a number of suggestions for improvements, such as better dampers, larger rear brake discs, things like that. I don't know what Mr Vandervell made of it, but they made the changes. He was not the easiest man to get along with. He was rather gruff and blunt. He had run out of patience with the BRM efforts and let that be known, as he thought they were 'too theoretical'. I found him a very practical person and he just wanted to beat the Italians. He was almost obsessed with beating them at their own game. He was patriotic, even chauvinistic, but I did admire his determination.

Moss further reflected on making his decision to go to Vanwall in one of his early books, *A Turn at the Wheel*:

> I made this decision finally in October after trying out two cars at Oulton. It was quite a tiring day. I flew up there with David Yorke from London Airport and we reached Oulton Park at 11 a.m. I drove the first car for one hour and fifty minutes, when the suspension broke, and then did two and a half hours on the other car, when a fuel-injector pipe broke. We took off for home at 5 p.m., and at 6.40 p.m. I checked in at Lime Grove for rehearsals for a television show that went out from 8 to 8.30 p.m. I had earlier tested the Vanwall at Silverstone, where I found that the new coil-spring rear suspension made it much smoother, though giving

more oversteer. My best time was 1min 40.8 sec, which compared well with the existing lap record of 1min 43sec, held jointly by me (in the Vanwall) and Mike Hawthorn (BRM). I really felt that with the Vanwall I might achieve my ambition to win the World Championship on a British car. However, as the Vanwall's first outing was to be in Sicily in the Syracuse Grand Prix, Tony Vandervell released me to drive for Maserati in the Argentine 'Temporada'. (Moss, 1961, pp.19–20)

Tony Vandervell had discussed his plans for 1957 with Harry Schell and had let him know that he was going to have top-line drivers for the following year. Schell would have happily stayed as number two to Moss, and, on reflection, the rationale for eventually having Stuart Lewis-Evans is not that easy to understand. Schell had shown not only how good the Vanwall could be, but had driven well beyond what was expected of him. Indeed, though

Stirling Moss

Stirling Moss was clearly seen to be at his peak when he signed for Vanwall in late 1956 at the age of twenty-seven. He already had a solid reputation as a great driver with a number of Grand Prix wins behind him, and both the experts and the public saw him as on the same level as Juan Fangio, whom Moss himself always considered to be the greatest. As publicly modest as he was, he did however recognize his own skills. He had worked his way up to Grand Prix racing via all the lesser formulae until his first GP race at the Swiss Grand Prix in 1951 in an HWM-Alta. He drove a number of essentially 'British specials' in F1 until he had his own Maserati 250F in 1954, had a successful season at Mercedes-Benz in 1955 somewhat in Fangio's shadow, and drove for the Maserati factory in 1956 before his two full seasons with Vanwall where he had fifteen races. He drove primarily Coopers and Lotuses from 1959 until his career ended at Goodwood in 1962. The popular cliché is that Moss was the greatest racing driver to not win a World Championship, which is undoubtedly true, though not something he has ever particularly dwelt upon, and in fact acknowledges that he retained much of his popularity because of this. His achievements in sports cars as well as a dabble in rallying helped to make up the picture of a true all-rounder, and his victory at the Mille Miglia in 1955 with Denis Jenkinson is probably the most well-known single race in history. He became Britain's number one sports personality for many years, and returned to racing in the 1980s with an unsuccessful season in the British Touring Car Championship, and then became a very popular and successful driver in historic races, which he continues today.

Vandervell's choice of the second driver, Tony Brooks, is understandable in retrospect, at the time his major Grand Prix achievement had been his win in the Connaught at Syracuse in 1955. Brooks was clearly demonstrating his ability through 1955 and 1956, even with the problematic BRM, but Vandervell must have sensed something about Brooks that he could not see in Harry Schell.

Shortly after Moss signed, Vandervell sent David Yorke to see Brooks, who had been almost universally referred to as C.A.S.Brooks in the press and at race meetings, and Brooks was more than happy to go anywhere other than BRM!

Tony Brooks talked to the author about his career at Vanwall, recalling his first experiences with the team after David Yorke had come to see him:

> I remember being invited to a test at Oulton Park and I flogged round there for quite a few laps and they seemed to be happy with that. I hadn't done much up until then except for Syracuse because the BRM was a disaster. If you think I was critical of them about 1961, well 1956 was worse. Most of

Tony Brooks

Much written about Tony Brooks indicates he rose from total obscurity to fame after his superb winning drive at the 1955 Syracuse Grand Prix in a works Connaught. This had indeed been only his first drive in an F1 car and fourth foreign race but he had raced seriously since the early 1950s, with a Healey in 1952 and a Frazer Nash in 1953–54. His name, C.A.S.Brooks, figures frequently in the results of many races during that period, and he did a number of saloon as well as sports car races. He drove for Aston Martin in 1955 and had several very good results in an F2 Connaught against much more powerful cars. Brooks was a works BRM driver with Mike Hawthorn in 1956, which proved to be a dreadful season in which he had a major accident at Silverstone, before going to Vanwall for 1957–58, where he and Moss made considerable motor racing history. He then was in the Ferrari team for 1959, again showing himself to be one of the truly topline drivers. As a qualified dentist, he stayed in the UK for 1960 and drove the Cooper T51 for the Yeoman Credit team before having a second try at BRM, which was as unrewarding as the first. He ended his career with a good third place at Watkins Glen in 1961, by which time he was also developing a thriving garage business. Throughout the 1950s, Brooks was a stalwart of the Aston Martin sports car team in international races. He is a regular visitor to historic race events and does occasionally demonstrate cars from the past though he doesn't compete. He remains an immensely approachable person, somewhat self-effacing about his achievements, though widely recognized as one of the fastest and most stylish drivers of the period.

the races they withdrew from, including Monaco at the start of the year. Apart from Syracuse, I hadn't done that much, so I was happy to regard Oulton as a test. I suppose it was me trying the car, but essentially it was them trying me, and it went well so they signed me up. They were very careful and I never heard them compliment drivers – they might have been drivers would up the retaining fee! Tony Vandervell wasn't at that test, it was just David Yorke and the team, but he was pretty tight-lipped and I didn't get much out of him – this is how they were, but it went well and they were happy enough to invite me to join the team the team. My impression was that it was thoroughly professional, in contrast to BRM, which was higgledy-piggledy with too many cooks, not enough doers and no good recipes for success, that was for sure. I felt very comfortable with Vanwall and thought the car was very well screwed together, which was my first requirement, so I was happy to accept the invitation to join them for 1957. I remember that my impressions from the test were favourable, even though I had such limited experience of F1 cars. The Connaught was a beautiful road-holding car and the BRM was diabolical, so I didn't have much of a yardstick to judge the Vanwall by. It seemed alright to me, though I didn't like it as much as the Connaught in terms of road-holding, but clearly it had much more performance, a much more powerful engine, but it wasn't as easy to drive. It wasn't a car that would naturally go into a drift. You had to corner it more geometrically than a Connaught certainly, and when I read the odd track test of the Vanwall where people have said it handled so well, the drivers were many seconds off the pace which makes all the difference. It didn't drift at all like the 250F Maserati would

I thought the team would be good, and I had respect for Tony Vandervell because he had thrown his arms up in horror over the BRM efforts to build a 'committee-car'. I admired his guts in going off and doing his own thing, starting with the Ferrari and then building up to a situation where he had a car capable of winning Grand Prix

races. So I had considerable regard and a certain amount of awe for him because he was quite a commanding figure. I always got on well with Vandervell and found him a very fair person. I always felt comfortable with him. We didn't meet very often in the early days, and I didn't do a lot of the testing then. Stirling did what was done, and of course most of the sorting in that period was done on the practice days prior to each race. But the Vanwall team was professional and probably did more testing than other British teams at the time.

Because Stirling had won with the car early in 1956, I certainly knew it had the pace, and I saw that through that season, though it still hadn't demonstrated reliability. When I got to know the team I was confident they would eventually get the reliability as well as the speed. I wasn't so aware of how the car had been developed until later, and I didn't have a relationship with Frank Costin, though I am sure I met him fairly early on. I was impressed with the Vanwall, and the applied principles of aerodynamics were evident to me when I saw and drove the car. I was impressed that it had the most aerodynamically efficient body. I wasn't aware of things like down-force, but it was not generally appreciated at the time. I do remember that when the car first appeared, there were people who thought it was ugly, or at least not beautiful. But that was a bit like when the Ford Mondeo came out, everyone said 'What an ugly car, it will never sell.' I think people are uncomfortable with anything they are not familiar with, and perhaps subconsciously rather than consciously resist change, and that was obviously a significant change for a Grand Prix car to look so sleek. I think it is considered an attractive car now, though it wasn't too often at the time.

Construction of the 1957 Cars

Engine testing at the end of 1956 had shown up weaknesses in both pistons and the hairpin valve springs, so two firms were producing pistons for testing. The springs were now reluctantly admitted to be less than satisfactory by

Vandervell, but to change them would have meant a complete redesign of the cylinder heads so further 'endurance' testing was undertaken, though failures still occurred. Pat Black was responsible for this testing, which could mean each spring was compressed 1.5 million times before being used.

With Moss' inclusion in the team came a long list of suggested areas for development and improvement, especially dampers, so new ones were being designed by the company that had done them for Mercedes. David Yorke had been concerned during early testing that the nose was not allowing enough cooling, something Frank Costin took exception to, and later when the car went into a wind tunnel, which it had not when it was first built, it was determined that the opening was indeed larger than it needed to be. However, it had worked so no one tampered with it. There was considerable long-distance telephone communication in mid February, about the time that Brooks' signing was publicly announced. Pirelli suddenly said it would not be able to supply tyres anymore, but Vandervell leaned on the company very hard, which helped to delay the decision, so tyres of the right size and type would be supplied, but Vandervell commenced testing with Dunlop tyres; comparison tests at Goodwood showed the Dunlops to be superior in the wet and the Pirellis better in the dry.

As early spring approached, all four 1956 cars had been transformed into 'new' machines, with considerable minor changes to the chassis, so many that these were in effect new chassis. The 1956 VW1, VW2, VW3 and VW4 became the first 1957 cars, and a total of ten 1957 cars were to be constructed. Jenkinson said that no more than four cars were fully assembled at one time, though this can be challenged further into the season. The transverse leaf-spring suspension was replaced with coil springs wound round the telescopic shock absorbers, which were also completely different by the time the season started.

While a total of seven complete 1957 engines would exist at any given time, there were spare parts for many more, including forty cylinder heads, of which some produced more power than others for no apparent reason. Vandervell became fairly obsessed with this phenomenon and spent huge amounts of time trying to work out why this happened. He never did, but this was probably the period when he started spending more and more time in the workshop, sometimes all night. His second marriage had ended in 1952, and he clearly lost himself in work, which began to take a toll on him, as well as on the mechanics and engineers who were coerced by example into working unsocial hours, though they were paid for these.

Vanwall Kicks Off 1957 at Syracuse

The Suez Crisis resulted in a number of races being cancelled or postponed due to lack of petrol, so GAV decided to make an entry for the Syracuse Grand Prix on 7 April, so that the team could begin seriously to shake down the 'new' cars. Three cars were sent to Sicily, VW1 for Moss, VW3 for Brooks and a spare listed as VW5, though other reports had only the first four cars built up by this time. The third car was a spare, as no third driver had as yet been contracted. Those were the days when getting to the furthest corner of Sicily was still a major event, though the Vandervell Products' own plane flew some members of the party, including Colin Vandervell, Tony's son by his second marriage, who was himself to become a respectable racing driver, especially in Formula 3. Some of those back at base were occupied with the building of a new transporter, and Frank Costin was working on the design for a streamline body for the French Grand Prix.

Fangio had won the first two races of the season in Argentina but didn't go to Syracuse. Ken Wharton had sadly been killed in a race in New Zealand in January so was no longer part of the scene, nor was Eugenio Castellotti, the Ferrari stalwart who had scored a great solo win at the Mille Miglia in 1956. He had been killed while testing the latest Grand Prix Ferrari at Modena. The ex-Vanwall drivers Schell, Collins and Taruffi were all employed, in works Maserati, Lancia D-50 and Centro-Sud Maserati respectively, and Denis Jenkinson was predicting a Moss victory at Syracuse.

The first practice on the 5.5km (3.4 miles) Syracuse road circuit was uncharacteristically wet, though the times were quick and Moss and Brooks were in the top three. Brooks had a spin within sight of the pits but carried on, and the second session was dry. Gear ratios were changed in the cars and Moss went out in the spare and set a quick lap, followed by Brooks doing the same thing, though the timekeepers seemed to have missed this. Brooks was then quickest for a time, until Collins went faster, and then Moss borrowed Brooks' car and improved on Brooks' time by two-tenths. The two D-50s of Collins and Musso ended up quickest of all, from Moss, Brooks and Schell. The race conditions were hot, and so were the Vanwalls. It wasn't long before they were 1–2, and before twenty laps, Brooks had set a new lap record. On lap 34, Moss came into the pits with a split fuel-injection pipe, while he had a forty-second lead. The pipe was replaced, but Moss lost a lot of ground; as he went back, Brooks was coming in, a water pipe in the head having broken, shorting the plugs and causing a misfire and retirement. Moss was driving like a man possessed, though it has to be said a very relaxed man possessed, and he set an all-time lap record on his way back up to third behind Collins and Musso.

Brooks was not terribly disappointed with the result, as he had seen how competitive the car was:

> I was confident that Tony Vandervell would get these things right. He was there on the spot and he

knew what was happening. I think there was only one race I recall competing in where he wasn't present, and that was because he had some major business commitment in Canada. But all other times he was there at practice and the race, and this gave me a lot of confidence as no one was going to pull the wool over his eyes. He was a forceful guy who hadn't got to where he was without problems. I was certain he would investigate and deal with them. He got involved with the team's work, but I think he was only rarely a negative force in this respect. He didn't tolerate fools, as they say, and he was the driving force. It would not have been the same team without Tony Vandervell. It's a shame that David Yorke is no longer alive, because he would have a clear view on this. You could say that any dictator does tend to steamroller through certain ideas of his own, but I think he got the vast majority of things right. Mind you, I didn't know that he actually was in the factory at night working on the car, but the true test was whether he got the job done, and in 1958 he certainly did. At races the team took its leadership from David Yorke, and Vandervell didn't interfere with this although David wasn't a technical man.

The gearbox in Moss' car was showing signs of breaking at the end of the race, partly because it had been driven hard, but also because the engine was delivering nearly 300bhp. It later turned out not to be the gearbox, but the clutch cracking. It was now clear what Vanwall could do with the best drivers on board. As the main part of the 1957 season approached, Vandervell had the fundamental arsenal he required to fight for the driver's World Championship in 1957, and for the Constructor's title which would be instituted in 1958. The engines used in 1957 featured a 96mm × 86mm bore and stroke, giving a capacity of 2,490cc. On this 'final' type of V254 engine, according to Karl Ludvigsen:

> Skirts of the smooth-sided crankcase extended well below the crankshaft centreline. A deep

bottom-finned sump capped the bottom of the V254, keeping the BP oil well out of the crankshaft's way. Ample support was provided for the five 70mm main bearings and the forged EN19 steel crank, with its four integral counterweights. Rod journals were 51mm in diameter and gudgeon pins – retained by circlips – were 25mm. Although the bearings were of generous width, the engine's length was such that the crank webs could be a reassuring 20mm. thick. (Ludvigsen, 2001, p.115)

In other words, this was a very robust and strong engine. Ludvigsen describes the design and specifications of the pistons, around which much work had to be done later when the regulations changed and methanol was banned and petrol had to be used. Moss' trouble at Syracuse with the broken fuel-injection pipe finally forced the team into action to solve it, and while companies were offering different types of pipe, Fred Fox went to Palmer Tyre Co. to try their Palmer 'Silvoflex' high-pressure rubber flexible pipe which was able to withstand the pressure that the Bosch pump could deliver. Vandervell had now grasped that the engine vibrations were tearing the pump mountings loose, but it was too late to redesign the whole layout. Palmer worked on this as quickly as possible, but not before the Goodwood Easter meeting took place. Ludvigsen analyses the problem and its solution:

> Initially fuel piping to the nozzles was by metal tubing, and as the big four [cylinder engine] had marked vibration periods at 4,500 and 7,000rpm this resulted in resonance-induced cracks and failures at unwelcome moments. Finally, an aircraft-type flexible hose did the job ... Leo Kuzmicki finally perfected this (injection system with Amal carburettor bodies) ... but drivers still had to apply the throttle with care to avoid the over-rich condition on sharp acceleration that would cause engine power to fade, creating a 'flat-spot'. (Ludvigsen, 2001, p.117)

At its best with nitro-methane fuel, the engine produced 295bhp, but could be run with wider torque for tighter circuits with 275bhp; the power output was seriously reduced to 265bhp in 1958 when the cars ran on BP-108/135 petrol.

Glover Trophy at Goodwood

Two weeks after Syracuse, the Glover Trophy for F1 cars was run at Goodwood and VW3, Brooks Syracuse car, was sent for Moss, while VW7, another all-new chassis, was for Tony Brooks. It was perhaps predictable that while frantic work was going on, the fuel system caused problems yet again, with both cars having the control rod between the Amal carb body and the injection pump control breaking; similar to the fuel pipe breakage, this was now clearly related to the same engine vibrations. Moss and Brooks had easily dominated the field and were two seconds quicker than the third car, Archie Scott-Brown's Connaught, and this made the result even more frustrating. Tony Brooks set fastest lap, but Moss was out after thirteen of the thirty laps, and Brooks was listed as sixth but not classified having done twenty-seven laps. Brooks really should have won:

> I remember that we had a lot of accelerator linkage trouble, and it surprised me that they didn't solve it, but as I have said, I thought they would. It was a question of vibration, and a four-cylinder engine is always going to be rough, so it's possible that to an extent it was expected. The Vanwall was good around Goodwood and similar at most of the circuits as regards its handling characteristics. As I have said earlier, and often before, it wasn't an easy car to drive. It wasn't a natural drifting car. It could drift, but it didn't do it easily. You had to be pretty precise, and the other thing was that the gearbox was not good news. It was rather heavy and difficult compared for example with a Ferrari or Maserati box. I think, or rather I know, that

Above *Vandervell confers with Tony Brooks during practice for the Glover Trophy race at Goodwood, April 1957. (Ferret Fotographics)*

Right *The nattily dressed Colin Chapman talks to Vandervell about the cars at Goodwood, 1957. (Ferret Fotographics)*

Above *Moss at speed at Goodwood. This photo was sent to the author by spectator Peter Davidson some forty-six years after the event. (P. Davidson)*

Below *Tony Brooks in VW7 at Goodwood in the Glover Trophy, April 1957. (Graham White)*

Above *Side view of Brooks at Goodwood, April 1957. (Graham White)*

Stirling also found it was quite a difficult car to drive. We aren't trying to pat ourselves on the back, but Stirling will tell you the same thing, and if you asked him to compare it with a 250F Maserati, he would eulogize about the Maserati. Part of it was that if the Vanwall's back end broke loose, it really broke loose. It wasn't gradual. It was a Colin Chapman feature, and I believe his Lotus cars were much the same, although I didn't drive them. It was a typical Chapman design and it didn't really want to be thrown around. That was true at Goodwood and at all the circuits, except for the disaster at the Nürburgring in 1957, when it bounced the drivers around and was unrecnisable as the same car.

Fortunately Moss had made a number of useful suggestions after the Syracuse race that were being taken seriously for the upcoming Monaco Grand Prix, which was long enough away so that some of these could be implemented. As Ludvigsen described it, the engine was modified to provide better torque at low speed, and this was useful as the steering lock had been increased, all with the intention of getting the power down earlier on Monaco's slowest corners. With Trintignant's 1956 episode of flattening the nose in the opening lap melee in mind, a new, shorter nose was designed, and this had a bar across the radiator to protect it from impact. When the cars arrived at Monaco, they had also been fitted with smaller windscreens, more aero screens than the wraparound arrangement. The Palmer flexible injection pipes had been thoroughly tested and during the course of this operation, it was decided that the Palmer 'Silvoflex' rubber could also be tried to replace the vulnerable joint in the connecting shaft, which had failed in the past, most recently at Goodwood. Amazingly, this worked perfectly when tested, leaving a few sheepish staff to wonder why this hadn't been thought of before. Other preparations for Monaco

Above *Stirling Moss at the Glover Trophy race. He retired.* (Graham White)

included changing cams to reduce the power output by 10hp at the top end. Moss' Goodwood car (VW3) would be ready for him at Monaco, and Tony Brooks would have another new chassis (VW7), as the production of new chassis and their spares was progressing very well, the month break between Goodwood and Monaco helping the team enormously. Moss and Laurence Pomeroy later carried out a substantial analysis of these improvements, especially the results of reshaping the ports and increasing available brake pressure, which was somewhat ironic in view of what happened to Moss at Monaco. (Moss and Pomeroy, 1963)

Clutch Trouble at the Monaco Grand Prix

Monaco in 1957 was particularly interesting because it meant that there would be a serious confrontation between four English drivers who could be considered of the top rank, and for once they were all in potentially winning cars: Moss and Brooks had the two superb and functional-looking Vanwalls, while Peter Collins and Mike Hawthorn, former Vanwall drivers, had the same two Scuderia Ferrari Lancia D-50s they had used a few weeks earlier to come 1–2 at the Naples non-championship race. The Monaco Grand Prix was the first 1957 World Championship round for the Vanwalls, as they had not gone to the Argentine. It has to be said that, other than Fangio, the rest of the field looked pretty weak in comparison, though Stuart Lewis-Evans was there again, having won the Goodwood race in the Connaught and he was getting some attention for his driving style.

The first practice on Thursday was at 5.45 a.m. and the Lancias had not arrived, so the field was largely green: Vanwalls, BRMs, Connaughts and Coopers. Collins talked himself into a Cooper as Brabham hadn't arrived and was lapping quickly. This was an F2 Cooper, which had made a few appearances already during the season, so the rear-engine phenomenon wasn't entirely new, but Collins' speed made everyone sit up and take notice. Moss was quickest and took the £100 prize, and the Vanwall was running very smoothly, both Brooks and Moss sitting around in the final two sessions waiting for good times to be set, which they would then go out and match. This was pretty relaxed for the Vanwall team. Even though Moss had thumped the chicane wall in the first practice, the bent suspension had been repaired, and when practice was over Fangio was fastest from Collins, Moss and Brooks. Fangio's pace in the very difficult V-12 Maserati was amazing as it was practically

Below Moss and Fangio fight for the lead on lap two of the 1957 Monaco Grand Prix. Fangio won.

impossible to get the power onto the road, but there he was on pole – again.

The fact that the BRMs weren't even in the hunt was not lost on Tony Vandervell. Poor Roy Salvadori hadn't even qualified. But Vandervell's joy was about to be dampened. Moss couldn't start his car on the grid so it was pushed and was nearly bogged down as the flag came down, but it suddenly took off into the lead. Fangio had confessed he was a bit concerned about the start, but he and Collins pursued Moss on lap 1. As the cars headed down to the chicane on lap 4, another famous Monaco incident occurred. Moss inexplicably went straight on into the barriers, and Collins, hot on his tail, swerved and hit the barrier on the left side of the road. Fangio missed them, as did

Brooks, but Hawthorn struck the rear of Brooks with his front wheel, which flew off and he sailed into Collins' parked car. All three Englishmen moved quickly and were very lucky not to be injured in the chaos, striding somewhat subdued back across to the pits. A pole had nearly fallen on Brooks as he cleared the wreckage, but his car didn't seem to be too damaged.

Fangio was off and away in the lead that he was never to lose. What no one realized was that Brooks was experiencing clutch seizure just as he was heading down into the turmoil of the chicane, and he was forced to drive the entire race with no clutch.

Brooks recounted the story of the race for the author:

The handling at Monaco wasn't bad – it was pretty good around the slow corners even though it was basically an understeering car. The difference in those days was that you had to adapt your driving to the car you'd got. You would experiment with tyre pressures, and springs and roll bars, but basically you'd got what you'd got! And so you drove accordingly. It wasn't particularly difficult there. I would say it was much the same elsewhere. The only place it was totally unsuited for was later

at Nürburgring. The real issue at Monaco was that the clutch had gone on about the fifth lap and I had 100 laps to do with no clutch, so I finished up with my left hand red raw after having to change gear without the clutch 2400 times. I followed Fangio for most of the race and finished twenty-some seconds behind him. I didn't think that was too bad because, first, it was Fangio, and second I had my own problems to deal with, and third, it was my first Continental grand prix apart from Syracuse, so I was reasonably happy with that.

I understand people sometimes say that was a great race for reasons which escape me although it was encouraging for Vanwall at the time. I was very satisfied in that I did a good job given the circumstances. Nobody needs an excuse to finish second to Fangio even if you don't have problems and the 250F Maserati was a lot more suitable at Monaco than the Vanwall because you could throw it around. Perseverance and determination came in useful that day. I was unfamiliar with the circuit as BRM had gone in 1956 and practiced little and didn't race because the car was not fit so 1957 was my first race there. I was a little surprised by the team's reaction after the race, or rather the lack of it. They didn't really say anything. I felt a little flat really and rather disappointed. The mechanics were always encouraging, but I don't remember David Yorke coming up and saying 'well done, sorry about the clutch'. Someone even suggested that Tony Vandervell was disappointed. I don't believe that, because I came to know him well enough. I heard that Denis [Jenkinson] suggested that it may well have been because he thought his was already a Grand Prix-winning car, but I felt that there weren't too many people, if any, capable of beating Fangio in a 250F Maserati even without problems. Perhaps he was just disappointed in that he thought Stirling had made a mistake in the heat of the moment, dicing with Peter Collins, but I would have been disappointed if he had been dissatisfied with my performance. Tony Vandervell was not the sort of person who would come up and slap you on the back and say 'well done' although I thought perhaps the team manager should have

Below *Hawthorn and Moss walk back to the pits after they had crashed, with Collins, on lap 4 at Monaco, 1957.*

Above *Tony Brooks drove a brilliant Monaco Grand Prix. The shortened nose aided cooling and avoided damage. (Ferret Fotographics)*

done a little more. If you see what Ferrari does today, it's almost obscene, jumping all over each other!

Stirling Moss later explained what had happened to him as he approached the chicane as being essentially 'nothing'. The front brakes did not appear to be working and under pressure the rears locked. He had managed to break his nose, though he didn't realize this until later. Collins told Moss that he could see the rears locking. Fangio's performance in missing the crash was one of the factors to convince Moss that Fangio was the greatest of drivers. He was also impressed at the precision of Tony Brooks in that race.

Mid Season Events

The following weekend saw Tony Brooks and Noel Cunningham-Reid win the Nürburgring 1,000 Kilometre sports car race for Aston Martin. In the July issue of *Motor Sport* Denis Jenkinson was very critical of the drivers whose 'strike action' over start money had caused the cancellation of the Dutch and Belgian Grand Prix, though he and Posthumus (1975, p.123) reported these cancellations as

Roy Salvadori

Roy Salvadori started racing in saloons and sports cars in 1946 and rose to become known as one of the best all-round British drivers. He had his first Grand Prix race at Silverstone in 1952 in a private Ferrari 500, and then drove for Connaught during 1953, retiring in every race, and then for Gilby Engineering in 1954/55/56 in a Maserati 250F. His 'season' with BRM in 1957 was limited to one race, and then he did events for Vanwall, before driving for Cooper for the rest of the season and into 1959, when he did a few Grand Prix races with the quick but out-of-date front-engine Aston Martin. He again drove both Coopers and Astons in 1960, a Yeoman Credit Cooper in 1961 and the Bowmaker Lola in 1962. Throughout this period he never won a Grand Prix though he was second at the German race in 1958, but he was very successful in sports and GT cars, winning at Le Mans in 1959 with Carroll Shelby for Aston Martin. Always a hard driver, he retired in 1965, became Cooper F1 team manager in 1966–67, and now lives in Monaco, with an apartment overlooking the start line of the Grand Prix circuit, and is a regular at historic events in the UK.

Above *Roy Salvadori*

being due to the fact that 'Europe was passing through another phase of financial instability about this time'. Very little space had been given over to reporting the Mille Miglia crash in the motoring journals, most of them not mentioning the deaths of ten spectators, while deploring how the daily papers had sensationalized the accident. That was the end of the Mille Miglia.

The French Grand Prix at Rouen was not due to take place until 7 July, to be followed a week later by the Reims Grand Prix, and this gave the team a long break to repair Moss' crashed VW3 and VW5, which had been less extensively damaged in his practice crash.

Later in June, Tony Brooks crashed his Aston at Tertre Rouge and injured himself painfully, and that would keep him out of the Vanwall until the British Grand Prix. Stirling Moss was driving the infamous Costin-designed Maserati 450S coupé at Le Mans. It was infa-

mous not because of the Costin work, which was very forward-thinking, but because of the manner in which Maserati had carried it out – the car ran second for a while and then fell apart. After Le Mans, Moss and his then wife Katie went to La Napoule near Cannes, and Moss had his famous water-skiing episode where much of the Mediterranean went up his already damaged nose. He was flown back to England by Tony Vandervell and put into a private clinic for his painful sinus condition until just before the British GP.

During this interval between races, the FIA had announced that the 2.5-litre formula would continue through 1959, but that from the beginning of January 1958, Grand Prix cars would have to run on 'pump petrol', something that upset a number of teams, and started the fuel companies on a programme of moving away from methanol. Shell-Mex & BP started this at once, testing new blends with the

Vanwall to prepare for 1958. Chassis VW6, the streamline Vanwall, was nearing completion and would go in the team's new transporter to Reims, while VW4 and VW1 would race at Rouen, and then the also new VW8, a lighter-weight chassis with twenty gauge tubing rather than eighteen gauge, would be joined by VW7 as the spare for Reims.

Though Jenkinson and Posthumus (1975) claim that there were never more than four Vanwalls built up at any one time, this appears to have been incorrect for a short time. American Don Capps argues that it would have been impossible to come back from Rouen, change over the cars and go back to Reims, so instead two cars were sent in each transporter, VW1 and VW4 to Rouen, and VW7 and VW8 to Reims and VW6 was flown to Calais after Rouen, VW1 and VW4 were put on the aircraft, flown back and dissembled for post-race inspection!

Roy Salvadori had left BRM after Monaco. The car was atrocious and the team would modify the brakes without telling the driver or Lockheed, which made them, and he had lost all confidence in the car. When David Yorke approached Roy, he agreed to drive at the two French races, and he was being paid a good fee. At Rouen he learned that Stuart Lewis-Evans was to drive the other car. Lewis-Evans was described by Roy, and virtually every other driver who knew or talked about him, as a 'slim and frail' person, though few of them knew why this was so. Yorke approached Lewis-Evans to drive, and it is not known whether he remembered that Stuart had written to him the previous autumn asking for a drive. He had come fifth at Le Mans in a Ferrari 315S with Martino Severi and was being considered for a Ferrari F1 drive, and that is why he was at Rouen, though a Ferrari never materialized for him, as they often didn't!

The author asked Tony Brooks how he rated Stuart Lewis-Evans:

> He could be very quick. I think he was basically not very strong in a health sense, as he had duodenal ulcers. He was very slight, slighter than me and that is going some! He could produce the odd flash of speed but was not very consistent. I did wonder

Above *Stuart Lewis-Evans*

Stuart Lewis-Evans

Lewis-Evans came onto the British motor racing scene at an early age. His father, 'Pop' Lewis-Evans, was a 500cc F3 racer and Stuart was a leading light of that formula for five years, winning many races from the greats of the time, including Moss. He got his F1 chance with Connaught in 1956 and won the F1 race at Goodwood in 1957 with the Connaught and was fourth at Monaco where Brooks was second, which brought him to the attention of Tony Vandervell. He moved into F2 racing while driving for Vanwall, and also had an ambitious sports car programme with Aston Martin. He also had a short spell as a Ferrari sports car driver. Lewis-Evans suffered from stomach ulcers, and this was sometimes seen as a contributor to his occasional off-the-pace performance in long-distance races. Whatever the truth of that, he was a masterful driver of the Vanwall, showing amazing speed at some of the faster circuits, and he played a major part in the team's 1958 season.

about him because he didn't do so well in the Aston team, and I always thought a good natural driver could drive anything quickly. He could produce some very quick lap times and he was fast at Zandvoort. He was a very pleasant guy and I got on well with him. I think stamina was the big question mark for Stuart but I guess we didn't know how well he was.

Hard Racing at Reims

Practice for the French Grand Prix saw only Salvadori in the car for the first two sessions, as Lewis-Evans was very much a last-minute signing. Roy had found the Vanwall very difficult to get into and to feel comfortable in because of his height, so the cockpit was modified to accommodate him. He found the car very much to his liking once he got settled in, especially the power, which was so much more manageable than that of the BRM. The handling was not quite up to what he wanted, preferring more understeer. Roy liked a car that he could throw round a bit, but was finding, as Brooks had said, that this was not what a Vanwall did. (Salvadori and Pritchard, 1985, p.108) Roy was sixth on the Grid after taking time to get used to the car. Lewis-Evans had even less time and was tenth, which caused some to say that the Vanwalls were back where they started. This was reinforced somewhat in the race when Salvadori lost oil from a loose cap on the oil tank, and this caused Flockhart to crash the BRM. Salvadori had apparently also over-revved during the slide while losing the oil, bending the valve springs, which forced him out on lap 25, and Lewis-Evans came in on lap 31 with stiff steering and overheating, with the result that the car was retired. The cracked cylinder head had caused the overheating, which expanded the radiator header tank and fouled the steering.

It was only a week until the non-championship Reims race, and there was some despondency in the camp, as Vandervell was expecting to be winning by this time. The beautiful streamline car was rolled out at Reims. This car was standard 1957 Vanwall underneath, but with a 280bhp engine, while the 'lightweight' VW8 had less top-end power but was better in the middle range. Lewis-Evans tried the 'streamliner' in the first practice but the gearing was wrong, and when both drivers tried it in the second, they were unhappy. Neither one could get used to it, and they didn't have prior experience of Reims to wring the most out of it, so it was put away, and would never reappear in streamline form. Everyone thought it was a striking car, with the body that was pure Lotus 11, and a carefully 'waisted' swoop back to the rear. It was never clear why nothing further was done with this after all the work that had gone into it. Fortunately the Donington Collection has a car built up with the streamline body, so it is still there to be admired. Karl Ludvigsen, writing about Vanwall at the time, referred to the streamliner as 'the most outlandish Vanwall machine'. (Ludvigsen, 1958, p.58)

Lewis-Evans, having moved back into his 'normal' car, was then stunning, especially as he had never been to Reims. He simply streaked around the circuit, heading the times for some while and Fangio had to work hard to displace him by only two-tenths of a second, with Behra third, and Roy Salvadori fifth. Things were looking up again, but Roy was nevertheless not happy:

I was rather slower [than Lewis-Evans] in 2min 23.3sec and there were good reasons for this. The car which I drove at Reims was so different from my Rouen mount that I could have believed that it was a completely different design. [It was a different chassis but not a different design.] It was oversteering appallingly and, as a result, weaving so badly down the straights that I was almost too frightened to move the steering wheel. The trouble may have been caused by the fact that my car was running on large, 17in wheels, whereas I believe Stuart's car was running on smaller wheels. I mentioned to David Yorke that the car was weaving badly, but I was merely told that most cars weaved on fast circuits (which to a certain extent is true), even in the slightest wind. I realize that I should have been more assertive and tried much harder to get my car sorted out, just as Stirling most certainly would have done. I had a very unhappy drive in the race and I probably should have retired. I had the speed to pass other cars but I had to choose the widest part of the course, for I could not be sure where the car was going! (Salvadori and Pritchard, 1985, pp.108–9)

Roy should have known that the team didn't believe there was anything wrong with Stirling's brakes at Monaco either! *Motor Sport* rather unkindly put Roy's troubles down to him being past his best, although *Autosport* did remark on the car's weaving. Lewis-Evans made a dazzling start to lead the pack, which had nearly run down race organizer Toto Roche, who had tried to stop cars from being push-started, and Jack Brabham drove 100yd down the road to John Cooper who gave Jack his helmet! For the first twenty laps, the Vanwall pulled away at the rate of a second a lap, averaging nearly 200km/h (124mph), but then Musso closed as Lewis-Evans was seen to be wiping oil from his goggles. Musso caught and passed Stuart on lap 34, who had lapped Salvadori at the halfway point. Towards the end, Fangio had his brakes lock and struck a post, so Lewis-Evans was third, though he too lost his brakes and sailed down the escape road at Thillois, but returned to third behind Musso and Behra, with Roy fifth, which was not bad considering his troubles. It was an interesting side note that some journalists continued to ask questions regarding how quickly the Vanwall would have gone if Fangio were driving it, the same journalists who bemoaned the perceived dearth of good young drivers. Actually,

it seems possible that Fangio would not have been able to or dared to go as quickly as Lewis-Evans, who had the capacity at times to make a car go quicker than it should have.

Roy Salvadori later regretted even more his failure to make demands on the team to sort out his car, when he discovered that Lewis-Evans had earned himself a drive for the rest of the season in a third car. Roy felt he got on with the team, and the two Vanwall drives were the 'highlight of the season'. He admired Yorke's management and described Tony Vandervell as being 'so wrapped up in his obsession to win the World Championship and hid himself so carefully behind a gruff, forbidding exterior that he was almost impossible to get to know'. (Salvadori and Pritchard, 1985, p.109)

The oil in Lewis-Evans' cockpit had come from piston ring 'blow-by' at the sustained high speeds, and it had also been getting on to the rear brakes, making the drive even more outstanding.

Victory at Aintree

As a large part of the team had been away from base for two weeks, and the all-important British Grand Prix at Aintree was coming up only a week later, the crew at Acton was working nearly round the clock to get the cars ready for Aintree, to be joined by the race team as soon as it returned from Reims. Some were perhaps wishing they were not running three cars. However, VW1, which Moss had driven at Syracuse and Salvadori at Rouen, was being prepared for team leader Moss, VW4 (the Rouen Lewis-Evans car) for Brooks, and VW5 was to run for the first time for Lewis-Evans. VW7 was prepared as the spare for Aintree, although little was done except to clean it, and it was to get considerable practice running at Aintree without any problems. Modifications had been carried out to the spare engines to improve breathing in the lower rev range.

While few drivers liked the twists and turns and somewhat grey environment of Aintree and nearby Liverpool, all the teams showed up for first practice. The Vanwalls were out first and Vandervell was determined to put on a good show, and to win. Moss was quickest from Lewis-Evans, while Brooks was still stiff and in pain and was taking it easy. There was time to try some new pattern Pirellis as well as Dunlops. Moss tried all three cars, perhaps four, on the first day, but was slower than Fangio and Behra. The engines were not pulling as cleanly as they should have in the mid-range but had tremendous top-end speed, with a touch of understeer, and the neutral handling meant the power had to be fed in progressively, while the Maseratis were much more at home with the tail hung out, and Behra was looking very strong. Brooks went quicker and ended up third, on the same time as Behra, but Moss was on pole, and Lewis-Evans was sixth, behind Fangio whom he shadowed in practice to get some lessons.

Moss charged out into the lead as the flag dropped in front of a huge crowd:

> I managed to lead at the end of the opening lap in VW1, and settled down to draw away. Stuart and Tony ran 5/6 by the twenty-lap mark, by which time I had nine-seconds lead from Behra. But a lap

Below *Stuart Lewis-Evans in practice for the 1957 British Grand Prix at Aintree. (Ferret Fotographics)*

Above *Jean Behra (4) and Moss at the start. Behra led and looked likely to win but his clutch exploded on lap 69. (Ferret Fotographics)*

later my engine fluffed and misfired. I stopped to have an earth wire ripped out and rejoined seventh, but the car was still sick so I stopped again. We had arranged for Tony to hand over his car – VW4 – to me if necessary, because he was not fit enough to drive the whole ninety laps. He came straight in and was helped from the cockpit so I could take over. The stop cost thirteen seconds. Tony took over my original car and soon retired it with magneto trouble, while I resumed ninth. (Moss and Nye, 1987, p.160)

Tony Brooks recalled the race:

The first time I was able to get up and about after my Le Mans accident was to drive to practice at Aintree. I should never have been allowed to race, and the reason I took part was simply because the cars still didn't have a good reliability record, and the idea was that we had a better chance with three cars in the race instead of just two. This thinking turned out to be exactly right. I had a great big hole in one thigh and abrasions all over my ankles and shoulders. I had big slabs of rubber to try to protect my thighs and shoulders against the high g-forces at Aintree. It was a very different thing doing one quick lap – I equalled the lap record as did Jean Behra (Maserati) but he happened to do

123

Above *Moss took over Brooks' VW4 on lap 21 and fought back to win the 1957 British Grand Prix. (Ferret Fotographics)*

it before me – two-tenths of a second slower than Stirling, which I was quite pleased about because I was a physical wreck. So I got onto the front row of the grid and the idea was that if Stirling's car had trouble, he would take over mine which was as it turned out. I was in about sixth place, not that far behind the leaders, but by the time he came in and we changed over, he was down to ninth. If I hadn't made that effort, there was no way we would have won the British Grand Prix. I then volunteered to get into Stirling's car, which was still misfiring. You never know what can happen until the chequered flag falls so I felt I owed it to the team to get in and keep going. It was not something I

wanted to do, it was a sense of duty. Again, I don't recall much being said about it afterwards. You never really knew what Vandervell or Yorke thought, you just had to guess. I adopted the view that I was pleased with what I had managed to achieve in very difficult circumstances and that was reward enough.done.

Stirling was the number one driver. I signed on as number two driver. It was all really a team for Stirling, and what he wanted, he got. Frequently he would try my car in practice, and want his engine in my chassis, or my engine in his chassis. He had the free pick of the cars and the equipment, which I never once complained about, because if I didn't like it, I shouldn't have signed as number two. I wasn't consulted, but I would tune my own car, to the limits of what you could do in those days – shock absorbers, tyres, roll bars and so on....working on the assumption that it would remain my car. We would both give feedback on the cars, but I worked more on the basis of speak when spoken to, because I was still inexperienced. This was really my first Grand Prix season because 1956 was such a disaster, and I was aware of being a new boy so I wouldn't presume to make dogmatic recommendations.

Below *Moss frightened the crowds when he came in for a late race fuel stop at Aintree. Left to right are mechanics Ron Sayer, John Rockell and Norman Burkinshaw. (Burkinshaw Collection)*

As Brooks has described, Moss went out and turned in a fantastic performance. Lewis-Evans had worked up to third behind Behra and Hawthorn, and Fangio and Collins had retired. Moss was cutting down the gap lap after lap, though Behra looked to be going too quickly to be caught. Moss got onto Stuart's tail and together they pulled back Hawthorn, then on lap 69 Behra's clutch exploded, and Hawthorn, right behind him, punctured a tyre. This meant Lewis-Evans took the lead past the pits, but then Moss was past him and the crowd rose as one to cheer the Vanwalls. Four laps later, Lewis-Evans stopped out on the circuit,

the ball joint in the throttle linkage gone, and he was trying to fix it. This joint had never broken before, and he affected a repair and was eventually seventh, but was later rather harshly disqualified. Moss stopped for a precautionary fuel top-up and went on to win, with Brooks, the greatest British Grand Prix ever. It was far more than Vandervell believed would actually happen, though he so much wanted it.

Moss and Brooks became, jointly, the first British drivers to win a World Championship Grand Prix in a British car following the first Grand Prix win by a British car (Connaught) and driver (Tony Brooks) at Syracuse (1955) since Seagrave in the Sunbeam at Tours in 1923. They would also be the last drivers to share a winning car. Moss considers it one of the best days of his career, and thousands of fans shared that view. Those who had been at Aintree and showed up at the forty-fifth

Below *Moss takes the flag for himself and Brooks, a monumental victory for Vanwall. (Ferret Fotographics)*

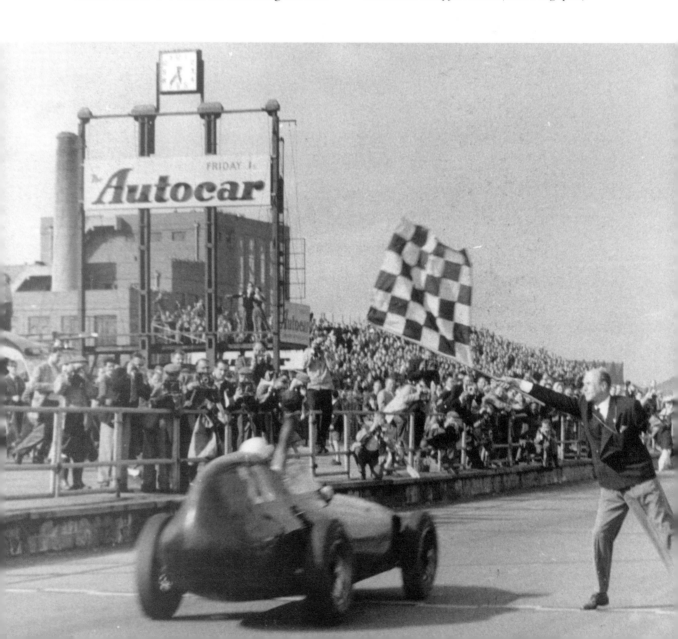

Right *Vandervell with
mechanic Arthur Pratt in
the pits at Nürburgring,
1957. (Esch)*

anniversary in 2002 said unanimously that it
had always been the very best racing day ever
for them.

The first person to greet Moss at the finish
was Norman Burkinshaw, who was the
mechanic for VW4, the winning car. He told
the author in a telephone conversation not
long before his death in 2002 that that was
probably his 'best day of work ever,' and that
echoed the sentiments of the team, even
Vandervell not hiding his pleasure in the
achievement. *Motor Sport*'s August editorial
headline read: 'Bravo, Vanwall; Bravo, Moss!'

Poor Handling at the Nürburgring

Two weeks went by before the German Grand
Prix, enough time for the victory to have sunk
in. VW5, VW1 and VW4 were sent to the
Nürburgring for Moss, Brooks and Lewis-
Evans. The Mahle pistons had been replaced
for Aintree and Nürburgring by those from
Hepworth and Grandage, though Mahle
didn't know about the change and advertised
accordingly! The engines were fine at the
Nürburgring and the fuel line problem was
gone, at last, but the team could not make the

Left *Nürburgring pits, 1957: David Yorke (left) and Tony Vandervell supervise the mechanics doing the hard work. (Ferret Fotographics)*

cars handle. Even a day's private testing before practice only served as a warning as mirrors fell off, bodies split, pipes came loose and the cars could not stay on the ground.

Tony Brooks had felt that there was a limited amount that could be done to alter the handling of the car, and thus the Vanwall performed in a fairly similar way at most circuits, and once you arrived, you could adjust but that was about it:

There was a limit in those days as to how much you could change the handling of the car, as it was intrinsic in the chassis design and you didn't have the million and one variations you can make to a car today. You needed to adapt your driving to the car. I would contest the odd comment I have heard that I didn't enjoy or perform on slow circuits. That's not true, it just happened that I won on the faster circuits, and I was second at Monaco in 1957 and 1959 and made pole position there in 1958. I

128

Above *Tony Brooks gets a rear wheel off the ground at the Nürburgring, 1957. (Esch)*

Right *Brooks on the pit counter at Nürburgring, 1957. (Esch)*

Below *Brooks practises VW1 at the German Grand Prix, 1957, where he finished ninth. (Fodisch)*

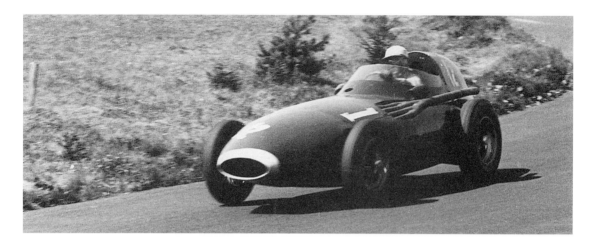

Above *Stuart Lewis-Evans tried hard in VW4 but crashed, German Grand Prix, 1957. (Fodisch)*

Right *Moss was characteristically smooth in an ill-handling VW5 at the Ring, 1957. (Esch)*

Left *Moss takes VW5 through the Karussell at the Nürburgring, 1957. (Esch)*

Right *Brooks in the Karussell at the Ring, 1957. (Fodisch)*

Below *Moss leads Brooks in the 1957 German Grand Prix, with the Schloss Nürburg in the background.*

Above *Lewis-Evans' car stripped in practice. (Ferret Fotographics)*

never particularly had much success at Silverstone. It wasn't that I couldn't drive Silverstone, or that I didn't enjoy Silverstone, I did especially before they messed it about. I did enjoy the faster circuits, and I got more satisfaction at Spa and Nürbur-gring than at Monaco, for example. But in 1957, we could not make the cars go quickly at the Nurburgring. It was absolutely terrible there. I was sick because I was still recovering from my Le Mans accident. I was still not fit, and I could have done with something less than a physical beating which was what it was. Stuart went off. I was ninth

Right *Lewis-Evans briefly leads Moss, but the team was out of luck at the Ring.*

and Stirling fifth. The suspension – the springs and shock absorbers – were totally unsuited and why they couldn't get it right in practice, I don't know. That was one surprise and a great disappointment. I guess they just didn't have the right shock absorbers and springs with them, I don't know, but I was surprised that they were caught out as badly as they were. With a circuit like that you need to bring the full range of options. But that was something I wouldn't know about. That would have been discussed with Stirling, and I'm sure that Stirling was giving them a very hard time, but I just accepted the car I was given. Really it was a case of mind over matter to finish there. When I finished that race, I was totally dehydrated, and I

went to Sid Henson's caravan, the Ferodo man who dispensed tea to people – not one of these three-million pound motor-homes – and I think I drank fifteen cups of tea! Vanwall was caught out, though they got it right the following year, so why didn't they have all the suspension options there in 1957?

Fangio won the 1957 German Grand Prix in what has generally been regarded as his best ever race, and arguably the best Grand Prix of all time, as it featured his fantastic comeback from a long pit stop to take the lead from Hawthorn and Collins. It was the race that certainly turned man into legend.

133

Moss Wins at Pescara

It is interesting that Jenkinson and Posthumus questioned the wisdom, then, of going all the way to the unknown Pescara circuit not long before the more important Italian Grand Prix, especially after Vanwall had gone to the Nürburgring without previous experience, and without apparently being ready for it, but Jenkinson and Posthumus had not questioned that trip. Whatever the reasons, Vandervell made the right decision, because the team won

Below *Stirling Moss scored his second of three victories on the daunting Pescara road circuit, in VW5.*

at Pescara and three weeks later conquered the field at Monza.

Moss had his Nürburgring car (VW5) for Pescara, but Brooks was in VW7 and Lewis-Evans had VW1. This was a circuit that Moss and Brooks really liked, a true road circuit of the early 1950s, on ordinary, untouched roads. Though Fangio was on pole and Moss second, Brooks and Lewis-Evans were on row three. The circuit was longer than the Ring and two of the three long stretches were very fast. Moss went into the lead on lap 2 and won, Brooks retired on the first lap with a piston gone and Lewis-Evans was fifth. Vanwall had won two Grand Prix races, and this one was in Italy – the next target was Monza.

Above *Norman Burkinshaw takes VW7 for some fuel in the Monza paddock in 1957. (Burkinshaw Collection)*

More Success at Monza

Vandervell's consultation with Harry Weslake had resulted in the decision to use an ethanol mixture of fuel rather than methanol, as this would improve reliability and a Grand Prix at Monza was likely to be a true endurance test. The cars for Monza were the same as at Pescara except that Brooks now had VW6, the car which had been developed with the streamline body, but had now reverted to 'normal' form.

The Vanwall vanguard sent shock waves deeper into Continental motor racing at Monza when the three green cars lined up one–two–three: Lewis-Evans, Moss and Brooks, all on the front, with Fangio, who had won the 1957 title, hanging on in fourth. Stirling Moss described the highlights of the race for the author:

Well, the Vanwalls had outclassed the opposition, that's all you can say. I had my gearbox give some trouble and I lost a bit of ground, but then it seemed to correct itself. Tony's throttle started to stick and he had to stop, and I was leading from Stuart, who then had a problem with the steering so he had to make a stop as well. This gave me a gap over Fangio, and I eventually was able to open that to about a lap and relax, and try to save the car. I needed to stop to put some oil in, and I changed the tyres, the rears, but I had plenty of time and managed to win the third race for Vanwall that year. I know Tony Vandervell really loved winning the Championship in 1958, but I believed that the race at Monza was almost more important to him. This made me second to Fangio in the World Championship, for the third time.

In spite of his problems at Monza, Tony Brooks recorded the fastest lap of the race and was still optimistic about his own chances in the team:

I still considered myself the new boy, so anything I achieved was good. I had faith in Vandervell getting it right, but it did require a certain act of faith because there was a strong psychological belief that only the Continentals could build winning Grand Prix cars. That was the big thing about Syracuse for me, which did sort of break

Left *Arthur Pratt signals that Moss has a big lead while David Yorke and Norman Burkinshaw look on. (Burkinshaw Collection)*

through that. But we were having difficulty initially building on that first brick for a while, and I was still sufficiently enamoured to think that I was in F1 racing and learning all the time.

By all accounts, Moss was right and Vandervell felt that deep sense of satisfaction in not only winning, but beating the best of the best by a big margin. The newspapers and even the more reserved motor racing journals were effusive in their total adulation of the Vandervell achievement.

There was then, as usual, a bit of backtracking on the part of some of the press when Vandervell withdrew his three-car entry for the International Trophy meeting at Silverstone, which had been moved to this later date in the season. The reason was largely that the team had done so much, it was failing to see the point of a big effort for a relatively minor race. The fact that the BRM of Jean Behra won this race seemed to have no impact on Vandervell, at least none that is recorded. A *Motor Sport* reader did later take Jenkinson to task for saying that the BRM was, more or less, the final nail in the Italian Grand Prix car coffin, or words to that effect! Vandervell did send one car for Moss to demonstrate at Goodwood on 28 September, and this was to please the crowds. This was Moss' Monza-winning VW5,

Right *Vandervell looks over Norman Burkinshaw's shoulder as Lewis-Evans comes in to retire. (Burkinshaw Collection)*

Below *Moss drove VW5 smoothly to a forty-two-second victory over Fangio at Monza. (Ferret Fotographics)*

but Stirling blew a plug out after five laps and damaged a valve, admitting that this was really his fault as he had convinced GAV that it was a good idea, but the car had not been touched since Monza.

The Season Ends in Morocco

This car was repaired, however, for the final 1957 race, a non-championship event, the Moroccan Grand Prix, which attracted a full entry because it would hopefully have Championship status the following year. Moss had the flu and was quite ill, so decided to fly home before the race. Four Vanwalls had been sent to the 4.4-mile (7km) circuit on the edge of the sandy desert near Casablanca. A new header had been fitted near the water radiator to act as a defrothing medium for the oil tank, and this also meant a greater capacity of oil could be taken on board, as the engine oil also circulated through the gearbox on the Vanwall. At first Tony Brooks set the pace, which Fangio would match, and then Brooks would go quicker. Moss got into his stride. This went on until Lewis-Evans went quicker and the whole process repeated itself. With Moss ill for the second session, Brooks took charge and tried all three cars, ending up on pole with Behra between himself and Lewis-Evans. Moss went home on Saturday, as he was too ill to do anything. After running near the front, Brooks was soon in trouble with a failed magneto and no spark, so the car wouldn't restart. Brooks had chosen to drive the car that was intended for Moss, VW10, a new chassis. The irony was that this car then returned to the UK, had a new magneto, and ran 300 miles of tyre testing without problem. Lewis-Evans chased Behra for much of the race but had to conserve his fuel and finished a good second. Thus the season ended, with Fangio World Champion and Stirling Moss second.

Brooks saw this as a very good first 'proper' season for himself: 'I was pleased for myself,

and Vanwall was looking like it was getting stronger.'

Before Morocco, Vandervell had signed an agreement to use Dunlop Tyres in 1958, as Pirelli was definitely out of the F1 business. Considerable testing was therefore to take place.

Fuel Changes

There were several major issues facing the team at the end of 1957. The FIA rule changes on fuel meant a great deal of work needed to be done to convert the engines from methanol to petrol. The FIA also shortened the length of Grand Prix races to 300km (186 miles), which meant that lighter cars, having better fuel consumption, would have an advantage. While the new Coopers were putting some worrying writing on the wall, Vandervell was not about to design a new car, but he would set the team to lighten the existing one. Drivers did not present a problem, though Vandervell sent Lewis-Evans to a Harley Street clinic to get his duodenal ulcer seen to. GAV wanted to try one last time to get Fangio, but the Argentine driver said no because he was thinking of retiring, and because he believed Moss should stay at the head of a British team.

Jenkinson and Posthumus described the means by which the fuel problem was dealt with, though it has to be said that innumerable experiments were tried:

> They found that the highest compression ratio they could use without running into detonation troubles was 11.5 to 1, and careful attention to piston shapes, port shapes and valve-timing meant that they got away with a loss of 17bhp at the top end, and 6bhp in the middle range, which was not too disastrous. Problems of pistons overheating were combated by a system of oil squirts on the underside of the piston, which worked well. The changeover to AvGas also involved alterations to the metering cams in the fuel-injection pumps, a

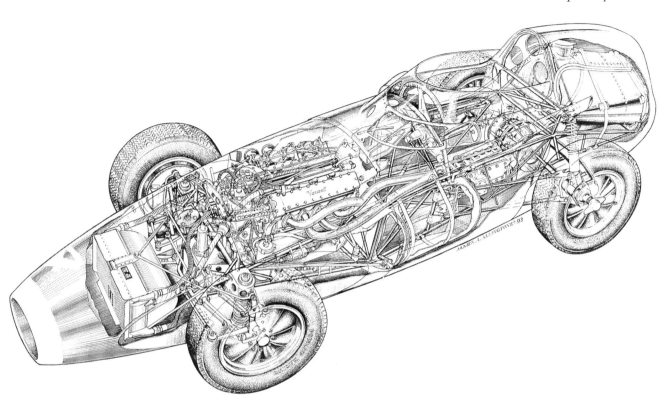

Cutaway of the 1958 Vanwall. (Christies)

Ready for 1958

job which the toolroom took on, after which the pumps were sent back to Stuttgart for modifications by Bosch. (Jenkinson and Posthumus, 1975, p.135)

Tony Vandervell had wanted to enter all the 1958 World Championship races as there was to be from this year a Constructor's Championship, and he wanted it. However, the lengthy process of converting the engines for the new fuel rules meant that he would not go to the Argentine race, and allowed Moss to drive a privately entered Cooper-Climax for Rob Walker. Moss thus became the first driver to win a World Championship race for Cooper, and the first won by a private entrant, Rob Walker.

In January 1958, Brooks and Lewis-Evans tested at Oulton Park and Silverstone, long-distance testing to see whether the first phase of modifications to the engines would work over the length of a Grand Prix. In early spring, Moss tested one of the new AvGas-altered cars at Silverstone, and this was also on Dunlops. He did a fastest lap of 1min 39.2sec, then eight laps at 1min 40sec, and found the car to be running well, though only producing 262bhp at 7,500 rpm, but he also found that the flat spot was less of a problem. He tested again in April with a car that incorporated further engine development, and also had lightening in the chassis, a reworked tail shape, and some lightening of suspension and brake parts, though attempts to use titanium brake discs were abandoned. Moss was well satisfied with

139

the result, as were Vandervell and the rest of the team. The work to present a winning 1958 team seemed to be reaching fruition. However, 1958 would be bittersweet.

Poor Start at Monaco

The team had a formidable armoury ready for the first race. The 1958 cars were all based on the 1957 chassis, with the same numbers, had had numerous detail changes to the suspension and to the bodies. VW1, VW2, VW3 and VW8 were not built into complete cars for 1958, and remained as spares in case they were needed. A significant change to the exhaust appeared at Monaco, with two tail pipes converging as they left the engine compartment, the single

pipe finishing just before the cockpit and feeding into a large sleeve running back to the tail.

At Monaco, Moss had VW7, Brooks VW10 and Lewis-Evans VW5. Tony Brooks was the star of practice and had gained his second pole position, while Moss and Lewis-Evans were struggling, Moss having steering and brake problems, so he then borrowed Brooks's car. Vandervell had said some months earlier that the team might have to stop the practice of swapping cars as it was not fair to the other drivers, meaning Brooks and Lewis-Evans. Moss is said to have 'got upset' about this and the idea was dropped. However, at Monaco, Moss asked to try Brooks's car and was at first refused by David Yorke, though Brooks later drove Moss' car, and Lewis-Evans drove Brooks's. The other drivers did not begrudge the team leader using their cars, but the cars often came back different than when they had last driven them, although on this occasion, the situation

Below *The Vanwalls appeared at Monaco, 1958, with the shortened nose with a support bar, and trimmed aeroscreen. This is Moss in VW7. (Ferret Fotographics)*

Above *Stuart Lewis-Evans lifts an inside wheel on VW5 before retiring at Monaco with overheating. (Ferret Fotographics)*

Right *Brooks in VW10 ran in second until a plug thread stripped. (Ferret Fotographics)*

was reversed. Tony Brooks had found Monaco somewhat odd:

> The plug problem on my car which caused my retirement from the race was a peculiar event. At the time I was told it came unscrewed, but having made pole position I was pretty unhappy about that explanation. It sounded very un-Vanwall to me. I don't really understand what happened there. Because I was a bit of an outsider I didn't get told technical information. I wasn't the type to go in and say 'What the hell happened there?' It wasn't my style and it wouldn't have got me anywhere anyway. But it was strange. I got great satisfaction from my second pole position, so I guess I took it as just one of those things.

Moss led the race for some laps, and then retired with valve gear problems. Brooks retired with the lost spark plug and Lewis-Evans with steering maladies. It wasn't a good start to the so-called Championship year. It was, however, the second British win for Maurice Trintignant who had won in Rob Walker's Cooper.

Moss Wins at the Dutch Grand Prix

The same three cars went to Zandvoort a week later for the Dutch Grand Prix, though Moss had VW10, Brooks VW7 and Lewis-Evans VW5. This was a much better race for the team, the green cars controlling practice, but with Stuart Lewis-Evans surprising everyone with pole position. A new arrangement for wheels had been tried at Monaco and at Zandvoort Moss had wire wheels at the front and light alloy 'wobbly' Lotus-type wheels at the rear. The alloys wouldn't work on the front, as they changed the outflow of hot air and gave an odd feel to the steering, because the alloys were much stiffer than the wire ones.

While Moss led from the start, Brooks was forced out with severe handling problems and Lewis-Evans with a broken valve spring holder in the engine. The win was a great boost to the 1958 hopes, but the retirements kept the shadow of unreliability hanging over the team, and it was clear there was still much to get

Opposite *Brooks pulls over and examines the engine as Schell goes by in the BRM P25. Schell was sixth.*

Right *Moss in VW10 corners hard at the 1958 Dutch Grand Prix. (Ferret Fotographics)*

Left *Stuart Lewis-Evans was on pole, but retired late in the Dutch Grand Prix with a broken valve spring holder. This is VW5. (Ferret Fotographics)*

right. Brooks was unsure what the handling problem was:

> Zandvoort is quite a peculiar circuit on the back section with quite quick curves and I wasn't satisfied that the car was right. I'd had two accidents at Silverstone and Le Mans, and I resolved that I was not going to race a car that was mechanically defective. It was dangerous enough without defects, so I wasn't satisfied that there wasn't something broken on the car. This was in the race, not in the practice, otherwise I would have sorted it. The handling problem must have been that serious for me to have brought it in, because usually I would continue if I possibly could.

Moss had found VW10 quite tricky on the fast swerves as well, but he recalled Brooks' car handling badly in the race and thought he had been nudged at the start. Moss also experienced the car weaving on the straights where there was a breeze, but, despite falling oil pressure on right-hand corners, he went on to win, setting fastest lap on the way. Thus, this was three wins in a row for British cars in the first three Grands Prix of 1958.

There was a rush of continuing development in the three weeks between the Dutch and Belgian races, and technical problems were occurring as quickly as they were being solved, with the increased diameter of the inlet and exhaust valves producing higher weights and breakages, though also improving the cooling. Valve timing and clearances were modified and again this produced some improvements as well as instances of the valves touching the pistons. Though much of this was known to team members at the time and to journalists later on, there is very little evidence that the question 'why' was asked, or, if it was asked, why it wasn't answered. Some journalists had very good access to people like Moss at the time, but don't seem to have asked him then or in retrospect why certain technical problems dragged on for months, or even years. One has to be speculative here, and surmise that much of this was due to Vandervell's *modus operandi*, where staff were in awe of him and were unable to or found it difficult to ask questions (thus implying criticism), and as a result soldiered on doing the best they could until another tactic appeared, usually from

Above *VW5 and VW7 in the Zandvoort paddock. (Ferret Fotographics)*

GAV himself. Many of the best ideas about the fuel problems would have come from Bosch and Daimler-Benz, some of which were acted on, but all of these came through Vandervell himself, so whether they were passed on was entirely up to him. Such was the weight of responsibility that he felt for 'his' team and 'his' car, that he did not delegate nearly enough, though he insisted that everything was done by a team. The author also suspects that many new and presumably sound ideas were tried but not tested, while others, such as the valve springs, were tested to death – without solving the problem.

First and Third for Vanwall at Spa

When the team went to Spa for the Belgian Grand Prix, it was with high hopes because it was felt that all the work would reap reward. In fact, it did, but it also reaped the consequences, as Moss' retirement was due to valves and pistons meeting in the very early laps of the race. The team had achieved better breathing through greater valve-lift, but had also created another problem.

But to imply that Moss' departure from this race diminished Tony Brooks' result would be unfair and inaccurate. For the first time, the team arrived at a Grand Prix as the favourites to win, Moss with his Dutch winner VW10, Brooks in VW5 and Lewis-Evans in VW4. The first practice was given over to setting up the handling and getting the gear ratios right for the high-speed sweeps of the Ardennes circuit, but they were surprised by the speed of the Ferrari 246 in Hawthorn's hands. The 246 Dino had been introduced at the beginning of the season, and the 1.5 F2 version at the end of 1957, but so far it had not been spectacular. Moss and Brooks then couldn't match Hawthorn's time, and Lewis-Evans was right behind them on the time sheets. Different size wheels and tyre combinations were tried to improve the Vanwall road holding. When Moss had 16in wheels on the front, he speeded up, and when 16in wheels went on the rear as well, he was the first under a four-minute lap

145

by some margin. In the final session, the Vanwall team felt its times were safe, and Brooks's magnificent 3min 59.1sec made a Vanwall one–two. But this was complacency in the team; as Moss' car was being race-prepared, Brooks went in to have the gearbox worked on and only Lewis-Evans was running when the Ferraris went out and Hawthorn and Musso annexed the first two spots. Moss was then third, Collins sneaked into fourth, Brooks was fifth and Lewis-Evans was three rows back. A new gearbox went into Tony Brooks's car.

The front row was lined up in reverse order to the normal position, as Hawthorn wanted to be on the left, though the other rows remained as they were. The start was totally bungled as the starter waited and waited for cars that could not get started, and the Ferraris particularly suffered, Collins boiling away. This all played into the Vanwall camp's hands as the flag came down, and Moss and Brooks were off and gone. As they accelerated out of Stavelot corner, Moss was flat out in fourth gear, tried to select fifth but found third instead, the revs rose and the valves and pistons met. The field rushed by and Moss was left in the silence of the Belgian woods, as Brooks led. Collins got past him. Brooks led again on lap 3, but Lewis-Evans struck the back of Gendebien's bright yellow Ferrari, spinning him and denting the Vanwall's nose. A few laps later Brooks went by with a gap to Hawthorn, as the start-line delay had caused Collin's irreparable damage.

Below *Tony Brooks (VW5) leads the Ferrari 246 Dino of Peter Collins at the 1958 Belgian Grand Prix, won by Brooks. Collins retired as a result of the start debacle. (Ferret Fotographics)*

He wasn't the only one, as Behra also lost oil pressure.

Brooks was flying, and had a thirty-seven-second lead by halfway, and had set a new lap record. Both of Colin Chapman's Lotus 12 Climax cars, which had also appeared this season, were doing better than usual, and Cliff Allison was in fourth, where he would finish. Brooks felt the gearbox tighten up in the final ten laps, and eased off, but Hawthorn was told to chase him, so he then set a new record. The oil pressure had been dropping, which wouldn't hurt the engine but limited the supply to the gearbox. Brooks was trying to keep the gap but go easy on the car, while Hawthorn was

sparing nothing. Brooks crossed the line for his second Grand Prix win. Hawthorn was revving every last ounce of power out of the Ferrari and the engine exploded on the line, spraying fragments everywhere. Lewis-Evans came in third, his fine drive capped by limping over the line with a broken right-front wishbone!

Tony Brooks was very pleased with his race:

I won the first three times I went to Spa, so it was a good circuit for me, and I was very happy with the win that year. I later felt it was a disaster they cancelled it in 1959 because I was with Ferrari then, and it was a Ferrari circuit, a circuit that I naturally quite liked. Stewart and Clark were both supposed to have disliked Spa and Jackie allegedly said that anyone who claimed they liked it was 'lying or crazy'. This always intrigued me, because

Below *Stuart Lewis-Evans takes VW4 around La Source hairpin at Spa, finishing a good third. (Ferret Fotographics)*

Above *Lewis-Evans accelerates down the hill past the pits at Spa. (Ferret Fotographics)*

if you were aiming at staying on the circuit, what was the problem? I wonder how much these guys were pushing themselves, because they couldn't have been confident in what they were doing. I never had to psyche myself up to produce my times. It was a satisfying race at the time and in retrospect, because it was my first Championship win without sharing the car, and I had especially enjoyed it. I have a solid silver cup, which Tony Vandervell had made for me because we had to hand the organizer's cup back, and there are some great names on it. It was a landmark day. I think Spa was an important day for Tony Vandervell and I got a tremendous kick out of it – the more challenging the circuit, the more satisfying the win.

Moss Comes in Second at Reims

The race results pattern at this point in the season was optimistic, in the sense that Vanwall was showing how good the car could be, but for several races it was only one car finishing, rather than the possibly over-optimistic one–two–three result Vandervell felt should be coming. The French Grand Prix at Reims three weeks later tended to reinforce this,

with Moss second but the other two cars retiring. Moss and Brooks had their Spa cars, VW10 and VW5, and Lewis-Evans was down to drive VW9, a recently built chassis. Moss had been concerned about front wheel 'flutter' at Spa, so there were struts bracing the top of the king pins to the chassis frame. While the Ferraris were flying, the Vanwalls were overheating and could not match the pace of the red cars. This may well have been related to Vandervell's war with his regular valve supplier whom he got into an argument with, then couldn't find anyone else to make the sodium-filled heads on the large valves that the Vanwall required. As a result, Vandervell Products became valve manufacturers along with everything else. This eventually worked well, but at the outset presented numerous problems. At the end of the final practice, Moss coasted down the long hill from Thillois into the pits, a valve having broken.

Fangio had not appeared since Argentina in

Above *Brooks (VW5) retired from the French Grand Prix with gearbox problems.*

Right *Fangio, Behra, Schell and Moss pass the pits at the 1958 French Grand Prix at Reims. It was Fangio's last race, where he was fourth, Moss second and Hawthorn won.*

January, and though his retirement had not been announced, it looked as though he had retired, until, there he was, fifty years old, in his own 250F Maserati. Hawthorn and Musso in Ferraris headed the grid from Schell (BRM), Collins (Ferrari), then Brooks and Moss, with Lewis-Evans tenth. Hawthorn and Musso led from Moss, and at one point Fangio was almost into the lead. On lap ten, Musso went off on the fast right-hand bend after the pits, over-turned and suffered injuries which would prove fatal. He was the last of the good Italian drivers. Brooks retired on lap 16 with a seizing

Below *Lewis-Evans (VW9) leads Jack Brabham's Cooper. The Vanwall retired and Brabham was sixth. (Ferret Fotographics)*

gearbox and he took over Lewis-Evans' car, which hadn't been running well, and retired on lap 35. Hawthorn won from Moss, but the second place was just not good enough for Vandervell, who felt he was 'losing ground'.

The results were overshadowed by news of Musso's death, a man who had been a hero a week earlier when he put a totally outclassed Ferrari on pole at the Monza banked oval against the American Indy cars and finished a mighty third in that Monza 500. It was a sign of the different times that *Motor Sport* (August 1954) ran an editorial condemning journalists who wrote about accidents and death in motor racing, and did not itself make any mention of Musso's death, except the line in the race report. Yet the season was beginning to exact a heavy toll on drivers. To be fair, there was a

tribute to Peter Collins in the September issue, though in that same issue D.S.J. was advocating a policy by Grand Prix teams not to allow their drivers to drive in other events, and was critical of advancing safety measures such as belts.

'British Supremacy Shattered' at Silverstone

Whereas the press coverage for several months had been very enthusiastic about the Vanwall achievements, at least one leader read 'British Supremacy Shattered' after the British Grand Prix at Silverstone on 19 July. Certainly expectations had been high after the 1957 Aintree race, and Moss put VW10 on pole but Lewis-Evans and Brooks were seventh and ninth on the grid. All the cars were now using alloy rear wheels and wire fronts. Moss led briefly and then drove at ten tenths to stay with the Ferraris, but his engine blew on lap 26. In fact, Moss was driving so hard that the car was in long drifts, whether he wanted them or not! Lewis-Evans just missed third by two-tenths of a second from Salvadori in the Cooper, and Roy was certainly not past his best, while Collins won from Hawthorn and Brooks was seventh.

> Tony Brooks views the British Grand Prix as something which showed his character: That's an example of where I soldiered on despite the problems, because some people at the time, rather than wanting to be seen as uncompetitive, would push their car too hard, inducing a failure, or would simply bring it in to retire giving the press some cock and bull story. I wasn't so proud that I was unprepared to appear uncompetitive by soldiering on and making the best of the equipment I was provided with provided the car was safe to drive. That was what I was paid to do.

Left *Tony Brooks at the British Grand Prix, 1958, where he took VW5 to seventh.*

Opposite, top *Moss led the 1958 British Grand Prix but retired.*

Opposite *Moss just gets the Vanwall to drift at Silverstone. (Ferret Fotographics)*

Left *Stuart Lewis-Evans at Silverstone, 1958. He was fourth in VW6.*

Below *Lewis-Evans at Silverstone. (Ferret Fotographics)*

Above *Brooks, smooth as ever at Silverstone. (Ferret Fotographics)*   **Below** *Brooks at the 1958 British Grand Prix.*

Brooks Wins the German Grand Prix in VW4

Yet again, Moss had VW10 at the Nürburgring, with Brooks in VW4 and Lewis-Evans absent because there were not enough engines. Not only had Moss lost his at Silverstone, but more had been damaged on the test bench in the intervening weeks. A spare car was sent but Lewis-Evans didn't drive it. The team, however, had done considerable preparation with springs, shock absorbers and settings, and had learnt from the 1957 debacle, whereas BRM was making the same mistake that Vanwall had made the previous year.

Brooks ended up four seconds quicker than Moss on the grid, though they were both on the front row, both behind Hawthorn and

Left *Norman Burkinshaw congratulates Brooks after his great German Grand Prix win in 1958, though the results are overshadowed by the death of Peter Collins.*

Above *Brooks on the way to winning the German Grand Prix.*

Right *Brooks drove a brilliant German Grand Prix to win in VW4. (Fodisch)*

Left *Moss leads Brooks in the 1958 German Grand Prix, which Brooks won. (Esch)*

Below *Moss in the early part of the race, before retiring on lap 4 with magneto failure. (Fodisch)*

ahead of Collins in a Ferrari 246 Dino sandwich with a Vanwall filling! Brooks was pleased with the practice:

I was usually on much the same time and faster than Stirling on some occasions, but at the challenging Nürburgring, it was very satisfying to put in a good lap because, after Fangio, Stirling was the bench-mark. I was also faster than him the previous year, even in the 'heaps', which was perhaps a more meritorious performance That had probably been an even more monumental performance! I had also won the 1000 Kms. There in the Aston Martin the previous year although I think I had won the respect of the team sometime back, though they didn't say anything. Perhaps I had their respect from the beginning, at Oulton Park, but the Nürburgring win did much for my status at the time. I reckon that was my greatest race, but my satisfaction was spoiled because Peter [Collins] was killed in that race. I was very much number two in the team, and I wasn't allowed to practise with full tanks for the Grand Prix. When we started the race with full tanks it was handling like the proverbial pig. I dropped way back from Peter and Mike Hawthorn, and at one stage I was thirty-five seconds behind them. Fangio, in 1957, had come back from about forty seconds behind, and I caught up with Peter and Mike quicker than he had according to the Ferrari time schedules. I am not comparing myself with Fangio. He had a less powerful car, I had disc brakes, he had drums and he was incomparable, but it helps to explain why I thought it was my greatest race. At the Nürburgring, which is as challenging as circuits come, I was catching them at about six seconds a lap. As the tanks emptied the car was handling much better and I caught up and had a great dice with both of them. I passed Mike into the first corner after the pits and Peter into the one behind the pits, but then he passed me on the straight. That was a bit of a myth about the Vanwall being fastest on the straights – not in 1958 on petrol. It was pretty quick, but the Ferraris had a lot of power. I passed him again into the same corner. Peter was trying

to hang on to me all the way around the back of the circuit where I wanted to build up a big enough lead to stay ahead on the straight when very sadly he overdid it at Plantzgarten. I was very pleased with the driving part of that race, but it was dampened, to say the very least, when I found out about Peter's accident. It was not until much later that we heard that he had died in the hospital. To win the German Grand Prix from behind against that opposition on that circuit was why it was my greatest race.

Moss' engine had just cut out on him, with a dead magneto, not for the first time, and that was on only the third lap. Hawthorn pitted with clutch trouble the lap after Collin's crash, so Salvadori and Trintignant were second and third in Coopers.

Moss Wins the Portuguese Grand Prix

An extra oil cooler was fitted to the three cars for the Portuguese GP at Oporto, with Moss in VW10, Brooks in VW5 and Lewis-Evans back with VW6 out for the second time during 1958. Moss took pole from Hawthorn, Lewis-Evans and Brooks. Moss led, with Lewis-Evans further back, but Brooks had an unusual incident: "I just got caught in the tram lines, and spun, which was pretty unusual for me, because I don't think I had more than three or four spins in my ten year's career.

Moss misread David Yorke's pit signal, which said 'HAW-REC', meaning that Hawthorn had set a fastest lap and would get a Championship point for that. Moss thought the signal said 'HAW-REG', meaning that he should ease up, which he did, first giving Lewis-Evans a tow, and letting Hawthorn unlap himself. Then Hawthorn spun and was facing uphill, and Moss slowed down and shouted to him to turn it round and point it downhill. When the officials later wanted to disqualify Hawthorn for driving against the

157

traffic, it was Moss who testified on his behalf that he had been on the pavement, not the road, so Hawthorn got his second place behind Moss and his fastest lap point, and at the end of the year, that would be the margin by which Stirling Moss lost the 1958 World Championship. (Moss and Nye, 1987)

Brooks Takes the Italian Grand Prix at Monza

In two weeks, the team was back to Monza, scene of Vanwall's great triumph in 1957, and the pressure was on for the team to stay at the top. The drivers had the same cars at Monza as at Oporto, and a bubble canopy was devised for Moss to try, but it only gave an additional 50rpm and Moss was very concerned that it would blow off or make the fumes in the cockpit unbearable. An extra sheet had been bolted to the rear of the car to bring the fairing up over the driver's head so that the perspex bubble could be bolted to it. The shape of the leading edge of the bubble meant no air went through the gap where the driver could see out, and in fact it extracted air from inside. Sadly, like the streamliner, it was put aside and never used again. The bubble was the first item

Above *Stuart Lewis-Evans was third in the 1958 Portuguese Grand Prix at Oporto.*

ever commissioned from a new company – Cosworth Engineering.

Moss, Brooks, Hawthorn and Lewis-Evans made up the front row of the grid. Tony Brooks comments:

> Vandervell was very happy with the result because he had taken the fight to the Italians and had won, twice. I got a tremendous kick because I had won the three classic races – Spa, Nürburgring and Monza, and I wouldn't swap those for any of the others. At that point I had no reason to think that the Vanwalls would do anything but carry on the following year.

In the race, Moss led the leading bunch of Hawthorn, Brooks, Lewis-Evans and Behra, and at lap 13 Brooks came in to report an oil spray at the rear, but it proved to be a minor leak from a drive-shaft gaiter, and then Moss went missing on lap 18 with the gearbox having started to tighten before finally breaking. Brooks had dropped to ninth, but had started a repeat of his German GP drive from a long way back. The Ferrari pit had failed to notice this for some time, and relentlessly Brooks moved up. Lewis-Evans went out on lap 30 with overheating, and as Brooks closed on Hawthorn, the Ferrari cooperated by losing its clutch and the Vanwall swept past. Phil Hill could have gone past too, but held station so that Hawthorn could finish second.

Below *Moss presses Hawthorn (14) in the early laps of the 1958 Italian Grand Prix at Monza, while Lewis-Evans (30) holds off the BRM of Behra (8). Brooks won his second Grand Prix in a row, while Moss and Lewis-Evans retired.*

Victory and Tragedy at the Morocco Grand Prix

It was nearly six nail-biting weeks to the last race of the year, the Moroccan Grand Prix at Casablanca where the team had gone in 1957 to learn their way round, which turned out to be a good idea. This time Moss' faithful – more or less – VW10 was given to Brooks and Moss had VW5, with Lewis-Evans in VW4. In simple terms, Brooks would have won if this swap hadn't taken place, and all the drama that did take place wouldn't have! But that is of course too simple.

The Ain–Diab–Casablanca circuit was 4.7 miles (7.6km) in length, and the Vanwall team arrived there in confident mood. The team's performance in the latter half of the 1958 season had been wonderful, and Stirling Moss still had a chance to win the driver's title – but he had to win, set fastest lap and Hawthorn had to finish lower than second. Moss was extremely tense during those weeks because he really wanted the title after finishing behind Fangio three times. Moss was behind Hawthorn on the grid, with a new engine

after his blew up in practice, Lewis-Evans was third, and Brooks was on row three. Moss led from the start and set fastest lap; in fact, he had done everything possible in spite of an incident in which he tapped Seidel's car, but Hawthorn refused to finish lower than second and again Phil Hill didn't go by when he could have, and thus Moss lost the title.

The author discussed this with Moss, showing him the photos taken within a minute of the finish, and the author suggested that he must have felt aggrieved, to which Moss replied: 'Why should I have been? I did everything possible in winning and setting quickest lap. There was no point in being upset with Mike.'

Below *Moss and Lewis-Evans on the front row for the 1958 Morocco Grand Prix.*

Above *Moss leads the early laps of the 1958 Morocco Grand Prix.*

Below *Tony Brooks in the opening stages of the Morocco Grand Prix.*

Above *Brooks chases Bonnier's BRM at Casablanca, 1958.*

Left *Moss on the right (8) overtakes Bruce McLaren's Cooper (52).*

Above *Brooks is past Bonnier's BRM on the long straight.*

Right *Brooks led Hawthorn before the Vanwall engine expired on lap 30.*

Above *Moss bent the Vanwall's nose on Seidel's Maserati 250F on lap 13.*

In fact, Moss said later that the loss had hurt, but he became philosophical about it within days. The whole event had been sobered by Stuart Lewis-Evans having a crash on lap 12, not a serious crash, but the rough ground ripped open the Vanwall and it burned furiously. Stuart had got out under his own steam, but he had been seriously burned and in fact died from his injuries seven days later.

Tony Brooks had retired on lap 30 with engine trouble. He described the aftermath:

I think that was a traumatic influence on Tony Vandervell, and I don't think he ever got over it. It was not his fault, but a driver had been killed in one of his cars and he very much took that to heart. My own guess, and I never discussed it with him, was that that was the biggest reason leading him to retire, but I also like to think that he had the sense to realize with the rear-engine Coopers coming on that he was going to have great difficulty in being competitive in 1959, as we did with the Ferrari. I think that was the second most important factor, but Stuart's death was the main one. If that had not happened, he might have continued, because he did go on developing the Vanwall.

This was the most bittersweet moment in Vanwall history, and whatever people felt about Vandervell as a person and businessman, there was no-one who didn't feel how difficult this was, to win the final race of the Championship you fought so hard for, to have his driver lose the driver's championship by one point, to win

Right *Moss setting fastest lap on his way to winning at Morocco.*

Below *The Vanwall mechanics tell Moss that he leads Hawthorn and Phil Hill by a large gap.*

165

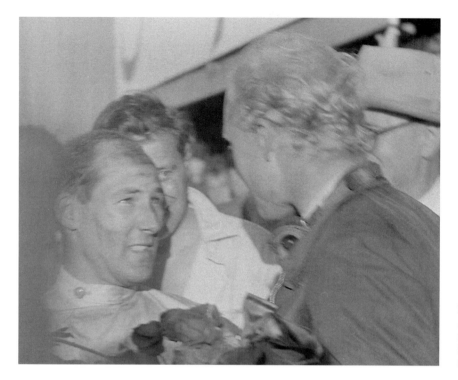

Left *Moss congratulates Hawthorn on winning the World Championship less than a minute after the finish.*

Left *Moss and Hawthorn discuss the race.*

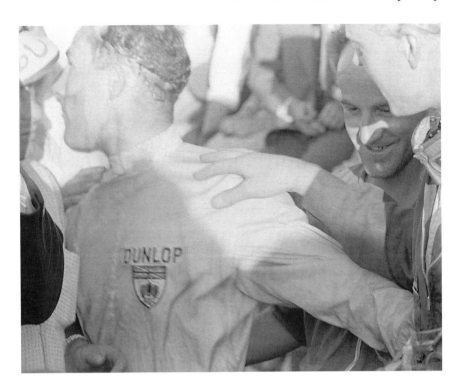

Right *As Moss looks away, Hawthorn makes a reassuring gesture.*

the inaugural Constructor's Championship from Ferrari, and to lose one of your drivers, all at the same time.

Vandervell himself took charge of flying Lewis-Evans back to England with a nurse in charge. Vandervell had been distraught from the moment he had learned of the crash, and he blamed himself, as this was the first time anyone had been seriously hurt in one of his cars. Lofty England from Jaguar tried to console GAV, but he did indeed seem to be inconsolable, and the strain of the last two years was now evident. He had worked endless hours on the car and the team; difficulty in delegating meant that he did an enormous range of jobs

himself, staying at the Acton or Maidenhead factories late at night. He was experiencing heart problems, and he was to a great extent a lonely man, whose first two marriages had ended in divorce – it is probably a cliché, though true, to say that he was indeed married to his work. It was the final insult that after succeeding, he should have to 'suffer' this blow, because, unlike others, he could not distance himself from the accident. Stuart Lewis-Evans died on 26 October, seven days after the crash, and for all that Vandervell had achieved, he found it almost impossible to put this ahead of what had happened. Real Vanwall racing ended in the final days of October 1958.

8   Vanwall Legacy

Through most of November and December 1958, the racing operation acted as if the 1959 season would see the team out again, as Vandervell had made no public announcements, nor did he share much with members of the team, though those closest to him on the development front knew that the end looked like it was coming, and that GAV was an ill man. On 12 January, he issued the announcement that he was going to 'slow down' on doctor's orders, and that meant that the racing was, essentially, over. Moss tells of how he was advised that there was nothing more that Vandervell could do for him. In January 1959, Mike Hawthorn had been killed in a road accident. Vandervell's response to this was not recorded, but it certainly could not have helped him to see a way of carrying on.

However, Tony Brooks gives a further insight:

> I didn't do any testing in 1959 as I was contracted to Ferrari, but Vandervell paid me a retainer for 1960. He was going to build me a rear-engine Lotus chassis with a Vanwall engine in it, and that was why I left Ferrari at the end of 1959. This would have been built to the Vanwall standards and would have been the forerunner of the situations which Stirling and later Jackie Stewart enjoyed with Rob Walker and Ken Tyrrell. I would have been the only driver and it would have been terrific to have a team of the calibre of Vanwall backing just me. I left Ferrari with a contract from Tony, thinking I was going to have potentially a Grand Prix winning car, but it appeared only once at

Snetterton I think, though he did come out with an old front-engine Vanwall which was given independent rear suspension, but it was hopeless. It was a car that was past its day.

VW5 Revamped

Though the racing operation was trimmed in the early months of 1959, the main team was kept on, and there was always a feeling that the team might be started up again, as Vandervell found it very difficult to move on. VW5 was taken into the workshop and rebuilt as a smaller and lighter version of the 1958 car. When Ferrari decided not to run his team in the British Grand Prix at Aintree, the car was entered by G.A. Vandervell for Brooks, but in a field full of Coopers it was well down the grid and five seconds off the pace, and it retired with a misfire. Moss had tried the car but did not want to race it. Brooks described this as a difficult time for his career:

> That race really cost me, because Ferrari didn't come because of a strike, and we had been first and second in the Aintree 200 only weeks beforehand. That and the cancellation of Spa were two of the three factors that cost me the World Drivers' Championship in 1959. I finished second, four points behind Jack [Brabham]. It was the best of six performances. Jack had counted all his six and I had at least one, maybe two, still to count, and the car was basically reliable. I should have picked up enough points at Aintree had the Ferrari been there. It was good of Vandervell to offer me the

Vanwall, but you could not appear on a one-off basis. The brakes didn't work and there were other problems.

The Low-Line VW11

In 1960, the team was asked to build a new car, mainly because Vandervell was still enthralled with racing and improving what he had done before, though clearly he was at a distance from the current F1 world, which was moving on very quickly. This new car was VW11. VW5 had been modified to accept an experimental Colotti independent rear suspension, but it had never raced with this and was broken up to supply the components for VW11. This became known as the low-line car for obvious reasons, and it had the Colotti suspension and gearbox.

Above *Brooks shows the three-wheel behaviour of VW5 at Goodwood, 1960. (Graham White)*

Very little fuss was made when the VW5 came out at Goodwood on 18 April 1960, and this was before it had the Colotti add-ons. It was lighter and lower but was not the low-line car, VW11. It was an interim development of the final front-engine car according to Mike Lawrence (Lawrence, 1998, p.262). Brooks described how he 'set the record for the fastest three-wheel F1 car,' as the car continually lifted a front wheel. He had qualified again down the grid but not that far off the pace, and went into the pits to have a plug lead replaced and finished seventh:

We went testing at Goodwood and one of the front wheels was off the ground most of the time,

169

Left *The tyre lifted on several parts of the Goodwood circuit. (Graham White)*

Below *Brooks still managed seventh in the outdated VW5, even though it had been lowered and lightened. (Graham White)*

the inside front wheel. Tony was persevering with this 1958 Vanwall and this made me think that he may have made the mistake of continuing in 1959 because of poor Stuart. This is all supposition, though, but it makes me wonder whether he still believed the car was capable of being developed and being competitive. There had been a complete change and without a rear-engine car you weren't going to get anywhere, and I don't think he realized that … yet. He decided then that he would provide me with a rear-engine car.

At the French Grand Prix at Reims on 3 July 1960 there was a single Vanwall entry, VW11, the 'low-line' Vanwall, which not only had reduced height but also had a small, round tail and no headrest. The rear suspension was comprised of double wishbones, the top

Below *Brooks in VW11, the 'low-line' car, at the French Grand Prix at Reims in 1960. Success was already past for Vanwall. (Ferret Fotographics)*

member having a long radius rod. The suspension used a coil spring and damper on each side. The gearbox was mounted behind the differential and there was a low prop-shaft line and a low seating position. There were alloy wheels, with thick spokes on the front and webbed solid discs at the rear. The car looked wider, and had a wider front opening, certainly wider than the current cars. Brooks's grid time was 2min 23.3sec, which was one-tenth of a second quicker than his 1958 time, so clearly the car was not much of a progression. But Brooks drove hard and then retired with transmission problems: 'There was no way I could be competitive with the rear-engine cars on any given lap.'

'Lotus–Vanwall': VW12

The team had gone to Lotus and bought a Lotus 18 into which they put a 2.5-litre Vanwall engine, and then refined the chassis, and this should have been a potent car, because it

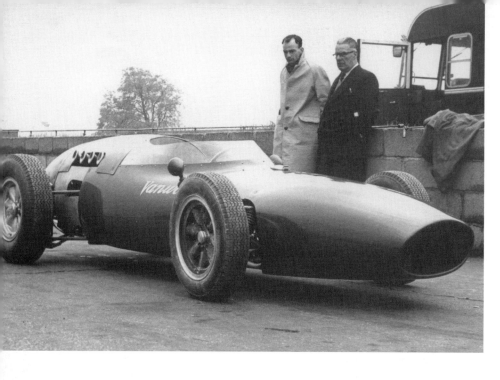

was more powerful than a Climax. Both Surtees and Brooks tested this car at various times and it was finally entered for the Lombank Trophy race in September at Snetterton, but it had valve trouble and didn't start. It was listed in Vanwall records as VW12, though actually Lotus 18 chassis number 901, which was later sold as a rolling chassis. Tony Brooks' wife Pina recalls that during this period Vandervell had said he was not going to race any more, but nevertheless had some projects going on, and would say that the 'new car just wasn't ready'. Vandervell's loyalty to his own staff also seemed to play a part in this, as he wanted to keep them in work, and kept coming up with things for them to do. While numerous references to Vandervell's health appear in all the Vanwall literature, Pina Brooks is one of the few people who was clear that Vandervell had heart trouble, and that he carried on for years in spite of this.

Sometime after the plan to run the 'Lotus-Vanwall' drifted away, it emerged that the engine in that car was not one of the 1958 2.5-litre units, but one that had been bored out to 2.6, making that project look like a launching pad for a car for the new Intercontinental Formula which was being supported in the UK. The FIA had announced back in 1958 that from 1961 Grand Prix races would be run to a 1.5-litre formula. The British teams in particular were against this, and to a large extent put their heads in the sand and thought it might not happen. They thought the fans would support a larger-engine series and indeed a number of cars contested this series, which lasted throughout the first half of 1961, until it was clear that the new rules were working and the smaller cars were quick.

VW14

At some point in 1960, with little fanfare, Vandervell had his team build a car for this formula, with the chassis number VW14. John Surtees was already part of the Vanwall story, though again, very few people knew this. He met Vandervell at the prize-giving for the 1958 Championship and Vandervell made a point of talking to Surtees:

'If you're going to drive a car, drive a Vanwall.' So when he heard that I'd tried the Aston Martin DBR1, he came on the phone and was quite

172

Above *Tufts of wool were used to test the airflow on VW14 at Snetterton. (Ferret Fotographics)*

Below *Surtees showed the promise of VW14 at the Silverstone International Trophy, 1961. (Graham White)*

Above *When photographers could get closer … Surtees at Becketts Corner, Silverstone. (Graham White)*

Below *The author drove fifteen laps in VW14, the last Vanwall, at Donington, 2001. (Peter Collins)*

annoyed. He said 'You should drive a Vanwall, and I'm sending David Yorke down and we'll get one ready.' So he sent two cars down to Goodwood and I sat in a Formula 1 car for the first time in January 1960. I did about 180 laps over two or three days, and his secretary, Marian Moore, said to me 'Keep him calm, he's getting too excited.' He said 'I'm going racing again, sign for me.' Sometime after that he told me that he had already bought a Lotus and was putting an engine in it. He said 'You can try that, and then I'm going to build you something safe.'

Well, the Intercontinental series got going and I did the one race for him. The car wasn't running well, and I overdid it as well, and spun it in the wet at Silverstone, and if it weren't for that we would have been second. That was not bad for a car with little testing. It had a problem with the fuel because of the injection. It would work very well on methanol, but not so well on petrol. That's how it was stillborn, and it never raced again. It stayed with the company for many years and when GKN sold the assets, it went. He had just said he was going to build a car for me, and I would go and see

him, and then one day it was ready. He was a man who did an awful lot for British motor sport. When I had my big shunt in Canada in 1965 and I was touch and go in a Canadian hospital, it was him who came into the hospital to see me, and sorted out getting a block of seats on a BOAC plane and flew me back to St Thomas' Hospital.

I wouldn't have missed out on my motorcycle racing, but I very much would have liked to have driven for him. I know Stirling was always doubtful about how good the car was, and I didn't have a lot to judge by. I knew the car didn't handle like the Maserati, but it was a very quick car. It felt fine to me when I drove it, though I didn't have anything to compare it with. It was amazing what he did, deciding to make everything himself, making his own engines, using direct injection, this was all a big achievement. When I joined Ferrari, I went through all that problem they had with injection, and I remember how hard it was to sort out. I felt the rear-engine car was basically sound, and if they could get and keep the engine sorted, and avoid those flat spots, it could have been well developed. I think the Vanwall engine was potentially better

Below *The 2.6-litre engine in VW14. (Peter Collins)*

than the Climax engine, but it was very finicky to run, especially on petrol. The car itself was not so bad and it could have been competitive. There was never any thought to run it as a 1.5-litre car. I very much would have liked to have that car, and Tony Vandervell promised it to me, but when the assets were sold it went to auction, and for several reasons I didn't get it.

This car, as Tim Scott quite rightly points out in his recent *Motor Sport* (May 2003, p.48) article, was unkindly and unjustly dubbed 'the whale' when it appeared at Silverstone, and Surtees himself says it was also referred to as 'the beast', because it was heavy and had some-

thing of a rotund shape, but these comments were unfair as it handled well.

A mystery remains over this entire period, because if Vandervell had Brooks under retainer and had clearly promised to build him a rear-engine car, what was he doing making a very similar offer to John Surtees? Both played a part in the short history of the rear-engine Vanwall episode, and, at least at the time, neither seemed to know the level to which the other was involved. Both Brooks and Surtees had other cars to drive and were busy anyway,

Above *Norman Burkinshaw with Vanwall history at the 1973 Reunion at Silverstone. (Burkinshaw Collection)*

Below *The 1973 reunion party: (left to right) Doug Orchard, Len Butler, Arthur Pratt, Phil Wilson, John Rockell, Denis Jenkinson, Harry Weslake, Cyril Atkins and Norman Burkinshaw. (Ferret Fotographics)*

Above *The 1973
Vanwall Reunion.*

Left *Tony Brooks
driving the Donington
Collection car with
streamline body.*

and by now had got used to Vandervell's spasmodic operation, so wouldn't be all that surprised when a car showed up. More significantly, no-one outside the factory seemed to know what plan, if any, Vandervell had for racing, and he still would not confide in journalists to any extent. His health, and heart condition particularly, worsened, and some people said he was drinking heavily, though that is mainly hearsay.

So, VW14 raced at the International Trophy at Silverstone in May 1961, and eventually ended up in the Donington Collection. Tom Wheatcroft took it out for very occasional outings, and in 2001 the author was allowed to do a number of laps at Donington in the very last Vanwall to race in period, a special honour indeed. It seemed very much like a car that could have been developed into a winner.

Below *One of the Vanwalls during an historic race at Silverstone, 1983.*

Coming to an End

As the 1960s progressed, there were no more serious racing projects going on at Acton or Maidenhead, and gradually the racing team began to shrink. David Yorke went off to work with another great and gruff character from British motor racing, John Wyer, and many of the mechanics went into research, development and sales areas of Vandervell Products. Some of them, like Norman Burkinshaw, maintained contact with the cars, and he was always there when the cars were run as part an historic event or a Vandervell promotion. Burkinshaw, with John Collins, had even bought the components for a complete car, which car restorer and vintage racer Tony Merrick raced, famously catching fire in an event at Donington, and Norman subsequently restored it. Tony Vandervell, who had married his long-time secretary Marian Moore, experienced worsening health and he died in

Above *John Surtees drove the Vanwall at Goodwood, 1998. (Steve Havelock)*

1967 at the age of 68. He was one of the few central characters missing when GKN had a Vanwall reunion in 1973 to celebrate twenty years of the first 100mph lap of Silverstone, and now most of those characters are gone as well. Vandervell didn't bring many 'young lads' into his race team. They had been experienced workers whom he knew, so they were already 'mature' in the 1950s when the team was racing.

There were occasional efforts to keep the Vanwall name alive in one form or another, and they are worth a brief mention here as part of the long and complex story, though to some extent they divert from the roots of Vandervell and his Vanwall racing venture.

The loss of Vandervell in 1967 was a huge blow to the company, though indeed it must have been expected. The executors sold Vandervell's share holding to the Guest-Keen-Nettlefold Group (GKN) and Vandervell

Products became a wholly owned subsidiary in 1968.

In the mid-1970s GKN announced what the motoring press called the 'belated Vanwall', a 4.7-litre Rover V-8-powered Lotus Europa, and though no claim was made to using anything Vanwall other than the bearings in the engine, the company was clearly making use of the Vanwall heritage. Other reports said this project had been ready as early as 1969, called the 47D and using the Lotus 47, the racing version of the Europa as its basis, with a 3.5 Rover engine giving 485bhp and ZF five-speed gearbox. This project did not succeed, but fifteen years later, in 1991, GKN again announced a project called 'Vanwall', which was essentially a Lotus Esprit copy two-seater in mid-engine format, with a 4.4 Rover V-8 and 330bhp. It was to appear in early 1992, but it was as successful as its 1970s predecessor.

Some of the remnants of the original team have come up for sale from time to time, and Moss' VW10, considered to be, aside from VW14, the only wholly original Vanwall Grand Prix car, has an interesting story con-

Above *Brooks and Moss demonstrate the Vanwalls at Goodwood, 1998. (Steve Havelock)*

Right *Brooks has a rest at Goodwood, 1999. (Steve Havelock)*

Above *VW2's exhaust. (Peter Collins)*

Below *VW2's engine with a good view of the Amal carburettor bodies on the left. (Peter Collins)*

nected to it. This car was in the USA in the Collier Collection in Florida from 1986 until sold at auction in 1989. During much of the 1990s VW10 was owned by Vijay Mallya and his Tierra Blanca Collection, and most of the substantial work done on the car was done by Tony Merrick. John Harper raced it at at least one Coys Silverstone meeting. The connection with Mallya is perhaps the most interesting one.

In 1995, *Formula 1 News* ran a short story concerning the possible re-emergence of the name Vanwall in Grand Prix racing, and it said that Nigel Mansell was involved in the project. In October 1995, the managing director of Glacier Vandervell Europe wrote to David Laird to say the Company 'has agreed in principle to grant VF One Ltd the right to use the Vanwall name for your proposed Formula 1 Team subject to the conclusion of a satisfactory trademark user's agreement'. David Laird and John Minett were founders of VF One, a company that intended to 'take Vanwall back onto the race tracks whilst at the same time prototyping our new engine technology'. VF One sent out a proposal to prospective financial backers, the key one being to Vijay Mallya, and in the proposal stated that links had already been made with an existing F1 team for supply of components and development assistance. There was also a plan for another Vanwall road car with a V-12 engine. Race car designer John Baldwin, team management expert Mike Earle and designer Robin Herd were all listed as members of the management team. The document also saw as an advantage the 'involvement of Nigel Mansell as a non-executive director to the company'. Vijay Mallya's financial position became a matter of public knowledge not long after these propos-

Below *Tom Wheatcroft drives VW2 at Donington in 2001. (Peter Collins)*

Above *The author tries VW2 at Donington, 2001.*
(Peter Collins)

als were made, and the project never got off the ground.

However, when motor racing fans and enthusiasts come to the Donington Collection or see Stirling Moss or Tony Brooks at an historic Goodwood meeting, they don't think of anything after the Vanwall heady days of 1957–58. Some of the surviving cars have subsequently been tested for historic magazines, by talented historic racing drivers, who all report the thrill of driving the cars. Tony Brooks has commented on how they all seem to find the cars easy to drive, an indication that no-one has driven one competitively since the 1950s. The reports remark that the gearchange seems 'easy and comfortable' these days, when in reality the gearbox always seemed 'easy' in the first few laps of a race, and as the oil warmed and thinned, the gearbox got harder and harder, because the engine oil had

to lubricate the gearbox internals, a Vanwall design problem that was never solved.

In many ways, that sums up the project. One man had a number of brilliant ideas and the means to turn them into action, but not always the patience and wisdom to do this in a way that would work. Tony Vandervell was a strong leader, and he was fortunate to have around him a team of competent people who could sort out most of the problems, and by sheer will and determination pushed his unorthodox engine into becoming a Grand Prix winner. The softer and lonelier side of Vandervell was hidden beneath this determination, and most of the instances of his kindness only emerged after his death. This drive to succeed has also meant that few people knew him, so the side that became public was assumed to be the whole man, and the caricature of him was thought to be Vandervell, the man who supposedly wanted to beat those 'bloody red cars'. This caricature did not serve him well, because his love of Grand Prix racing was largely based on his admiration, knowledge and intimate contact with those 'bloody red cars', and it is the author's final argument that the caricature was invented by people who failed to get to understand him and his ways, not by Vandervell himself.

Perhaps a fitting last word should come from a Grand Prix driver who had a particular affinity for Vanwall, and whose view explains why the mention of Vanwall still raises the temperature of the enthusiast. New Zealander Howden Ganley was, of course, a driver for BRM in the 1970s:

> My wife Judy and I were both involved in Chris Amon's engine business, Chris Amon Engines Ltd, and the factory was in Reading, but we did all the dyno testing at Vandervell Products in nearby Maidenhead, and the fuel tank which they pushed from dyno cell to dyno cell was a complete Vanwall tail tank, one of the big riveted ones, with four castors on the bottom so it could be pushed around, and that was what they ran the engines on. I gave them a hard time, trying to buy it from them, saying 'Here, I'll give you the money, you can buy a brand new one.' But they wouldn't part with it. Then a couple of years ago I noticed the old factory was being demolished and the last thing standing was the front wall which faced onto the road, and every day I would go to work and see the big Vandervell Products sign on the wall, and I thought I should go in there and give the workman £10 and have him put it in the boot of my car. Well, I put it off, and one day it had disappeared. I missed the sign and the fuel tank. The reason it was important was that I was, in my youth, besotted with the 250F Maserati, and when that was no longer the car, the Vanwall came along with Tony Brooks and Stirling driving, it was the great dream car. When I lived in Maidenhead later, I realized how close I was to where the engines were built, but I was always a Vanwall enthusiast. Still am.

Appendix
Vanwall Chassis

1954

Vanwall Special – This was the Cooper-built chassis which used 2.0-, 2.3- and 2.5- litre engines. It did not have a chassis number. Crashed and not rebuilt.

1955

VW1, VW2, VW3, VW4 – These cars were used in 1955 and broken up with numerous parts used in the 1956 cars. VW2 was reconstructed with original parts and is in the Donington Collection.

1956

VW1/56, VW2/56, VW3/56, VW4/56 – These were the cars built to the Chapman/ Costin design. The numbers do not correspond with the 1955 chassis. They were stripped at the end of the season and modified and improved with new components for 1957.

1957

VW1/57, VW2/57, VW3/57, VW4/57, VW5/57, VW6/57, VW7/57, VW8/57, VW9/57, VW10/57 – Four of these cars were based on components from the 1956 cars, but the chassis numbers were not the same. VW2 was never completed; VW6 was the streamline car, converted back to normal configuration; VW8 was a lightened chassis; VW9 was not completed in 1957; VW10 is now in private ownership.

1958

The 1957 cars were used in 1958. Only VW4, VW5, VW6, VW7, VW9 and VW10 were used in 1958. VW4 was destroyed in Morocco, 1958; VW6 was broken up; VW7 was broken up; VW9 was rebuilt as a show car;

1959

VW5 was rebuilt into a lower and lighter car, raced at the British GP in 1959 and Goodwood 1960. It was broken up to provide components for VW11. It had a Colotti-design rear suspension and gearbox but was not raced with these.

1960

VW11 was built up from some components of VW5. It was known as the 'low-line' car, and had a Colotti rear suspension and gearbox design. It raced only once at the French Grand Prix. It was subsequently dismantled. VW12 was Lotus 18 chassis 901, fitted with a 2.5-litre engine for testing, and the chassis was then sold.

1961

VW14, the only rear-engine Vanwall and the last Vanwall to be built, raced once, and was rebuilt with body modifications during 1961; it is in the Donington Collection.

Bibliography

Bacon, R., *Norton Twins* (Niton Publishing, 1995)

Bamsey, I., *Vanwall 2.5 Litre – A Technical Appraisal* (Haynes Publishing, 1990)

Cooper, J. with J. Bentley, *John Cooper – Grand Prix Carpet Bagger* (Haynes Publishing, 1977)

Crombac, J., *Colin Chapman – The Man and His Cars* (Haynes Publishing, 2001)

Edwards, R., *Stirling Moss – The Authorised Biography* (Cassell & Co., 2001)

Hawthorn, M., *Challenge Me The Race* (William Kimber, 1958)

Jenkinson, D., *A Story of Formula 1* (Grenville, 1960)

Jenkinson, D. and C. Posthumus, *Vanwall – The Story of Tony Vandervell and His Racing Cars* (Patrick Stephens, 1975)

Klemantaski, L., *The Vanwall Story* (Hamish Hamilton, 1958)

Lawrence, M., *Grand Prix Cars 1945–65* (Motor Racing Publications, 1998)

Lawrence, M., *Colin Chapman – Wayward Genius* (Breedon Books, 2002)

Ludvigsen, K., 'Vanwall Vindicated', *Sports Cars Illustrated*, March 1958

Ludvigsen, K., *Classic Grand Prix Cars – The Front-Engined Formula 1 Era 1906–1960* (Sutton Publishing, 1998)

Ludvigsen, K., *Classic Racing Engines* (Haynes Publishing, 2001)

McDonough, E., *Ferrari 156: Sharknose* (Sutton Publishing, 2001)

Moss, S., *A Turn at the Wheel* (William Kimber, 1961)

Moss, S. and L. Pomeroy, *Design and Behaviour of the Racing Car* (William Kimber, 1963)

Moss, S. and D. Nye, *Stirling Moss – My Cars, My Career* (Guild Publishing, 1987)

Mundy, H., 'Man and Machine – The Vanwall Achievement', *The Autocar*, 2 January 1959

Nixon, C., *Mon Ami Mate* (Transport Bookman Publications, 1991)

Nye, D., *Autocourse History of the Grand Prix Car 1945–65* (Hazleton Publishing, 1993)

Nye, D., 'How Went The War?' *Historic Race & Rally*, Issue 4, Vol. I, February/March 1993

Rous, C., 'Manx Norton and the Vanwall', *Classic Racer*, Number 29, Spring 1990

Salvadori, R. and A. Pritchard, *Roy Salvadori – Racing Driver* (Patrick Stephens, 1985)

Setright, L.J.K., *The Grand Prix Car 1954/1966* (George Allen & Unwin, 1968)

Setright, L.J.K., *The Designers* (Follett Publishing, 1976)

Sheldon, P. and D. Rabagliati, *A Record of Grand Prix and Voiturette Racing*, Vols 4–6, (St Leonard's Press, 1987)

Surtees, J., *John Surtees – World Champion* (Hazleton Publishing, 1991)

Taruffi, P., *Works Driver* (Bandiera and Scacchi, 1964)

Williams, R., *Enzo Ferrari* (Yellow Jersey Press, 2001)

Yates, B., *Enzo Ferrari – The Man and the Machine* (Bantam Books, 1991)

Journals

Autosport
Classic & Sports Car
Classic Racer
Historic Race and Rally
Motor Sport
Road and Track
Sports Cars Illustrated

Index

Ain-Diab Casablanca circuit 160
Aintree 10–15, 53, 59–60, 72, 121–3,
    126–7, 149, 168
Aintree Trophy 59
Aintree 200 51, 168
Airspeeds 82
Albi Grand Prix 40
Alfa Romeo 17, 20–1, 24, 30–1, 35
Alfa Romeo Alfetta 158/9 20, 30–2,
    34
Allison, Cliff 75, 147
Amal carburettors 27, 34, 44–5, 55–6,
    65, 87, 110
Annis, Casey 12
Argentine Grand Prix 88
Argentine Temporada 105
Army Service Corps 18
Ascari, Alberto 17, 24, 30, 40, 46, 47,
    50, 56, 60–1, 65, 68–70, 88
Aston Martin 12–14, 53, 106, 117–20,
    157, 172
Austin Seven 66, 79
Automotive Products Ltd 20
Autosport magazine 37, 46, 121
AvGas 138–9
Avon Trophy 78

Baldwin, John 183
Bamsey, Ian 9, 20, 49
BARC 46
BARC Autumn Trophy 39
BARC International Trophy 74
Bazzi, Luigi 20
Behra, Jean 51, 59, 65–6, 72, 98, 100,
    120–3, 125, 136, 138, 147,
    158
Belgian Grand Prix 53, 63, 70, 93,
    117, 144–5
Berthon, Peter 17, 19, 21–2, 25
Bertocchi, Guerino 81
Bira, Prince B. 37
Black, Pat 108
Blackbushe airfield 21
Board of Trade 21
Bordeaux circuit 66
Borrani wheels 55
Bosch fuel injection 46, 52, 64–5, 72,
    83, 110, 139, 145
Bowmaker team 119
BP Oil 39, 50, 66, 68, 110, 118
Brabham, Jack 9, 75, 121, 168
Brandon, Eric 48
Brands Hatch 16
BRDC *Daily Express* Trophy 49, 50–2
BRDC International Trophy 17, 20,

24, 30, 47, 65–6, 68, 72–3,
    88–9, 104, 136
Bremgarten 53
British Grand Prix 10–14, 22–3,
    32–3, 38, 40, 52, 70, 72–3,
    101, 118, 121, 124, 126, 150,
    168
British Touring Car Championship
    105
British Wire Producers Ltd 20
BRM 12, 14, 17, 20–4, 26–8, 30,
    32–40, 42–4, 47, 51–4,
    59–60, 63–4, 67–8, 73, 77–8,
    84–5, 88, 91, 93–4, 96, 101,
    103–7, 114–16, 118–20, 136,
    154, 185
BRM P25 77
BRM Research Trust 19, 21, 25,
    32–3, 39
BRM V–16 20, 25, 34, 36, 65–6, 78
Brooklands circuit 74
Brooks, Pina 172
Brooks, Tony 10–13, 15, 32, 53, 59,
    75, 77, 90, 94, 101, 106–10,
    114–18, 122–8, 134–5,
    138–40, 143–8, 150, 154,
    157–60, 164, 168–9, 171–2,
    176, 184–5
Brown, Alan 11, 47–53
BTH magnetos 29
Buck, Chris 12
Buenos Aires Grand Prix 88
Bugatti 88, 96, 98
Burkinshaw, Norman 10–11, 42, 45,
    70–1, 127, 179
Busso, Giuseppi 20

Campbell, Malcolm 18
Capps, Don 118
Castellotti, Eugenio 10, 69–71, 76–7,
    91, 94, 98, 100, 109
Castle Combe circuit 78
Castrol Oil 68
Challen, Keith 40
Chapman, Colin 10–11, 44–5, 51, 55,
    78–9, 81–7, 89–90, 93, 96, 98,
    113, 147
Chapman, Hazel 98
Charterhall circuit 39, 42
Chimay GP de Frontieres 88
Chiron, Louis 91
Chris Amon Engines Ltd 185
Clark, Jim 147
Clayton–Still radiator 45
Clements–Talbot car 18

Collier Collection 183
Collins, John 179
Collins, Peter (driver) 10–11, 42,
    51–4, 56–64, 67–8, 76–8,
    90–1, 93–4, 96–8, 100, 109,
    114–17, 125, 133, 146,
    149–50, 157
Collins, Peter (photographer) 11
Colombo, Gioacchino 20–1
Connaught 11, 14, 51, 67, 72, 75,
    77–8, 84–5, 91, 103, 106–7,
    110, 114, 119, 126
Cooper 14–15, 40, 46, 53, 72, 75, 77,
    79, 88, 105, 114, 119, 138,
    143, 149, 157, 164, 168
Cooper-Bobtail 75
Cooper-Bristol 37, 39, 45, 48, 51, 63,
    66
Cooper-Climax 139
Cooper-Climax T51 73, 106
Cooper-JAP 66, 73
Cooper, John 38–40, 45, 47–8, 121
Cooper, John (*Autocar*) 79
Cooper Manx 27
Cooper-Norton 79
Costin, Frank 10, 44–5, 55, 56, 79–83,
    86–7, 89, 91, 93, 107–8, 118
Costin, Mike 11, 79, 82
Costin, Ron 11, 81–2
Cosworth DFV engine 16
Cosworth Engineering 158
Coventry Climax engines 35, 175–6
Coy's Silverstone meeting 183
Craig, Joe 26, 28, 44, 58, 104
Crombac, Gerard 'Jabby' 85
Crystal Palace circuit 74–5
Cunningham-Reid, Noel 12, 117

Daily Graphic Trophy 34
Daimler-Benz 65, 93, 145
DeHavilland Aircraft 79, 82
Delahaye cars 73
Delamont, Dean 79
Dennis Motors 48
Donington circuit 52, 74, 179
Donington Collection 11, 27, 89,
    120, 179, 184
Dreyfus, Rene 73
Duckworth, Keith 16
Duke, Geoff 26–7
Dundrod circuit 31–2, 36, 77
Dunlop tyres 55, 84, 108, 122, 138–9
Dutch Grand Prix 63, 71, 117, 143–4

Earle, Mike 183

Ecclestone, Bernie 14
Ecurie Bleue Team 73
Emery, Paul 75
Emeryson-Alta 75
Empire News Trophy 78
England, Lofty 167
ERA 17, 19, 39, 66
Esso Oil 68
Eves, Edward 28

Fagioli, Luigi 37
Fairman, Jack 10, 67, 75
Fangio, Juan 10, 12, 24, 30, 37, 40, 42,
        52–3, 56–7, 60, 63, 69–72, 76,
        85, 87, 90, 91, 93–4, 96–8,
        100–1, 103, 105, 108,
        114–15, 117, 120–2, 125,
        133–5, 138, 148, 157, 160
Farina, Giuseppi 'Nino' 31–2, 34,
        39–40, 52, 77, 87, 96
Ferodo brakes 133
Ferrari 17, 43–4, 50–1, 53, 55–6,
        61–3, 66, 70–3, 76, 88, 91, 94,
        97–8, 100, 106–7, 109–10,
        117, 119, 146–9, 157, 159,
        164, 167–8, 175
Ferrari 125C 21, 23–4, 33
Ferrari 156 10
Ferrari 315S 118
Ferrari 246 53, 145, 157
Ferrari 375 31, 34, 36, 38, 40, 45
Ferrari 500 119
Ferrari 553 Squalo 60
Ferrari 555 Super Squalo 76
Ferrari 625 71–2
Ferrari, Enzo 20–1, 23–5, 30, 31,
        33–4, 36, 39–40, 70
Ferrari-Healey 53
Ferrari Monza 66, 70
Ferrari Thinwall Special 11, 17, 22–4,
        30, 31–7, 39–40, 43, 45–6,
        49–54, 58, 60, 62, 65
Ferret Fotographics 11
Festival of Britain Trophy 31
FIA 118, 138, 172
Fitch, John 75
Flockhart, Ron 54, 78, 120
Fodisch, Jorg Tomas 11
Ford 67
Ford GT40 33
Ford Mondeo 107
Ford 105 engine 16
Fox, Fred 44, 46, 110
Frazer–Nash 66, 106
French Grand Prix 14, 52–3, 63, 73,
        97, 108, 118, 120, 148, 171
Frere, Paul 94, 96

Ganley, Howden 12, 185

Ganley, Judy 185
Gendebien, Olivier 146
George Salter & Co.Ltd 20
Gerard, Bob 39, 75
German Grand Prix 102, 127, 133,
        157–8
Getrag gearbox 86
Gilby Engineering 119
Gilera motorcycles 26
Girling brakes 33–6, 39, 54
GKN Stampings 29, 175, 180
Glacier Vandervell Europe 183
Glover Trophy 40, 110
Godia, Francesco 94
Gonzales, Froilan 36, 38–9, 51, 53, 61,
        101
Goodwood 30, 31, 34–6, 39, 42,
        46–7, 49–50, 52–3, 58, 60, 64,
        87, 96, 104–5, 108, 110,
        113–14, 119, 169, 175
Goodwood Festival of Speed 36, 184
Goodwood Trophy 42, 59
Goodyear Co 32, 35, 39, 50, 54–5, 65,
        69
Gordini 11, 56, 64, 73, 88, 91
Gould, Horace 75, 78
Graffenreid, Emmanuel de 22
Gran Premio Di Siracusa 88
Gran Premio Napoli 68, 114
Grand Prix of Europe 32
Gray George 87
Guest-Keen-Nettlefold Group 180
Gulf Porsche 33

Harper, John 183
Harrison, Dexter 12
Havelock, Steve 11
Hawthorn, Mike 10–12, 37, 39–40,
        42, 46–8, 52–3, 58–60, 62–5,
        67–72, 75–8, 90–1, 94, 96–7,
        98, 100–1, 103, 105–6, 114,
        116, 125, 133, 145–7,
        149–150, 154, 157–60, 168
Hay, Neville 12
Healey cars 106
Heinzelman, Ed 11
Hemingway, Ernest 9, 43
Henson, Sid 133
Hepworth and Grandage pistons 29,
        34, 93, 127
Herd, Robin 183
Humber cars 104
HWM cars 34, 53, 105
High Duty Alloy pistons 93
Hill, Phil 63, 159–60

Indianapolis 500 73
Intercontinental Formula 172
International Gold Cup 76

Italian Grand Prix 33, 53–4, 75, 80,
        102, 104, 134, 136

Jaguar 62, 66–7, 71, 77, 79
Jano, Vittorio 70
Jenkinson, Denis 9, 12, 20–1, 23, 30,
        47, 53, 62, 66, 85, 90, 103–5,
        108–9, 116–17, 134, 150
JBS cars 53
Jiggle, Mike 12
Joseph Lucas Ltd 19–20, 35
Joscelyne, Brian 11
JW Automotive 33

Karlskoga circuit 75
Kieft 500 79
Klemantaski, Louis 9
Kling, Karl 52
Kop hill climb 18
Kuzmicki, Leo 26–8, 46, 58, 71, 78,
        85, 91, 104, 110

Laird, David 183
Lampredi, Aurelio 23–4, 30, 36
La Napoule 118
Lancia 44, 50
Lancia D-50 10, 44, 53, 60–1, 66,
        68–71, 77–8, 89–91, 94,
        97–8, 109, 114
Lancia-Ferrari 53, 89–90
Lancia, Gianni 44, 46–7
Lawrence, Mike 11, 45, 49, 79, 85
Lehrer, Tom 83
Le Mans 12–14, 53, 63, 71, 74, 76,
        118–19, 123, 132, 144
Leston, Les 78
Levegh, Pierre 71
Lewis-Evans, 'Pop' 119
Lewis-Evans, Stuart 11, 14, 67, 85,
        105, 114, 118–22, 125, 127,
        132, 134–5, 138–40, 143,
        146–8, 150, 154, 157–60,
        164, 167, 171
Leyland Motors 35
Le Petoulet 88
Lockheed brakes 118
Lola cars 119
Lombank Trophy 172
Lotus 14, 79, 98, 105, 113, 168, 171,
        175
Lotus Esprit 180
Lotus Europa 180
Lotus-MG 51
Lotus MK 7 Clairmonte 86
Lotus MKVIII 79, 82
Lotus MKIX 79, 82
Lotus-Vanwall 172
Lotus 'wobbly' wheels 143
Lotus 11 81–2, 120

Lotus 12-Climax 147
Lotus 18 171
Lotus 47 180
Lucas, Oliver 19
Ludvigsen, Karl 28, 110, 113, 120
Luxembourg Grand Prix 48
Lynton House 18

Macklin, Lance 75
Maddock, Owen 45–6, 50
Maglioli, Umberto 13
Mahle pistons 93, 127
Mairesse, Willy 80
Mallya, Vijay 183
Mansell, Nigel 9, 183
Manzon, Robert 64, 91
Marimon, Onofre 61
Marston radiators 46
Martin, Ray 79
Maserati 14, 17, 21, 40, 58, 61–2,
        66–8, 73, 76–7, 80–1, 85, 89,
        91, 93–4, 103–5, 109–10,
        122–3, 175
Maserati A6GCM 73
Maserati V-12 115
Maserati 4CLT 22, 73
Maserati 250F 10, 15, 52–3, 57,
        59–60, 62, 67–8, 72–3, 75–6,
        78, 80, 91, 105, 107, 113, 116,
        119, 149, 185
Maserati 450S 73, 118
Maserati 2513 62
Mays, Raymond 17, 19, 21–2
Mercedes Benz 10, 21, 52–3, 56, 61,
        65–6, 76, 105, 108
Mercedes Benz W196 60, 65, 69, 70,
        72
Merrick, Tony 179, 183
Mieres, Roberto 72
Mille Miglia 46, 50, 66, 105, 109, 118
Minett, John 183
Monaco Grand Prix 11–12, 37, 64–5,
        68–70, 73, 80, 88, 91, 93, 107,
        113–14, 119, 127, 132, 140,
        143
Monaco Historic races 88
Montovani, Sergio 59–60
Monza 11, 33, 53, 56, 75–6, 81,
        134–6, 138, 158
Monza 500 149
Moore, Marian 175, 179
Moroccan Grand Prix 63, 138, 159
Morris Oxford 54
Moss, Stirling 10, 11, 13–15, 34,37,
        51–3, 57, 59–60, 62–3, 66–7,
        69–72, 75, 77–81, 84, 87–8,
        90–1, 93–4, 96, 98, 103–4,
        106–10, 113–19, 121–2,
        124–7, 133–6, 138–40,

        143–6, 148–50, 154, 157–60,
        164, 168, 175, 184–5
Motor Sport magazine 17, 37, 44, 50,
        52–4, 59, 74, 121
Mundy, Harry 35
Musso, Luigi 68, 77, 91, 93, 109, 121,
        146, 149

Nassau 53
National Motor Museum 11
Nixon, Chris 51, 52–3, 64
Norton 9, 18, 25–9, 39, 44, 46, 55, 58,
        83
Nürburgring 53, 113, 116, 127, 132,
        134, 157–8
Nürburgring 1000 Kilometer race
        117, 157

O & S Oilless Bearing Co 19
Odiham Aerodrome 47, 64
Oporto circuit 157
Orsi, Omer 80–1
Oulton Park circuit 10, 76–7, 79,
        84–5, 104, 106–7, 139, 157
Owen, Alfred 19, 37
Owen Organisation 39, 67, 78

Palmer Silvoflex 110, 113
Palmer Tyre Company 110
Parnell, Reg 17, 30–4, 39, 51, 77, 91
Pau circuit 64
Pau Grand Prix 65–6,88
Pedralbes circuit 60
Perdisa, Cesare 96
Pescara circuit 134–5
Peugeot car 28
Pilette, Andre 94
Pirelli tyres 84, 108, 122, 138
Pomeroy, Laurence 114
Porsche 13, 59, 79, 86
Portago, Alphonse de 101
Portuguese Grand Prix 157
Posillippo circuit 68
Posthumus, Cyril 9, 12, 20, 134
Pratt, Arthur 45, 60
Protos F2 car 82

RAC Trials 66
Ramponi, Giulio 21
Redex Trophy 75
Reims 11, 14, 31–2, 52, 63, 96–8,
        101, 118, 120–1, 148, 171
Reims Grand Prix 118
Reims 12 Hour race 96, 100
Richardson, Ken 19, 22, 36
Richmond Trophy 36
Richter, Eric 25, 28, 33–4
Riley sports cars 63
Roche, 'Toto' 121

Rolt, A.R. 'Tony' 51
Rosier, Louis 40, 75
Rouen 11, 118, 120
Rous, Charlie 26
Rolls–Royce 9, 28, 35, 44, 55, 83
Ross, Peter 79–80, 82, 86
Royal Aircraft Establishment 91
Rubery Owen & Co.Ltd 19–20

Salvadori, Roy 11, 14, 67, 115,
        118–21, 150, 157
Schell, Harry 11, 59–60, 71–3, 75–8,
        80, 85, 87, 89–90, 93–4, 96–8,
        100–3, 105–6, 109
Schell, Lucy 73
Scherdel springs 28
Scintilla magneto 35–6
Scott, Tim 176
Scott-Brown, Archie 91,110
Scuderia Centro Sud 91, 109
Scuderia Ferrari 77, 114
Seagrave, Henry 126
Seidel, Wolfgang 160
Setright, L.J.K. 25–6, 45, 50, 64–5
Seven-Fifty Motor Club 79
Severi, Martino 118
Shawe-Taylor, Brian 32
Shelby, Carroll 119
Shell Mex 39, 50, 60, 118
Shell Oils 39
Shelley Company 18
Silverstone circuit 12, 20–1, 24, 30,
        32, 38, 40, 47–50, 52, 64, 66,
        68, 71–3, 75, 79–80, 84–5,
        89–91, 101–2, 104, 106, 119,
        132, 136, 139, 144, 149, 154,
        175–6, 179–80
Smith, Gilbert 26
Snetterton 53, 75, 168, 172
Sommer, Raymond 24
Spa 11, 70–1, 93, 97, 132, 145, 147–8,
        158
Spanish Grand Prix 46, 60
Specialised Pistons Ltd 20
Stacey, Alan 75
Stewart, Al 11
Stewart, Jackie 147, 168
Suez Crisis 108
Sunbeam cars 126
Surtees, John 11, 172, 176
Swiss Grand Prix 48, 53, 73, 88, 105
Syracuse circuit 62–3, 126
Syracuse Grand Prix 78, 105, 106–10,
        113, 135

Talbot cars 73
Taruffi, Piero 11, 37–8, 40, 71, 76–7,
        103, 109
Tecalmit Ltd 20

Thin wall bearing 19–21, 23, 44
Tiera Blanca Collection 183
Titterington, Desmond 10–11, 77, 91
Tourist Trophy 77
Tours circuit 126
Trintignat, Louis 88
Trintignant, Maurice 11, 51, 71, 80,
    85, 87–9, 91, 93–4, 96, 98,
    101, 103, 113, 143, 157
Tulip Rally 66
Turnberry airfield 38
Tyrrell, Ken 75,168

Uhlenhaut, Rudolph 93
Ulster Trophy 31, 36, 38
United States Grand Prix 73

Valentine Grand Prix 65
Vandervell, Anthony 28
Vandervell, Charles 'CAV' 18–19
Vandervell, Colin 108
Vandervell, Geoffrey 'Ned' 18
Vandervell Products 15, 17, 19, 21, 25,
    29, 40, 54, 58, 78, 108, 148,
    179–80, 185
Vandervell, G.A. 'Tony'9, 10–11,
    16–17, 20–33, 35–40, 43–8,
    50–6, 59–60, 62–5, 67, 70–4,
    77–82, 84–8, 91, 93, 96–8,
    100–10, 115–16, 118–20,
    122, 124, 126–7, 134–6,
    138–40, 144–5, 148–9, 158,
    164, 167–9, 171–2, 176,
    179–80, 184–5
Vandy car 19
Vanwall Special (Cooper T-30) 11, 42,
    45–51, 53–4, 57–60, 62

Vanwall VW1 67–70
Vanwall VW1/56 89–91, 97, 101, 103,
    108, 118, 121–2, 127, 134,
    140
Vanwall VW2 11, 27, 67, 72, 75–8, 84,
    89
Vanwall VW2/56 89–91, 97, 101, 103,
    108, 140
Vanwall VW3 72, 75–6
Vanwall VW3/56 97, 101, 103, 108,
    110, 114, 118, 140
Vanwall VW4 75–6, 78
Vanwall VW4/56 101, 103, 108, 118,
    121, 123, 126–7, 145, 154,
    159
Vanwall VW5/57 108, 118, 121, 127,
    134, 136, 140, 143, 145, 148,
    157, 159, 168–9
Vanwall VW6 'streamliner' 118, 135,
    157
Vanwall VW7/57 110, 114, 118, 121,
    134, 140, 143
Vanwall VW8/57 118, 120, 140
Vanwall VW9/58 148
Vanwall VW10/57 138, 140, 143–5,
    148, 150, 154, 157, 159, 180,
    183
Vanwall VW11/60 'Lowline' 169, 171
Vanwall VW12/60 (Lotus 18/901)
    172
Vanwall VW14 11, 172, 179–80
VF One Ltd 183
Villoresi, Luigi 38, 68
Volonterio, Ottorino 75
Von Trips, Wolfgang 96

Walker, Graham 18
Walker, Murray 18
Walker, Peter 33
Walker, Rob 63, 88, 139, 143, 168
Walker, Ted 11
Warsaw, University of 26
Watkins Glen 33,106
Wellworthy cylinder liners 28
Weber carburettors 34, 40
Weslake, Harry 135
Wharton, Ken 11, 38, 40, 42, 59,
    65–9, 72, 75–6, 85, 108
Wheatcroft, Tom 11, 27, 36, 179
White, Graham 11
Whitehead, Peter 33, 64, 79
Williams, Frank 10
Williams, Richard 20
Wills gaskets 52
Wilson, Phil 44
Winfield airfield circuit 34
Woodcote Trophy 39, 59
Wootton, Derek 11, 15, 75, 79, 82
World Championship 11, 15, 35, 57,
    63, 85, 105, 109, 114, 121,
    126, 135, 138–9, 158, 167–8,
    172
Wyer, John 33, 179

Yates, Brock 22–3
Yeoman Credit Team 73, 106, 119
Yorke, David 33, 47, 64, 71, 79, 85,
    96, 104, 106–7, 109, 116, 118,
    121, 124, 140, 157, 175, 179

Zandvoort circuit 73, 120, 143–4